BUILDING EVALUATION

for Adaptive Reuse and Preservation

BUILDING EVALUATION

for Adaptive Reuse and Preservation

J. STANLEY RABUN

RICHARD M. KELSO

JOHN WILEY & SONS, INC.

Copyright © 2009 by John Wiley & Sons, Inc. All rights reserved.

Published by John Wiley & Sons, Inc., Hoboken, New Jersey.
Published simultaneously in Canada.

For general information about our other products and services, please contact our Customer Care Department within the United States at (800) 762-2974, outside the United States at (317) 572-3993 or fax (317) 572-4002.

Wiley also publishes its books in a variety of electronic formats. Some content that appears in print may not be available in electronic books. For more information about Wiley products, visit our web site at www.wiley.com.

Design and layout by Jeff Baker

Library of Congress Cataloging-in-Publication Data:
Kelso, Richard, 1937-
  Building evaluation for adaptive reuse and preservation / Richard Kelso, J. Stanley Rabun.
     p. cm.
  Includes bibliographical references.
  ISBN 978-0-470-10879-6 (cloth)
 1. Historic buildings--Remodeling for other use. 2. Architecture--History. 3. Buildings--Repair and reconstruction. 4. Architecture--Conservation and restoration. I. Rabun, J. Stanley. II. Title.
  TH3411.K427 2009
  721.028'8—dc22
                            2008018989

Printed in the United States of America.
10 9 8 7 6 5 4 3 2 1

Contents

Preface

When considering the feasibility of a building for adaptive reuse, there is no widely accepted method for the early stages of the process when clients and the professionals they enlist to inspect properties and structures intended for development must answer many questions. Is the structure sound? What has to be done to make it safe and meet building codes? What components can be used and what must be replaced? Will construction costs allow the desired return on investment? Many historic buildings have had updates and systems added that may or may not be adequate or compatible with the new planned use—what can be salvaged? What is needed to bring them up to modern standards?

The list is endless, and knowing some of the answers will tell the interested parties whether a project is economically possible or prohibitive. In too many instances, developers and inspectors encounter problems that translate into increased construction costs and reduced profits. Up until now, experience and intuition are often the only guides to making decisions for adaptive reuse. Too often developers and businesspeople need the expensive services of design professionals to determine the spatial fit and the financial expenditures necessary to complete the construction and occupy the space. A reference manual outlining inspection and assessment methodology is badly needed—and this is the objective of this book. It provides both the seasoned veteran and the novice with a systematic method for determining the condition of a building's structure, its systems, and the cost of improvements to make the building functionally and aesthetically pleasing—and profitable. The "Pro Forma Analysis" included here can be an initial indicator of project feasibility. Upon its completion, a decision to buy or lease can be made with a minimum expenditure of time and monies. If a project is feasible, the next step in the process, the more expensive programming or spatial allocation phase, is now easily justified.

Existing material assessment books are available. However, each is focused on specific materials and considers primarily deterioration or failure. So it is obvious that a systematic method of investigation and assessment is needed. To address this, we have developed a book that comes after *Structural Analysis of Historic Buildings* (John Wiley & Sons, 2000) by coauthor J. Stanley Rabun. We take a different route by giving you a clear, comprehensive method of investigation and assessment for making that critical decision whether to reuse, build anew, or pass up on an unsuitable structure. The authors utilize many years of experience in the construction industry. Both are responsible for many projects of the type discussed in this book. They have encountered many of the variables that go into making informed business decisions. This is necessary because every existing building contains systems that need to be assessed to determine if replacement or updating is necessary. This volume fills the gap in asking the right questions, finding the right answers, and making the right decisions to make adaptive reuse a profitable as well as rewarding venture in preserving the structures that so often provide our cities and towns with their identity.

Acknowledgments

We are grateful to our friends, real estate developers David Dewhirst and Mark Hines, who always made their urban building projects available to us as needed. Special thanks are due Karen Melia and Barbara Melia Morris who contributed infrared photographs from the work of Ms. Morris and Bob Melia for Real-Time Thermal Imaging. We also thank Lee Raines, PE, who reviewed Chapter 3, and Dr. Andy Kelso, who contributed photographs.

Our editors, John Czarnecki, Ava Wilder, and James Reidel were instrumental in developing and completing the book. Our publisher, John Wiley & Sons, encouraged Dr. Rabun to begin the project and have been supportive and helpful throughout its creation.

Lastly, without the tolerance, support, and encouragement of our wives, Dr. Josette Rabun, FASID, and Sarah S. Kelso, we would have never completed this work. We also thank our children and grandchildren for allowing us to take some of the time we would have had together for this effort.

Introduction

Expenditures for renovations of buildings rival that for new construction in the United States. Of these expenditures, a large portion is for preparing an existing building for a new use. This book is intended as a guide for those who are considering such a project. It focuses on the existing building and its internal systems. It should be on hand—and in mind—during walk-through inspections of the building and during the conceptual design stages of the work.

Dr. Rabun's book, *Structural Analysis of Historic Buildings*, explained the rationale behind the structural support systems in existing buildings and identified the need for additional information on existing buildings. John Wiley & Sons was the natural publisher for this volume as the recognized leaders in technical publications.

The authors have chosen to organize this book by the systems that serve a building much the way we are organized by our skeleton, internal organs, arteries, and veins. That is, by a building's systems—structural, electrical, mechanical, and plumbing. One reason for this organizational pattern is that the systems are, under current practice, usually designed by specialized professionals. Another reason is that each system to some extent can be evaluated separately. Construction work is typically handled by trades focused on each of the systems. Costs can be broken down by subcontracts in the same way.

This is not to say that the systems are independent of each other—those analogous systems in a human body we know are not. The systems of a building are linked and intertwined. They function together. Keeping to this principle, the parts of this book are intended to function together as well as to give an overview of the status and condition of an existing building and assist in decision making regarding potential reuse.

Specialized professionals can analyze and evaluate the systems in an existing building without much assistance from a work such as this. However, even for specialists, it is a checklist of things to consider and a source for background information on older ways of designing and building—that is, it provides various expertise beyond their own experience. This book also provides information on how systems are related, another area where being too specialized can be a limitation.

Real estate developers, architects, contractors, and building owners are the primary readers and users the authors have in mind—especially those who are new to the field of adaptive reuse. Such professionals learn to identify the historic horizon of a building, its probable system types, what systems can be reused, and the upgrades or new systems that may need to be installed to achieve profitability.

There is a trend in progress for teams of professionals to cooperate in the survey, analysis, design, and construction of adaptive reuse projects as contrasted from the traditional owner-developer/architect/contractor arrangement. The older organization was based on competitive and adversarial relationships between these individuals.

A more effective and sustainable organizational pattern is for all to be on board from the beginning and to contribute in all phases of the project. In this way sustainable features can be incorporated from the very inception and can often result in cost-saving measures in other areas.

The system chapters, 3 through 5, are arranged with a description of the historic development of that system by eras. This is followed by guidance in identifying the system and advice on evaluating the performance of that system and its suitability for continued use in the new occupancy. The chapter then recommends choices for replacement or upgraded systems in lieu of existing systems. Chapter 6 and 8 respectively discuss the sustainability of the building for reuse and the tests that can be employed to gain further information on the condition and performance of systems.

Chapter 7 features a "Pro Forma Analysis," that is, a Microsoft Excel worksheet designed to accept simple data inputs from initial square footages, rental rates, taxes, mortgage rates, and the like for the building. Estimates of construction costs by square foot and other specialty expenses are a part of the input data. The pro forma analysis worksheet can provide a number of different rates of return on the investment. It is a valuable tool for earliest stage feasibility analysis, which is all that is needed to determine if the project as conceived provides a positive return. If the project is proven feasible, then as consultants become involved and a more comprehensive set of construction estimates and rental rates evolve—with an accurate determination of the net rentable square footage—a more sophisticated set of worksheets and other kinds of computer applications will be appropriate.

This book includes detailed instructions that enable the reader to construct a pro forma spreadsheet identical to the one in Chapter 7. Adapting it to another project is simple as the variable input data is all set to be entered on sheet one (even additional items of expense or income can be set up on the first sheet). Sheets two, three, and four automatically generate the information and comparisons needed to evaluate the financial feasibility of a project.

Architectural Character CHAPTER 1

Any building considered for adaptive reuse, remodeling with change of use, or simply cosmetic change while its current use continues must be evaluated—both the exterior and the interior—for its future configuration. The evaluation must consider every factor that involves physical changes to the building as well as the economic ramifications of such actions. The assessment of any existing building with a new use or continued same use requires knowledge of buildings, building utilities, code requirements, and financial implications.

The assessment of an existing building must be done in a comprehensive manner. The owner, the architect, and several kinds of engineers must work as a team in order to arrive at a comprehensive assessment that yields the information required for accurate decisions about the compatibility of a building for its intended use. The assessment is the tool for decisions concerning the required modifications and other modifications that are desirable to enhance the building aesthetically. The pro forma analysis allows the owner to explore the purchase price and to what extent modifications are cost effective and thereby produce a positive return on the investment. Work of any kind on a building in today's economic climate will be expensive and may entail unforeseeable costs. A detailed assessment eliminates many of the unknowns.

When considering a restoration or rehabilitation, architectural decisions not only involve program decisions, they also involve the evaluation of existing structural and architectural details and whether they are to be kept intact, modified, removed, or replaced. Original details, even building massing, are the very essence of the architectural composition as conceived by the original designer. The preparation of any restoration project or adaptive reuse project must include a series of considerations concerning the original architectural concept.

Buildings Prior to 1850

The inventory of pre-1850 buildings is limited and those that tend to possess the purest architectural character are located in the major cities of the Eastern portion of the United States, that is, in what were the thirteen original American colonies. Many commercial buildings, churches, and houses still exist from this period and most have distinct architectural character and styles that go back to roots in the Middle Ages. In addition to the population centers of former American colonies in New England, add the Mid-Atlantic states and other areas that have pre-1850 structures—e.g., Charleston, South Carolina; Mobile, Alabama; New Orleans; and San Francisco. Many of these structures have federal landmark status and are listed in the inventories of the National Landmark Program (part of the Historic Sites Act of 1935) and the National Register of Historic Places formed in 1966. Christ Church in Providence, Rhode Island (Figure 1.1), is an example of a national landmark. There are numerous such landmark

FIGURE 1.1
Christ Church, an eighteenth-century structure, Providence, Rhode Island.

church structures that feature tall spires in former colonial centers that are important to American history. These structures are protected by state and national legislation and maintained by their owners or preservation divisions of the state and federal park services. Others are maintained by private organizations formed for the purpose. When confronted with the possibility of an adaptive reuse project on these buildings, and when any federal money is involved, the applicable *state historic preservation office* (SHPO) must oversee the project plans and the actual work. Also needed is the approval of the National Park Service, which is secured through the SHPO. The supervision and approvals ensure that the actual use of federal funds complies with legislative requirements.

In the American Southwest, there are pre-1850 structures that are in specific-use categories such as the Spanish missions of Texas, New Mexico, Arizona, and California as well, which have given rise to thematic styles. Landmark status has been awarded to these structures, which often consist of churches, schools, and other support structures (see Figure 1.2).

FIGURE 1.2
Mission San Jose, about 1720s, Mission District, San Antonio, Texas.

The Colonial Period: 1630–1780

Initially shelter from the elements and protection from Native Americans were the primary considerations for erecting homes, barns, stockades, and the like. The earliest settlers used medieval and folk traditions in their building schemes. Regional characteristics distinguished the colonial structures of the northern and southern colonies. In the north the colonial houses were basically one to two room structures with central fireplaces. Some were one-and-a-half stories or two stories, with the same plan on the second floor. Later developments would extend the second floor roof to the rear, down to first floor wall level, which formed a structure known as a *salt box* (see Figure 1.3). At the same time the South had basically the same plan with fireplaces on the gable ends to prevent overheating in the summer. Initially, both northern and southern colonial structures used small casement windows with heavy "blinds" for fortification.

FIGURE 1.3
Typical saltbox house,
Nantucket, Massachusetts.

Georgian Period: 1720–1780

Georgian, an outgrowth of English Renaissance, was the first formal style imported to America. Georgian buildings are highly symmetrical and contain specific details both inside and out. Such structures became one of the first projections of wealth as it developed in the colonies. The architectural composition and the status and ornate lifestyles of the homeowner was made tangible by the lavish use of wood and the carpentry and craftsmanship of its details.

Palladian or high-style Georgian consisted of a central element flanked by symmetrical wings. Engaged columns with classical orders are also characteristic, as are such decorative details as dentils and quoins. Windows were larger, double hung, and divided into multiple smaller panes typically in a 6 over 6 or 8 over 8 pattern. Interiors repeated the use of the orders, heavy moldings, decorative window and door casings, and fireplace surrounds and mantels of elaborate detail (see Figure 1.4).

Vernacular Georgian was, as the name implies, a vernacular adaptation of the Georgian style utilizing symmetry and details. The flanking wings, however, may or may not exist, or they may not be attached to the main element.

Federal Period: 1780–1830

Commonly referred to as the architecture of the New Republic—or Adam style after the architect Robert Adam (1728–1792)—Federal architecture is a purely American type of architecture that borrowed elements from Georgian and Classical styles. Buildings typically have a semicircular or elliptical fanlight over the entry door. Entry doors are always six-panel classical doors, and often vertical sidelights are located on each side of the door. Door trim included formal pilasters. Porches often featured a pedi-

FIGURE 1.4
Home of Col. John Vassal, British Army, Brattle Avenue, Cambridge, Massachusetts.

FIGURE 1.5
Harrison Gray Otis House No. 3, Beacon Hill Historic District, Boston, Massachusetts.

ment and columns. The roofs of Federal period buildings are typically low-pitched and often include a balustrade with coping located at the eaves.

A "light" form of architecture, the Federal style followed Roman Classical style. The architectural details and proportions were delicate, refined, and classical. A low-pitched roof might often be found on Federal-style buildings as well as Palladian windows, fanlights, sidelights at the doors, and proportional rectangular windows with plain lintels (see Figures 1.5 and 1.6).

Jeffersonian Classicism is a romantic architecture that uses pure Roman classical form and details.

FIGURE 1.6
The historic Custom House in Salem, Massachusetts.

FIGURE 1.7
Second Bank of the United States, Philadelphia, Pennsylvania.

Greek Revival Period: 1800–1850

Greek architecture can be said to be a symbolic gesture of American liberty and democracy. It used classical temple forms, for example, a lower pitched roof with decorated pediments (following with the tradition of the Acropolis) and the Greek orders on correctly scaled columns with entasis. In keeping with ancient Greek architectural style in this revival architecture, ornamentation was used on the street-facing, or formal, pedimaent. The more formal structures were not only suited for religious buildings, their templelike plans were used for institutional and government buildings as well as banks (see Figure 1.7). Greek Revival was adaptable, however and could be used for residential architecture whether in whole or in part.

Early Victorian Period: 1820–1860

This marked the beginning of a playful period in architecture. Many styles of the past were revived and adapted—sometimes in subtle ways to create a new look. The Early Victorian Period was true to the styles being revived in the design and construction of houses: Gothic and Italianate. Although in many instances, the form and massing of residential structures would not always lend itself to the form and proportions of the pure form.

Gothic Revival

The Gothic Revival preferred to compliment nature rather than conquer nature. Buildings express individual needs through individual designs. Gothic Revival expressed the material and finishes and structural composition. Pointed, Gothic, and lower-profile Tudor arches were used on window and door framing. The following are variations on this style:

Castellated Mode Varied elements and circular and rectangular shapes were used to express asymmetry. Massive, rough texture, and crenellations along parapets were used (see Figure 1.8).

Tudor Revival This so-called English style often utilized the half-timber methods of the English Jacobean style in England. It even copied the cantilevered second story of half–timber over a brick first story. Ornamental, clustered chimneys were often included.

Carpenter Gothic This style featured smaller predominantly wooden houses utilizing gothic details, steep-pitched roofs, gable ends, and board and batten. The exterior walls of moderate-sized churches could be constructed in the Carpenter Gothic style.

Italianate Style

This fashion started later in the same picturesque movement as the Gothic Revival. It copied the vernacular rural estate architecture of Italy. Many row houses were designed with the facades in the Italianate style. Variant forms included the following:

Tuscan Villa Here an asymmetrical mode utilized towers, arcaded porches, and a low-pitched roof with wide, bracketed overhangs.

Italian Villa This symmetrical mode can be identified by its use of cubic proportions and, in some structures, a central tower.

FIGURE 1.8 *(left)*
The Furness Building,
College of Architecture, the
University of Pennsylvania,
Philadelphia, Pennsylvania.

FIGURE 1.9 *(right)*
Venetian Gothic building
owned by the Junior League
of Galveston, Texas.

Buildings from 1850 to 1900

The inventory of buildings constructed in the half century from 1850 to 1900 increases tremendously as does the type and quality of structures. Many architectural styles literally criss crossed the country in parallel with the development of railroads and such communications technology as the telegraph and telephone.

Interestingly, architects were not plentiful in medium-sized cities and nonexistent in small cities and rural locations. For this reason, a lot of the construction in the smaller cities and rural areas was done with mail-order plans and in the local building vernacular. Gentleman architects, without the formal training of those architects operating in large urban centers, took ideas and visions from their travels and brought them home. The scales in which they built, however, was more often than not abbreviated. There were several sources of building components and details that could be ordered and shipped to the job location; therefore, some components standardization existed during this time.

The affluent owners of country estates and summer getaways in remote locations could afford to commission formally educated architects.

High Victorian Period: 1850–1880

This was a period that, despite an incredibly bloody civil war in which thousands died and much property was destroyed, nevertheless saw not only a growth in urban and rural populations but also a growth in commerce and the wealth it generated. A concommitant need for the replacement of structures lost during the Civil War, structures for business, and housing for low, middle, and upper income people intensified construction during these three decades. It is not uncommon to see different styles used for the same building. The following surveys many of the styles in this mix (see Figure 1.9).

Renaissance Revival: 1845–1865

Designers of the Renaissance revival, like their counterparts in the Pre-Raphaelite movement, were inspired by the Italian High Renaissance, namely the palaces of Florence and Venice, which resulted in two variants:

Tusco-Roman mode The palaces of Florence served as models for their classical plans with flat roofs and balustrades.

North Italian mode The Palaces of Venice served as models and used cast-iron ornamentation, porch details, and railing assemblies.

Second Empire Period: 1850–1875

Designers turned to the architecture of Napoleonic France and Paris in particular for their massing of a large central block with wings, horizontal layering, mansard roofs (hence the term "Mansard style," another name for this movement), ornamental dormers, and the classical orders. The Second Empire style also employed such ornate details as cast-iron columns, porch railings, and roof cresting of decorative ironwork (see Figure 1.10).

High Victorian Gothic: 1855–1880

Victorian Gothic utilized larger, sprawling plans and complex compound-like arrangements. The emphasis was on verticality, with steep roofs and towers. Facades were varied in material and colors, and belt courses of cut stone mixed with red brick surfaces and heavy window surrounds all helped distinguish this style (see Figure 1.11).

High Victorian Italianate: 1860–1890

More elaborate than the earlier Italian Revival architecture, this style emphasized ornamentation and larger surface treatments.

Egyptian Style: 1845–1885

The Egyptian style was widely accepted as the architecture of the dead. Thus it was very appropriate for cemeteries, cemetery gates, mausoleums, tombs, and other funerary structures. The style was also used for prisons as the sloped walls fit the internment concept. Other institutional buildings saw the use of this style, including houses of worship (see Figure 1.12).

FIGURE 1.10
Second Empire style house,
Austin, Texas.

FIGURE 1.11
Gothic architecture,
Tarrytown, New York.

FIGURE 1.12
Egyptian style building occupied by the University of Virginia Medical School, Richmond, Virginia.

FIGURE 1.13
Eastlake (or Steamboat Gothic) style used in Calvert, Texas.

Eastlake Style: 1855–1885

The Eastlake style, named for its proponent, the architect Charles Eastlake (1836–1906), used sculptural elements, including elaborate three-dimensional scroll-work usually applied to gables, cornices, and porches of residential buildings for the most part—which gave the houses a look similar to Mississippi steamboats (hence the name *Steamboat Gothic*). The *stickwork* (small wood decorative pieces) was applied in patterns to reflect ornament like "Gingerbread Decoration" (see Figure 1.13).

FIGURE 1.14
Grissom House, currently the "Bishops Palace," home of the Roman Catholic Archbishop of Galveston, Texas.

FIGURE 1.15
The Richardson Romanesque post office in Washington, D.C.

FIGURE 1.16
Late Victorian style house,
Memphis, Tennessee.

Chateauesque Style: 1865–1900

This style featured a combination of the French Gothic and Renaissance vernacular with very elaborate details, forms, and massing to emulate the great French chateaus of the sixteenth and seventeenth centuries. For this reason, the style was mainly seen in the construction of mansions for the newly wealthy (see Figure 1.14).

Romanesque Revival: 1845–1890

A revival of forms and details of an early Christian era, Romanesque buildings were inspired by the pre-Gothic architecture of churches in Rome and elsewhere in Italy. In the nineteenth century this style was often used for institutional buildings such as those designed by H. H. Richardson, who popularized the style, and churches, once again, utilized the bell towers and heavy building shapes— characterized by semicircular arches with low spring lines that made for short fat columns and rusticated stone walls on lower levels. Upper levels would convert to a less rusticated stone with elaborate details (see Figure 1.15).

Late Victorian Period

From 1880 until well into the new century, a new thought process attempted to design with more attention to the purity of revived styles. At the same time, new Industrial Age inventions and technologies became available for buildings and building systems. Hence, as designers tried to carefully emulate the past, they also facilitated client demands for "progress" in the way of new inventions such as electrification, heating systems, and modern bathrooms and kitchens with running water (see Figure 1.16).

FIGURE 1.17
Shingle style house, Cambridge, Massachusetts.

Queen Anne Style: 1870–1890

This was the name lent to a revival of English rural and vernacular traditions from the seventeenth and early eighteenth centuries. The massing is traditional square block, often with round towers. The roof dominates the appearance of the Queen Anne–style buildings and utilizes half-timber upper facades, shingles, and multiple facade treatments, typically of wood construction, in various examples.

Shingle Style: 1875–1900

Shingle style, as the name implies, is a unique use of massing and combinations of form with shingle facades to compose a new style of architecture that followed the Queen Anne style. Uniquely American, Shingle style does not emulate European paradigms. The new architectural form has both organic and vernacular massing. Open space is emphasized in the typical plan of a Shingle style residence with the rooms organized around a central hallway (see Figure 1.17).

Beaux-Arts Classicism: Union Station, Washington, D.C.

Buildings from 1900 to 1950

Beaux-Arts Classicism: 1890–1915:

The Beaux-Arts Style is derived from the academic classical architectural style taught at the École des Beaux Arts in Paris. The École was founded to train artists and architects for the French crown and later the civil government. This style reintroduced monumental architecture, axial references, and symmetry to the American scene as well as an emphasis on the sculptural and the integraton of the other arts into the composition, that is, the building. The Beaux-Arts style utilized classical orders and featured heavy cornices, arches, and stone balustrades, which would normally hide the low pitched roofs (see Figure 1.18).

Second Renaissance Revival: 1890–1915

The New York architectural firm of McKim, Mead, and White brought this style into prominence with their notable buildings such as the Boston Public Library. Derived from Italian Renaissance forms of the fifteenth century, the Second Renaissance Revival is exemplified by buildings of monumentality, symmetry, and very little ornamentation except for the use of the classical orders.

Georgian Revival: 1890–1930

The Centennial celebrations that began in 1876 brought about a revival of colonial Georgian architecture. Georgian became the preferred architecture of the middle classes, given its perceived elegance and a distinctive style, and its popularity has really never diminished as new homes testify to the endurance of this style.

Late Gothic Revival: 1890–1930

The Late Gothic Revival saw new building types that adapted Gothic forms and details in very useful ways to buildings that do not resemble the Latin cross plan of cathedrals and the like. This style also adapted itself very nicely to skyscrapers of this period immediately before and after the turn of the century. Collegiate buildings also adopted this style as it symbolized scholasticism as well as a noble and intellectual atmosphere.

Mill Construction: 1850–1930

Mill construction is the name given to structures that were essentially formed by the technology that they facilitated with the Industrial Revolution. Such buildings were most often utilized for textile factories, warehouse buildings, and the like during the nineteenth and early twentieth centuries. Examples of mill construction are easily identifiable by their structural systems as well as their utilitarian form and appearance. Most structures are one to four stories and made of brick masonry. They feature large window openings and skylights as well as "sawtooth" roof systems. Variations include the following:

Standard mill construction Floors are of heavy plank laid flat upon heavy timber girders spaced 8 to 11 feet apart on centers. These girders are supported by wood columns spaced 16 to 25 feet apart.

Mill construction with laminated floors Floors are of heavy plank laid on edge and supported by heavy timber girders spaced 12 to 18 feet apart. These girders are supported by wood columns spaced 16 to 20 feet apart.

Semimill construction Floors are of heavy plank laid flat upon large beams spaced 4 to 10 feet apart on centers and supported by girders spaced as far apart as the loading will allow, These girders are supported by wood columns that could be spaced 25 feet apart if the loadings are light.

Fireproof Construction: 1875–1930

Beginning in the mid-nineteenth century, *fireproof construction* attempted to eliminate the use of smaller, thinner structural wood elements that burned easily. Fires were a constant hazard in the traditional buildings because of combustible structural members and floor systems. Floors were the most vulnerable to fire, especially in buildings of 3 to 12 stories that used lighter-weight planking and the like—exactly the type of building found in the core of all cities and towns in the United States in the 1870s and 1880s. The Great Chicago Fire of 1871 and other large urban conflagrations pointed to the need for a new type of construction that could minimize fire losses. The Chicago Fire caused the largest loss of property and materials of any fire to that date and maybe even to this date. Wood structural elements were subject to heavy damage or total loss in an intense fire. They needed to be replaced; thus engineers developed noncombustible floors that were constructed of an inventory of railroad rails, wrought-iron or

steel beams, and brick or terra-cotta arches (sometimes termed flat arches). These components were very successful and many variations were developed until modern construction introduced the concrete slab supported by concrete beams or fireproofed steel beams.

Skyscraper Buildings: 1890–1920

Skeletal frame construction did not have the height limitations, both practical and physical, that existed for buildings that relied on masonry load-bearing walls (see Figure 1.19).

The parallel development of the elevator made access possible for the newer, taller buildings given the public's reluctance to climb flights of stairs above certain levels (four to six floors). People were also hesitant to accept claims that such buildings were safe from being toppled by the wind or that the air was not really thinner and not unhealthy to breathe. Even though the claims for unlimited heights were made for skeletal frame technology, the first skyscrapers were only 16 to 20 stories.

The skeletal frame allowed for a number of changes in how buildings were assembled. Since walls no longer had a load-carrying function, curtain wall systems could be attached to the frame rather than support the next story.

Prior to the skeletal frame, masonry load-bearing structures had height limits based on the capacity of the masonry in compression and the wall thicknesses at ground level to keep the compressive stresses within allowable limits. The Monadnock Building in

FIGURE 1.20
Skeletal frame with terra-cotta curtain wall system, Austin, Texas.

Chicago, the last great masonry load-bearing structure, had wall thicknesses of seven feet at ground level. The building was so heavy that it sank into the ground. The loss of rentable prime commercial space at ground level on the Monadnock Building due to masonary wall thickness was nearly 40 percent.

The skeletal frame was very practical. Buildings constructed this way were much faster to erect, and it was possible to leave the curtain wall off at ground level while constructing from the second floor to the parapet. Each level of the curtain wall was supported by framing at the floor level. With the first floor being open, construction equipment and materials were not impeded by narrow entrance ways, a feature still important today.

Terra-Cotta Architecture: 1890–1920

The period of architectural terra-cotta construction parallels that of the skeletal steel frame. Entire building facades and details were done in terra-cotta, which is very similar to brick in composition and manufacturing process. Terra-cotta is molded, unfired clay that is baked in a kiln for a period of time and then baked a second time with the glazing compound. It is then cooled and shipped to the job site for use. Its joints are mortared like conventional brick masonry joints. Terra-cotta, however, is not a load bearing material in the true sense. Instead, it is used for the curtain wall and thus supported by the steel frame—or it is hung on the steel frame by a series of hooks and rods attached to the steel frame. Void areas (holes or grooves) on the reverse of the terra-cotta shapes are then filled with mortar to secure alignment (see Figure 1.20).

There are three types of terra-cotta: architectural terra-cotta (unglazed), decorative glazed terra-cotta, and glazed terra-cotta. The first two are primarily used for exterior work and some interiors such as lobbies and the like. The third is mainly a glazed brick used in interior spaces for wainscoting that needed to be cleaned frequently such as institutional building hallways, bathrooms, and so on. The glazing utilized was a slip glaze incompatible with the masonry base material in expansion and contraction coefficients, and the glazing cracked and crazed. Terra-cotta buildings and other decorative elements were very popular with architects and clients, as it was one of the first curtain wall system materials that accompanied the new skeletal frame technology.

Architecture from 1900 to 1960

Architecture from 1900 to 1960 is sometimes referred to as the period of "Organic Architecture," because designers attempted to use materials that harmonized with nature and structures and spaces that integrated the indoors with the outdoors. The period 1900–1960 was also a time span that included some revival styles at the early portion of the period and was followed by some fairly nondescript forms and little architectural character.

Art Nouveau: 1890–1920

Art Noveau was a relatively short lived style that was mainly used for decorative interior details. It was very popular in Europe and flourished in buildings, interiors, and graphic design such as wallpapers, etc. Art Nouveau in America saw a limited number of buildings and a larger number of interior details such as stair railings and guardrails.

Art Deco: 1925–1940

The Art Deco period was relatively short and ended with the outbreak of World War II. After the war, architects, influenced by modernists fleeing Nazi Germany and Nazi-occupied Europe (e.g., Walter Gropius and other Bauhaus architects), embraced more modern forms.

Late Gothic Revival: 1900–1940

From 1900 through 1940, many churches were constructed in a nearly pure gothic style while embracing modern construction methods. Such methods included steel-framed trusses that were encased in wood below the arches or bottom chord so as to look gothic in style but modern in technology.

Office buildings, too, were constructed in Late Gothic Revival style as the scale and verticality of their height suited the style nicely as shown in Figure 1.21 (see also Figure 1.19).

FIGURE 1.21
Sterrick Building, Memphis, Tennessee. When built in 1925, it was the tallest building in the South.

Colleges and secondary schools embraced the Late Gothic Revival style as a way to link themselves to the traditions of Oxford and Cambridge universities as well as other centers of learning, hence the substyle Collegiate Gothic for such institutional buildings.

Architectural Character

All buildings have certain elements that project their style of architecture and give the building its architectural character. Architectural character is that collection of features that gives the building its uniqueness and authenticity. The character itself is not necessarily the style as previously discussed. It is rather a combination of things that make a building "architectonically correct," ranging from a local interpretation of the style (i.e., the *vernacular*) to the following:

- Footprint on the site
- Form, massing, rhythm, and symmetry
- Materials, primary and secondary, type, texture, and color
- Craftsmanship
- Degree of articulation, details, and finishes
- Color and finishes
- Roof type
- Windows (their patterns and reveals)
- Solids-to-voids ratio
- Doors, including the "celebration of the entrance"

Identify Character Defining Elements

The following is a list of architectural elements that define a structure. If any of the following are removed or altered, the architectural character of the building is lost and, in cases were restoration is impossible, irrevocably destroyed.

- Towers, including details, articulation, windows, parapets, and roofs
- Roof shape (gabled, hipped, mansard, flat, etc.)
- Roof treatment (tile, slate, cedar shake, metal, skylights, etc.)
- Strong horizontal and/or vertical shape—both provide a dominant character
- Curtain walls, including material and delineation
- Load-bearing walls, including material and delineation
- Terra-cotta (i.e., architectural terra-cotta, glazed terra-cotta, etc.)
- Windows, including window surrounds and reveals, window type, and pattern
- Skylights (i.e., decorative skylights and lanterns)
- Doors, including door surrounds and reveals
- Row houses (primarily the front facade)
- Warehouse row (primarily the front facade)
- Nineteenth-century skyscraper (front and side facades)
- Modern-era building (primarily the front facade)

- Interior features such as lobbies, elevator doors, floors, etc.
- Interior features such as decorative plaster, moldings, paneling, ceilings, floors, and other elements
- Staircases such as monumental stairs, details, materials, etc.
- Spatial definitions and core arrangement

Defining the Work, Procedures, and Regulations

Landmark Structures

Work on landmark structures should be limited to purist restoration work in which features are repaired and restored to their original condition. Replacements should be limited to damaged or rotted elements, preferably in hidden locations. If it is necessary to replace elements that are visible, exact material matches must be utilized. For this process, the applicable State Historic Preservation Office (SHPO) and U.S. National Park Service (NPS) must be involved and approve all substitutions. Compliance with various regulations is especially crucial when federal funds are included in the restoration package, either directly or indirectly, such as a grant for rehabilitation of an overall municipal district in which the building is included. In cases where Section 106 review by the President's Advisory Council is activated, the Standards for Rehabilitation issued by the National Park Service apply as well as a thorough NPS review, all of which is submitted to the Advisory Council.

Architectural decisions concern the existing details as well as the interior and exterior finishes. Windows and doors are items that may need an upgrade, rehabilitation, and replacement. Great care must be exercised in considering their replacement. The applicable SHPO and the NPS see the craftsmanship of original items as just one of many important criteria that go into preservation of an entire structure. Even in the name of energy conservation, original single-pane windows are not to be replaced with more thermally efficient factory-made windows. This is why architects consider interior storm windows made of Plexiglas. Internal storm windows are efficient, have good sound-reduction qualities, and are very inexpensive to clean and maintain while not altering the exterior facade or harming the interior window frame.

National Register Properties

National Register properties may or may not be landmark structures. Because such land and buildings can be privately owned, the rights of ownership and improvement are not superseded by a National Register status. Likewise, various state or city medallion programs do not protect a property from change. The only protection that has any meaning is historic zoning. In municipalities, permits can be denied for demolition or alteration of an H-overlay or historic-zoned property.

Inclusion on the National Register of Historic Places is an honorary listing, a prestigious honor roll that designates the property as "contributing to the history of the nation." Properties located in a National Register Historic District are treated identically to individually listed structures unless the National Park Service and the State Historic Preservation Office act formally to decertify or declare the structure as noncontributory to the historic district. When a National Register property is contemplated for an adaptive reuse project, if inappropriate alterations or additions of any kind are allowed by the governing planning authority, the only recourse for preservationists may be removal from the National Register.

Work on these historic structures can take many forms. A total modernization of the building, for example, can involve installing modern conveniences such as air conditioning, lighting, and convenience outlets, additional bathrooms, kitchens, material finishes, floors, and so on. These are a minimum of what is expected in a contemporary rehabilitation. In this sense the developer may deal with only the codes enforcement office within a municipality or no authority at all.

Certain federal tax incentives exist when a developer or owner follows rigid guidelines and procedures that protect the integrity of the property. Property tax abatements exist, too, for approved rehabilitation work on listed properties, when local or state guidelines are workable. These incentives and programs are very successful when the preservation forces and the developers and owners work in a cooperative spirit. Remember, however, if federal funds are included, the Section 106 review process is enforced.

Buildings Not Listed as Historic and Modern Buildings

There are literally hundreds of thousands of buildings of all ages in the United States that need to be investigated and assessed for adaptive reuse projects. The process is much more than simply a match of the right prospective owner or developer and a building. Program requirements are always a factor; at their simplest level they ask the question: Does the building have the needed square footage to meet the programmed needs? The assessment process is identical for all categories of buildings. The prospective owner, developer, and professional consultant look at the same elements and building systems that define historic character. They determine what portion of the useful life remains. A life-cycle analysis determines this, and it entails evaluations for each element and system, addressing the economic feasibility and desirability of keeping them intact or upgrading them. The process requires discipline and knowledge of each system to be assessed. In most instances the assessment requires the thorough examination of several consultants.

In his pamphlet *Designing for Change in Building Use*, David Rock describes the right approach for adaptive reuse:

The structure of an existing building together with its character and service systems can and must form a base for creative solutions. To understand the full implication of what exists and how to use it creatively as a base for something new requires empathy and sympathy with the situation, attitudes which are currently strengthened by the revised interest in architectural history and the study of the vernacular. It is an interesting and perhaps disturbing thought that, when working on the redesign of an existing building, one is in effect, probably working in partnership with a dead architect or engineer. (Rock 1979)

Project Initiation

Once a developer (or development group) initiates a project concept, a number of steps are needed. There are financial considerations such as rental rates, sales projections, and project costs. There are a number of overlooked considerations attached to these costs as well. Together, the overall economics of an adaptive reuse project can tilt the scale of profitability. Therefore, it is critical that an economic analysis of all costs should be included in any comparative evaluation. Many developers are astute in the financial aspects of a project, and it is always desirable if the project can approach 100 percent lender financed. Borrowing money and controlling costs, while maintaining a sellable project, is mandatory to the development "game." Financing a project is affected by the following criteria:

- Interest rates are the key to development.

- High interest rates mean no speculative development.

- Rates above 9 percent control inflation but are not suitable for development.

- Rates below 9 percent are where development begins (but inflation can cause problems if it rises, and generally interest rates rise and construction costs increase).

- At 6 percent interest and around 4 percent inflation is where development flourishes.

The ideal scenario is to use borrowed money to make money, a concept that is in keeping with the principal of "putting money to work."

Any project has players who contribute in various ways, real or intangible. Among them, and least of which, is the financial sponsor, banker, insurance executive, or corporate head. A project team must be assembled that includes that financial person along with the architects and engineers who provide the plans, details, and estimates, however preliminary or detailed they may be.

Project Development

Any project must go through several steps before the reuse enters the construction phase.

The floor plan translates to a yield of rentable or sellable square footage per floor. It provides the tool necessary to project sales amounts or rental income. Comparisons of rental and sales data can come from a number of sources: knowledge of the area in which the building is located, real estate sales data, and information from appraisers records is fairly reliable but must be interpreted, that is, equal size, equal quality, location, and the like. The comparisons must be made from buildings of the same general construction and use type.

An important question is the current inventory figures in the city where you contemplate a project. An excess of quality rental office space drives rental rates down and makes new projects impossible. In this atmosphere, no project can be undertaken unless it contains a large amount of prerented or presold spaces— or it is a single-tenant scheme. The same applies to residential units. If the market is flooded with rentals and condos, there is no profit in the construction of additional units. Such conditions dictate whether you develop (i.e., spend money).

Construction costs also factor in the pro forma analysis (or, simply, the *pro forma*). It is composed of every variable in the development game, especially where the construction costs are involved. Typically the pro forma is a computerized analysis that takes the project costs and weighs them against sales or rental data. It is an invaluable tool in the decision-making process. The pro forma is a reliable method that allows the development team to analyze the project. The pro forma lets them creatively play the what-if game with the project's financial performance character to test the rates of return in a number of ways.

To do this, a pro forma analysis collects all of the data attributing to the annual expenses of a building, including construction, long-term interest, utilities, taxes, federal income tax implications, and the rental incomes (or sales projections) to calculate a series of rates of return. If the project is rental, a forecasted selling price (after a five-year holding period) compared with discounted cash flows also produces an internal rate of return. (A typical pro forma analysis is discussed in Chapter 7.)

The pro forma provides the developer with information to maintain a strong position. If construction costs run higher than projected at any stage of the project, the developer's only recourse is to change the quality in such a way as to make the project cost effective (such as the use of less expensive finishes). If the project is competitively bid, a "lump sum" or "turnkey," and the price comes in too high, the plans and specifications can be changed and the project rebid. If the price is being negotiated, specification changes can be made as preliminary totals are generated. The negotiations then produce a price that is the best under the circumstances. There are other types of construction projects, such as "cost plus" or "cost plus with a fixed fee," but neither produces a known or final cost at the beginning of the project, which can be used in the pro forma analysis before the commitment is made.

Economic feasibility is part of any evaluation of a real estate purchase for business use and for any redevelopment project. An owner or developer requires that an investment produce a return. Typical developers may evaluate two or more possible projects and choose the one that provides the greatest return. As the economy cycles, there are periods in which real estate is not the best investment.

Survey of Existing Conditions CHAPTER 2

The survey of and assessment of the condition of any building that is under consideration for purchase or long-term lease is a complicated undertaking. It needs to be comprehensive with an emphasis on identifying good points as well as problems. Each system must be evaluated and the determination made as to whether the system is "out of date" or "within the present" as to availability of replacement parts. The most elementary consideration is the structural and construction type where several questions must be answered. The condition of structural walls and elements is identifiable with relatively little effort even for a nonprofessional. An obvious problem that must be evaluated by a professional is the change of use that significantly increases the code-dictated live load on the floors or part of the floors of the building.

Embedded systems such as plumbing, electrical, heating, and cooling present special problems; while they may still function, they may be outdated; and it may be more practical to replace before covering up with the modern finishes. It may save a significant amount of money as a dated system may "go out" only a short time after completion of the revitalization.

Identifying the Construction Type

Initially, a *survey of the existing conditions* is required to identify the various systems and materials used in the original construction of the structure to be preserved. This survey should also include any additions or alterations. The architectural style or approximate date of construction may provide clues as to the systems that make the building a functional enclosure. To some extent the date of the building or the architectural style should provide basic system expectations. For instance, pre-1860 structures are often either load-bearing masonry or wood-frame type (i.e., mortise and tenon, or heavy-timber frame), which, together with related construction methods, are discussed in the following subsections. After 1870 newer types of construction were introduced as well as other advances in building technology. Because of the Civil War, the 1860s saw limited construction activity in the United States save for the advances in building railroads and other structures associated with the war effort.

Load-Bearing Masonry

Load-bearing masonry is stone or brick masonry walls, single or multiple story, with the wall thickness coordinated with the height of the building or number of stories.

The actual *load bearing* comes from using the masonry walls to support floor joists and the corresponding floor itself. In a more complex building the floor joists can be supported on one end by a girder and on the other end by pockets in the side of a masonry wall. The pockets are recessed areas in a masonry wall that allow the joist to be

FIGURE 2.1
Details of wood timber frame
construction.

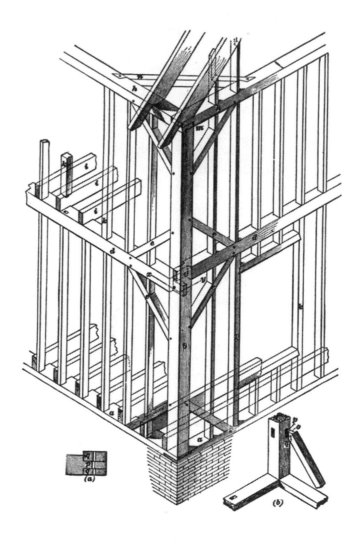

supported by the wall. The girder, typically a heavy-timber member, can also be supported by masonry end walls; for buildings of some depth (front to back), a series of
columns are used to give support along intermediate points, breaking up the length of
the girder into a series of simple spans.

Heavy-Timber Frames

Heavy-timber frames constructed of wood are a type of medieval construction that
European craftsmen introduced to the American colonies, taking advantage of the ma-
ture, plentiful timber available in the New World. The heavy-timber frame consisted of
top and bottom wall plates and vertical corner posts as shown in Figure 2.1. The timber frame utilized mortise-and-tenon joints and a series of studs spaced 24 to 30 inches
on centers. The infill between the studs can be masonry or masonry with stucco. In
some cases, the exterior of the timber frame can be covered with horizontal siding. For
either type, the interior face of the exterior walls is lime-sand-and-gypsum plaster. On
the structures with wood exterior siding, the interior face uses wooden laths to hold the
plaster. All interior walls are wood lath and plaster. Some formal spaces, in more expensive structures, have wood paneling and decorative woodwork.

FIGURE 2.2
Section through a typical mill building of masonry and wood.
Source: Huntington 1947, 347.

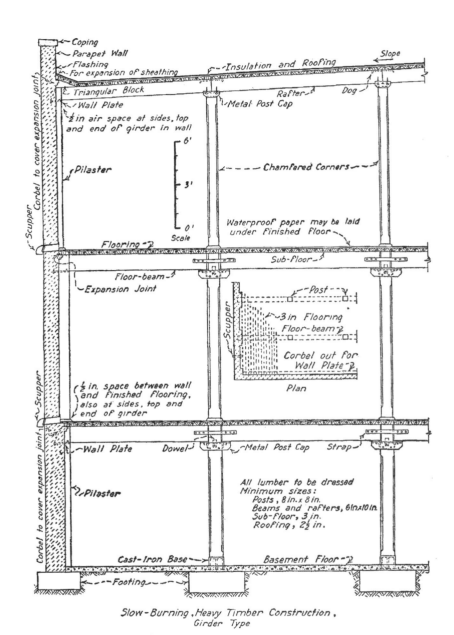

Slow-Burning, Heavy Timber Construction,
Girder Type

Mill Construction

Mill construction, as used in the late nineteenth century and early twentieth century, usually referred to buildings that utilized heavy-timber girders, beams, and columns as framing inside load-bearing masonry walls. Such structures were called *mill buildings,* or *slow-burning, heavy-timber construction,* due in part to their predominant use as factories and for their shape, plan, and height (see Figure 2.2 and 2.3). This period also saw the introduction of cast-iron columns as well as timber, wrought-iron, and

FIGURE 2.3
Details of several types of mill buildings of masonry and wood.
Source: Voss and Varney 1926A, 92.

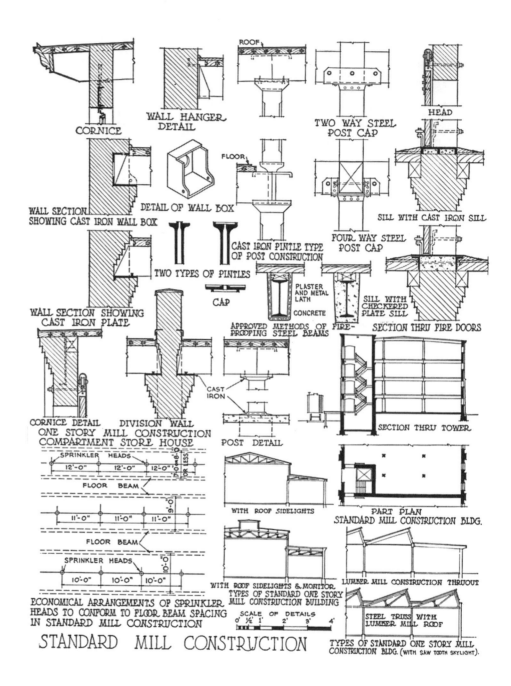

structural steel beams and joists. The masonry exterior walls, however, remain a constant feature. Mill buildings were created to house textile mills and other kinds of industrial uses. They had large windows to facilitate natural light as well as skylights, which were elevated sections of the flat roofs with sidelights called *lanterns*.

Fireproof Construction

Fireproof construction attempted to eliminate the use of smaller, thinner wood elements such as floor decking and average-sized wood joists that burn easily. Wood beams and girders were not the first element to burn in a fire, because their thickness was harder to ignite. A fire of any magnitude and intensity, however, would quickly engulf the entire floor system. Wood girders and large wood columns that contain chamfered corners (linear edges of intersecting planes) are very slow to ignite due to their bulk and the lack of sharp edges.

Brick masonry and terra-cotta arches (sometimes called *flat arches*) spanning wrought-iron or steel joists were introduced in progressive urban areas as early as the 1870s. One isolated example of brick masonry arches using railroad rails as joists occurred at Cooper Union in New York City in the mid-1850s. The use of the arches and wrought-iron beams produced a building that could not be completely destroyed by fire in the way that wood floor systems were. The contents of such buildings could burn, but the intention of the fireproof construction was to prevent fire from destroying the building entirely. However, the heat of a fairly intense fire could partially melt the wrought-iron beams, or its heat could weaken the beams and cause excessive deflections if not failure. A solution was quickly designed, as the use of a protective terra-cotta shape and mortar to protect the bottom flange of the beams provided an insulation barrier that kept the intense heat away from the beams until the intensity of a normal fire reduced itself. Cast-iron or wrought-iron interior columns also required terra-cotta or brick masonry (both with plaster), because they too had to be protected from intense heat. Superheated cast-iron columns actually shattered or exploded when hit with a surge of cold water from fire hoses.

Skeletal Frame Buildings

Skeletal frame buildings began in the 1880s and differed from what had been built earlier in that new materials—first cast iron and wrought iron and then structural steels—were used to construct a building "skeleton" of columns, beams, and joists. The skeletal frame served as the main structural element and the enclosure (exterior walls) were hung on the exterior beams like "curtains," hence the name, *curtain walls*. These skeletal frame, buildings allowed for more height than buildings that used the heavy masonry load-bearing walls, which had height limitations. The development of the reliable elevator coincided with the skeletal frame. With the development of the skeletal frame, the *skyscraper* of 12 to 16 stories became a reality. Wrought-iron brought about the taller skeletal frames as cast-iron was best suited for columns. The cast-iron column had to be axially loaded, as the material would not take the tension loads or shear encountered by beams and beam connections. Wrought-iron members, especially the larger ones, were a composite of several shapes and plates riveted together to make beams, girders, and columns. The framing had to be insulated to protect it from the heat of fire. Masonry, terra-cotta, and plaster were the materials of choice.

Building Construction

For the most part the construction of new buildings in the United States from 1917 to 1919 and 1942 to 1945 had to be put off due to shortages of manpower and material diverted to win World War I and II, respectively. In the years following both conflicts, there was a surge in building as well as new developments in building technology. At the end of World War II, buildings began to utilize lighter-weight forms of enclosure and interior materials than used during the era of cast-iron and wrought-iron construction. Structural steels quickly became the primary material for the skeletal frame and curtain wall support systems. Cast-in-place reinforced concrete construction grew in popularity. A cheaper alternative, reinforced concrete nevertheless took longer from start to completion due to the curing time of concrete.

The Decades of the 1960s, '70s, and '80s

Few architectural advancements took place during the 1960s and the following two decades. Building styles were nondescript, neither following old precedents nor innovating. Glass facades were one of the few new systems introduced during this period. Structural steels continued to be the material of choice for skeletal frames, and these improved as higher-yield stresses were developed. In the latter part of this 30-year period, concrete became a more specialized, free form of construction. The increasing cost of labor made cast-in-place reinforced concrete buildings more costly than structural steel buildings in comparable building sizes, and it remains a much slower construction process. Prestressed precast concrete is a viable option that was used for buildings of lower height, because this method does not have the positive joint system to allow for high-rise buildings. The post-tensioned concrete system is considered viable for mid- to high-rise buildings; but it is also labor intensive and has the same curing time as cast-in-place concrete.

The 1990s and the Twenty-First Century

Following the 1980s, a commercial form of construction appeared that many called *disposable architecture,* because such structures conformed to a "life cycle" not only of usefulness but durability. As construction costs have risen to new levels, owners now look at building-performance data and utilizing materials that last only through the initial use of the building. This is what is meant by the life cycle; after this time span is met, the next use typically requires a remodel, and the life cycle begins anew.

The original plans for the building plus the plans of any alterations or additions from the past are an invaluable asset in the evaluation process. Unfortunately, the plans are not available on a very large percentage of the existing inventory of buildings. When the owner or realtor cannot provide a set of the original plans, another source can be the building's architect, whose office, if still around, may have the original drawings or microfilm copies. Building code officials may have the plans on file, as they review them during the permit process. If the building is of any importance, historical commissions or local preservation groups could have a set of the original plans and specifications.

The Walk-Around and Walk-Through

The *walk-around* and *walk-through* provide a thorough visual inspection of the building that is being contemplated for purchase or long-term lease. The walk-around is a critical look at every square foot of the building from the ground through to the roof. It is not a random approach to finding flaws. It is an organized inspection.

The following list of equipment is used to perform a building inspection. Not everything here is necessary for the investigation. However, it is best to have every item to be fully prepared.

- Recording paper pads, preferably with 1/4-inch grid lines.
- Plenty of sharpened drafting-type hard black (HB) pencils or 0.7 mm automatic drafting pencils.
- A voice recorder with several blank tapes or similar storage media.
- A notebook or laptop computer can be useful if a folding table and chair or the seat of a car is available. However, some feel that the burden of using a computer on-site is not good for the process, as one is struggling with the computer while not concentrating on the building.
- Two or more film or digital cameras with a telescopic feature that can take both color and black-and-white photographs. Film should be 125 speed. Digital cameras should have extra batteries and large capacity memory cards of 512MB or better.
- An infared camera.
- Moisture meter.
- Monocular eyeglass.
- Tape measures in 25- and 100-foot lengths.
- Levels, including three-foot carpenter's level, torpedo level, and a string level with a 200-foot-length of string.
- Ladders, including an eight-foot step ladder and, if possible, a 32-foot extension ladder.
- Tools, including screwdrivers (Phillips and flat blade), carpenter's hammer, crowbar, and pliers.
- Portable lighting, including a flashlight and high-intensity lantern.

The Walk-Around

The *walk-around* is an organized walk around the building. Each facade must be inspected thoroughly to identify gross problems. Each facade must be sketched and photographed to identify problems such as evidence of settlement and cracks in masonry, as well as the condition and alignment of windows and doors. Cornices at the second-floor level and the roofline need to be assessed. If the building is more than two or three stories tall, the monocular proves useful.

The physical integrity of the building must be checked. Here the telescopic feature on the camera can also make it easier to get photographs that help with the assessment. You need to identify also missing elements and make a determination as to the feasibility of replacement and reconfiguring the building to return it to its original form.

Every facade available must be treated in the same manner. In the center city core, some buildings have common side facades with an adjacent neighbor. Asking the owners of these neighboring structures may provide useful information about the condition, thickness, and other issues affecting the party wall.

Obviously the wall between a building and its neighbor should be a double wall, one for each building; so if one structure is lost, the adjacent building has its own wall. It is necessary to ascertain the location of the property line that ideally should run between the two walls.

The same approach to each facade of the building is required to make a successful, comprehensive inspection. To be deliberate and accurate, the starting point for each facade of the inspection must be the same, say, from the left corner of the wall for each facade. The direction of movement and method of observation should be the same for each facade as well, starting at ground level and working up the building in approximately 10-foot zones. Notes, and observations recorded by photographs, sketches, and recorded verbal descriptions, are limited to that area. The next and successive zones follow the exact same procedure, using the same starting point and looking at the next ten foot of the wall.

Three forms of damage can exist on the typical building:

1. Human-inflicted damage on the facade, alterations to be removed, and the like.

2. Inherent damage to building materials from moisture. Brownstone and terracotta buildings, for example, are susceptible to moisture and the freeze-thaw cycle. Wood trim and siding are affected by moisture if the protective paints are neglected.

3. Pervasive structural damage such as settlement of foundations, fire damage, and the like.

The determination that the building meets, at least initially, the required new use's square footage can be made by obtaining the overall size of the building's footprint. The interior *walk-through* will provide the answers as to the compatibility of the interior spatial configuration or the ability to reconfigure the space(s) to meet program needs.

The Walk-Through

The walk-through is important first for establishing the feasibility that the building's interior space is physically compatible or can be made compatible for the planned use. If the space is too small and the overall footprint too small, the building is not going to work or will require an addition. If the building is a good fit, then the assessment of the interior becomes vital to the planned project. The walk-through is also important because it is a continuation of the walk-around. The same structural damage issues, along with interior building system issues and related aspects, must be assessed as a part of the evaluation. The degree of the assessment depends upon the compatibility of the building to the planned use and the condition of existing active systems and material finishes. The assessment will take on a specific direction depending upon the types of enclosure systems, substructural systems, and material finishes on walls, floors, and ceilings. Early buildings, erected prior to 1900, may not be equipped with electrical or mechanical heating systems. These systems, if they exist, are later additions and may be out of date when compared to what is available today. The only comfort system found in early structures was generated heat. Before the steam radiator served this purpose, heat was acquired through fireplaces or cast-iron stoves. These systems are specialized and are addressed in later chapters.

FIGURE 2.4
Masonry wall foundation on mortared earth.
Source: ICS 1923, sec. 5, p. 25.

Identification, Assessment, and Evaluation

Pre-1860 Buildings

Buildings from this era are very simple. Most are load-bearing masonry walls with wood joists and girders. They can have heavy-timber or cast-iron columns that are easy to analyze structurally. The cast-iron columns are found in buildings after about 1840. Pre-1860 construction can also be of heavy-timber frame.

Foundations

Pre-1860 buildings may or may not have actual foundations. In some instances the brick or stone was laid directly on a bed of mortar placed at ground level in the bottom of a trench (i.e., at bottom of wall). It was a common practice to provide a reverse corbel or belling-out of the width of the wall at foundation level to reduce the actual soil pressure as shown in Figure 2.4. For a given load, the wider the wall bearing on the soil, the lower the actual unit pressure on the soil. For some masonry walls, brick or stone was also belled-out and laid on heavy flat stones prepared for this purpose or an early form of unreinforced concrete called *béton*, a French word for a rich lime-sand mixture with both large and small aggregates. As long as water did not come into contact with the foundation, this material would set and make a good hard-bearing course.

Soil, at the load point of foundations for a building, compresses under the load of any heavy building. The normal compression of this substrata allows the building to settle, and typical settlements are very small and do not effect the building as the movement is uniform. Building settlement is an initial occurrence that takes place in the first 12 to 18 months of the structure's life. A localized foundation failure can occur if due, for example to a rising water table saturating the bearing strata, an external water source such as a leak in a waterline or downspout, or an overflow due to a stopped-up drain pipe.

The foundations are difficult to assess as they are normally inaccessible and a visual inspection below ground or below the basement is not possible.

Questions to address when assessing the building's foundations include:

- Does the foundation system show any signs of settlement visible in masonry walls above the ground? Are windows and doors in proper alignment?

- Are there any cracks in the foundation walls? The lower walls?

- If visible, are all of the piers in sound condition? Are they all plumb?

- Does the ground around the building slope away from the building?

- Is any moisture present in the crawl space or in the basement?

- Does crawl space or basement smell of dampness?

- Are there any signs of rising damp in crawl space, in basement, or on interior or exterior wall surfaces above the ground?

If there are signs of a localized foundation problem, and if the building is free standing and accessible, a soil investigation is required to determine the condition of the soil at point of bearing. If the soil is moist, wet, or is not at optimum compaction, the soil test will provide invaluable data.

If loads on the structure—dead loads and live loads—are not going to change with the new use, and no visual difficulties are evident, the foundations are best left undisturbed. Foundations are visually impossible to inspect on the typical pre-1860 load-bearing masonry structure. In many instances the foundations are inaccessible due to the building being situated in the middle of a row of zero-lot-line buildings where another building wall exists immediately behind the wall of the building being assessed. Some investigative efforts can be made by hand excavation from inside the structure's basement. Again, if no visual problems exist and the loads are not going to be significantly increased, it is probably best to leave the foundations unexcavated. A trench or other excavation utilized to expose the foundation may actually damage the foundation or result in loose backfill, both of which can allow water to penetrate.

Differential settlement can adversely affect a structure because one end settles more than the rest of the building, which causes cracked walls. In a row of columns where one column is on softer ground than the others, the building can and will move nonuniformly.

The performance of building foundations are directly related to the following variables:

- Loads on the structure

- Type and dimensions of the foundations

- Soil condition at point of bearing

- Groundwater and water table location

- External interference with any of the above variables

FIGURE 2.5
Improperly placed windows in a masonry wall causing wall cracks.
Source: ICS, 1899B, sec. 7, p. 134.

Load-Bearing Masonry

Cracks in Masonry Walls

Pre-1860 load-bearing masonry walls that utilized traditional lime-sand mortars have a unique ability to withstand loads and building movement without significant wall failure. Some small cracks can and will self-heal as the lime-sand mortars chemically reconstitute in a manner known as *autogenous healing*. Window placement on a masonry wall can be a problem if they are randomly placed as shown in Figure 2.5. These windows are scattered all over the wall without regard to any form of alignment. When aligned, the walls adjacent to the windows inherit the role of columns and the stresses are concentrated in one line rather than in several nonconnected lines.

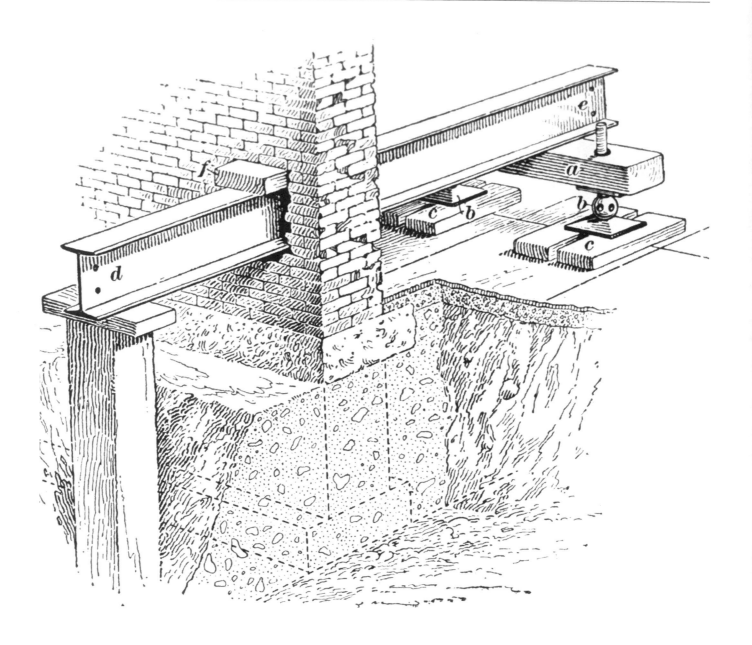

FIGURE 2.6
Foundation revisions or replacement utilizing needle-
beam technology.
Source: ICS, 1899B, sec. 7, p. 77.

Cracks and Evident Settlement

Masonry load-bearing walls that have wide cracks and obvious vertical movement
show signs of foundation failure. It may be localized and the result of changes in subsurface soil water content or running water undermining the foundation by washing
water from beneath the footing. If it is necessary to work on the foundations or completely replace a section of the foundation using a system of needle beams. The needle
beam can hold the building up or even raise it to its original position, while a replacement reinforced concrete foundation is constructed (see Figure 2.6).

The needle beams are inserted into the walls at points about five feet on center as
shown. The beams are jacked "tight," lifting the upper portion of the wall very slightly.
The lower portion and the footing where the damage exists are removed and the new
concrete footing is provided at a lower depth. A new lower portion of the wall is laid up

to the bottom of the upper section. Stone blocks are then inserted in the wall between the needle beams, and flat jacks (also called *waffle jacks*) are used to raise the wall to release the pressure on the needle beams. The needle beams are then removed and inserted in new locations if necessary. The flat jacks are then hydraulically pressured to lift the wall and allow mortar to be placed in the open joints at the top of the new lower wall. The jacks are left in place, pressured, and remain in the wall permanently. The new foundation system bears on a lower and more stable strata that is undisturbed and capable of carrying the required load. The needle-beam system is very difficult if not impossible to use on the sidewalls of urban buildings in a zero-lot-line area. The neighboring building is built to the property line, and the needle beam cannot penetrate through to the interior of the adjacent building without the cooperation and approval of the adjacent building owner.

Rising and Descending Damp

Rising damp is the migration of moisture from the subsurface material upward through the pores of the masonry wall by capillary action to a point where it is released, usually on the inside face of the wall at a point two to four feet above the floor. The capillary rise will be higher for thicker walls than thin. Evaporation of this moisture at the faces of the wall results in the deposit of efflorescent salt crystals. Evaporation can and will occur on both the inside and the outside of the wall as shown in Figure 2.7 and 2.8 (see the color plates). Air-conditioning can lower the humidity within the interior space and thus bring about the evaporation. Exterior walls that have sun exposure also experience evaporation of the dampness as do other exterior walls in periods of low humidity. The moisture that enters the wall takes up soluble salts from the ground, salts from the masonry and mortars, and deposits them when the moisture evaporates in the wetting-drying zone. When these salts crystallize, they expand and cause damage to the wall.

Installing impermeable wainscoting on the interior wall, to cover up the area where the salts form, is ineffective. The covering stops the evaporation in the original wetting and drying zone. However, the deposition of salts eventually moves above the wainscoting.

The five characteristics of rising damp include the following. The dampness:

• Is not seasonal.

• Does not rise far up the wall, only two to four feet.

• Impregnates the entire thickness of the wall.

• Takes moisture from the ground (either from the groundwater table or from improper surface drainage, leaking pipes, etc.).

• Is eliminated in a few years after the water source or permeability of wall is changed.

There are specialty consultants and contractors who can inject silicones into the lower portions of the walls (just above ground level) and correct the upward flow of dampness. To do this, the silicones fill the open pores in the masonry and mortar and provide the barrier as needed. Most injection tubes are inserted in holes that are angled downward to about the one-third point of the wall. The silicones spread laterally as well as by gravity which gives predictable wall coverage. As shown in Figure 2.9 (see the color plates), the injection holes are spaced about three inches on center both inside and outside of the wall. In some instances the installation of an impermeable membrane in the wall, just above or below the ground line, is required. Contractors saw a joint at or near the ground line approximately one-half the thickness of the wall and physically insert a membrane, such as a copper sheet, into the wall. The sawn joint can usually be done in five- to six-foot segments. After a copper segment is inserted, the joint is then "pointed" with mortar. This method requires a second line of cuts on the interior walls at the same level and the insertion of a copper sheet on the inside half of the wall. Obviously, this method is both expensive and only about 80 percent effective, as the dampness can get through gaps in the copper or other inserts.

At the time of the original construction, most experienced builders used asphalt or slate as the impermeable membrane laid within the wall to prevent the occurrence of rising damp.

Descending damp is a moisture intrusion into the top of the wall. It is usually caused by leaks in the roof, flashing malfunction, or failure in the joints in copings on parapet walls. Descending damp flows down the wall from the top, and the efflorescent salts occur two to four feet below the ceiling nearest the intrusion zone. The salts crystallize at this higher level and damage the upper area of the wall. The moisture and the salts travel within the wall. However, they are pulled to the surface by the lower humidity within the space. The source of water intrusion into the top or upper section of the wall must be repaired before the problem goes away.

Signs of rising or descending damp in a building are relatively easy to identify. If the interior wall finishes are plaster applied directly to masonry, the damp areas blister as the water, laden with salts, is drawn to the surface by lower humidity environments. The blisters crack open and the damp salts resemble cotton. The walls that are infused with damp salts will not hold paint or other finishes (see Figure 2.10, the color plates). The wall with the rising or descending dampness cannot be cleaned, scraped, sanded, or refinished, as the dampness reoccurs and damages the wall as before. Many well-intentioned building owners have fought the problem by cleaning, sanding, plastering, and painting again only to have the same problem reoccur in just a few months. Covering up the rising damp areas with something like an impermeable wainscot is also not the solution, as the damp with its efflorescent salts just rises above the wainscot.

After a wall has been equipped with an impermeable membrane, a *poultice* can be used to draw the moisture out of the walls faster than the normal drying out process, which can literally take months. A poultice is a raw clay that is highly absorbent and draws moisture from the wall. It is applied to the damp wall to a thickness of one to two inches. When the poltice is saturated with water, it can be scraped off and discarded. Successive applications can be used to dry the wall further, as required before the final cleanup and the reintroduction of repairs and new wall finishes.

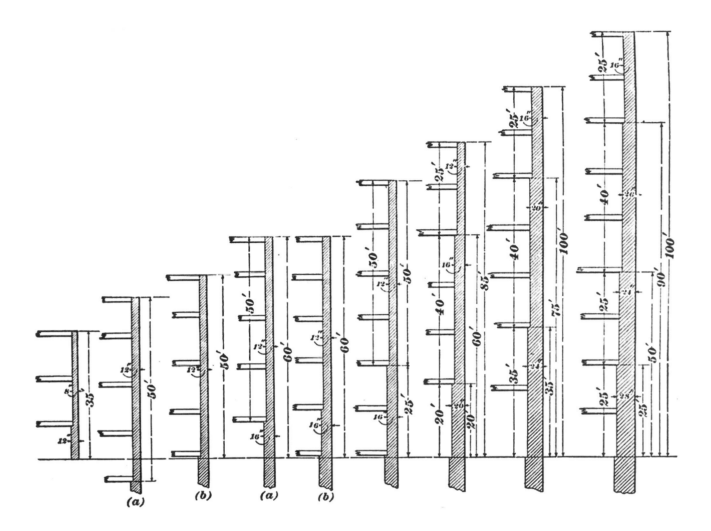

Interior Load-Bearing Walls: Things to Consider

It is important to identify the load-bearing walls on the interior of a building as well as the ones on the exterior. All masonry walls are heavy and produce large loads on their foundations. Load-bearing walls are the walls that carry the floor or roof joists. Obviously, one-half of the exterior walls will almost always be load-bearing walls. If joist direction is side to side, then the sidewalls are load-bearing and the front and rear walls are nonload-bearing or they carry at least minimal loads. The thickness of the walls, the wythes of brick, or the stone thickness is often an indicator of the type of wall. Load-bearing walls will be thicker than nonload-bearing walls. And often nonload-bearing walls will be made of wood with wooden lath and plaster in older buildings. Early building laws dictated the thickness of masonry based upon the number of stories of the building (see Figure 2.11).

FIGURE 2.11
Early building law graphic representation of wall thickness requirements for masonry load-bearing walls.
Source: ICS, 1899B, sec. 7, p. 97.

FIGURE 2.12
Trussed partitions acting as lateral load stiffeners in a masonry load-bearing wall building.
Source: ICS 1923, sec. 5, p. 27.

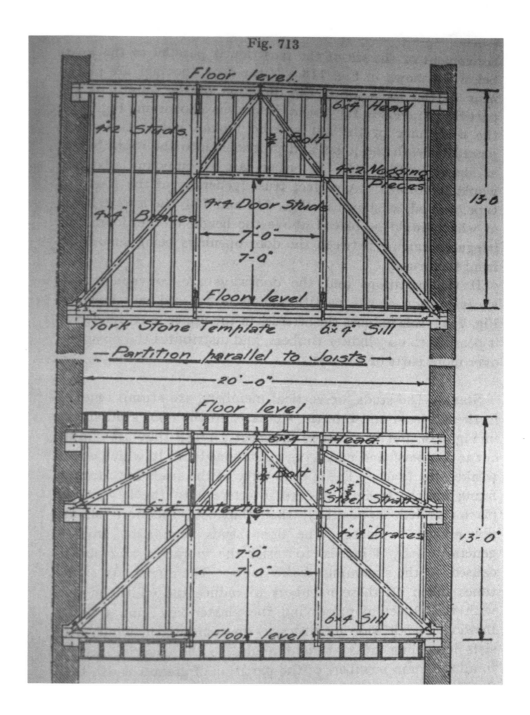

In narrow buildings, typically buildings in an urban setting are narrow and deep, cross partitions were trussed in such a manner as to allow passage. The trussed partitions, however, provided structural support for the long masonry walls that had no other form of lateral resistance. The truss action allowed floor joists to be supported on the trussed partition (see Figure 2.12).

The following items should be observed and documented when assessing masonry walls:

• Assess the type of brick or stone laying pattern. Are there any visible masonry headers that tie the wythes together? Patterns most often reveal the header courses.

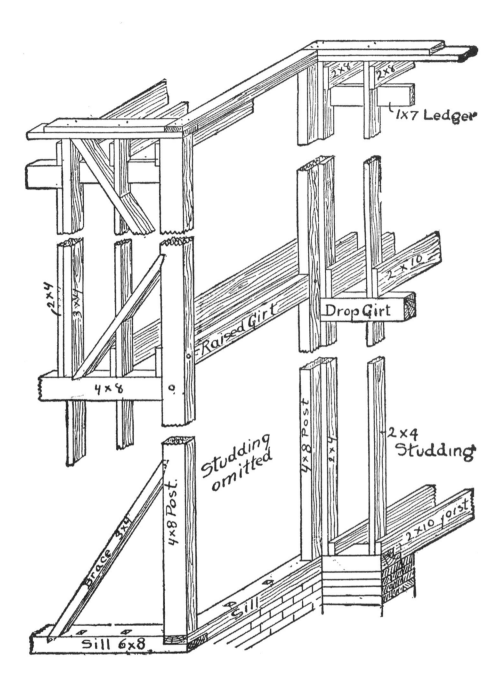

FIGURE 2.13
Details of wood-braced frame construction showing heavy-timber bracing.
Source: Kidder 1904, 51.

- Are there cracks in the masonry walls: vertical, horizontal, lacing? Photograph and sketch the crack patterns and locations.

- Which walls are load bearing? Which walls are nonload bearing?

- Note the thickness and type of every wall: masonry or other.

- Water is the worst enemy of lime-sand mortars, because it often erodes the joints if it is allowed to run down the wall such as from a stopped up scupper that overflows. Are there any signs of eroded or washed-out mortar joints?

- What type of tooled joints are used in the exterior walls?

FIGURE 2.14
Balloon frame construction showing continuous studs.
Source: Huntington 1947, 366.

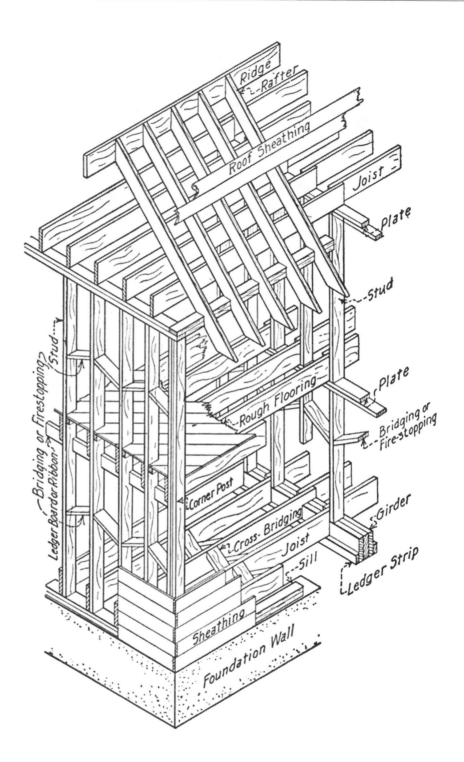

- Is there a need for pointing the mortar to secure the weathering ability of the wall?

- Because people of the pre-1860 era considered exposed brick or rock unfinished, they embraced the style of painted plastered walls. Thus the interior sides of the masonry exterior walls are often plastered with a lime-sand-gypsum plaster and painted.

FIGURE 2.15
Platform or Western frame construction showing a platform at each floor.
Source: ICS 1905B, sec. 20, p. 1

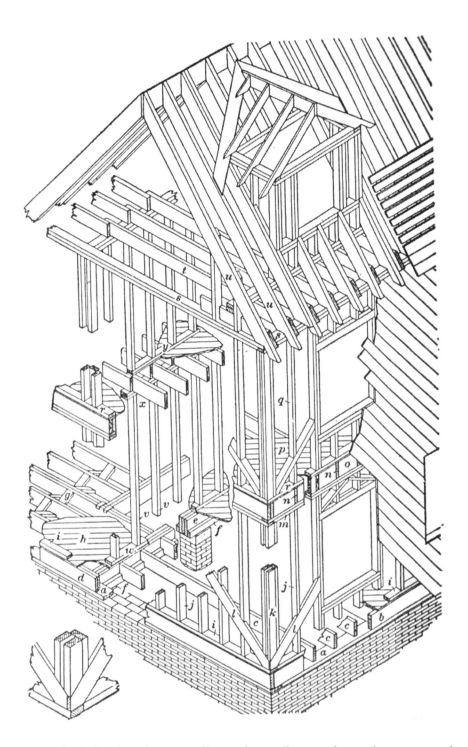

- Door and window locations can affect and contribute to the crack pattern on the walls.

- Are the lintels or headers arched, round, curved, or flat?

- Do relieving arches exist on any walls?

- Do any walls contain a series of arches that are not terminated by a shear wall or buttress?

Wood Framing Systems

Wood for building was very abundant during colonial times (and still is today). During this period, before the Industrial Revolution, trees were felled and logs fashioned as required to construct a small building.

In Colonial America and the early United States, the *braced frame* was a continuation of methods utilized in medieval Europe. Logs were hand hewn into the columns, studs, and beams required by the system. The joints were mortise and tenon, and often the foundations were stacked stone or mortared stone piers at corners and points along a wall. The braced frame system has a large, hewn sill plate that easily transferred loads to a number of piers (see Figure 2.13).

The processing of wood for building systems became commonplace with the advent of the circular saw in the 1840s. Prior to that time, planks were fairly irregular in thickness as they were cut from logs with a two-man, crosscut saw with one man in a pit, hence the term *pit sawing*. The circular saw was powered by a steam engine and cut lumber from logs. Thus an era began of producing sawn lumber for commercial purposes. The *balloon frame* came into popular use in the 1870s after the Great Chicago Fire (see Figure 2.14). The *platform* or *western frame* came into popular use at about 1900 (see Figure 2.15).

In the more than 100 years of framing wood structures with sawn lumber columns, stud walls, wood joists, and girders, the wood framing members have undergone a very deliberate evolution of sizes to create a nominal-size wood member. In the beginning, circular sawing lumber sizes cut members slightly larger than required, and as expected, each member would shrink a small amount during the air- or kiln-drying process. The target size was a width of 1" × and 2" × and 4" × and larger, in two-inch increments. The thickness also came in two-inch increments; that is, sawn lumber would be 1" × 4" (full size, rough sawn) through 2" × 14" and larger members in this category through 4" × 24". Anything larger than the four-inch members was classified as heavy timber, which were also rough sawn, true sized as named.

In the 1940s sawn lumber and heavy timber were reduced in size by planing, which resulted in a smoother, more uniform surface. Another size reduction occurred in the 1960s as further planing provided the kind of lumber product still in use today and known as S4S (surfaced four sides). The reduced lumber sizes are covered in later sections. The significance of this discussion now is that sawn lumber sizes can be used in estimating a building's age.

Items to consider, observe, and document when assessing wood framing systems to 1860 and before include the following:

- Is the structural system a braced frame or possibly log with siding on the exterior and an interior finish of some type? One may not be able to ascertain this information without some semidestructive, invasive method into the area of the framing.
- Species of wood framing system.
- Locate the load-bearing and nonload-bearing walls.

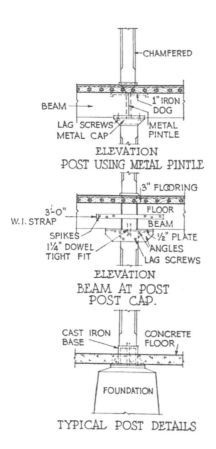

FIGURE 2.16
Details of heavy-timber wood columns.
Source: Voss and Varney 1926A, 91.

FIGURE 2.17
Heavy-timber column with metal cap and later reinforcement.

- Sheathing type (underlayment type) of wood siding.

- Siding or enclosure type and species: ship lap, ship lap with beaded bottom section, board and batten, horizontal tongue and groove, cedar, cypress, oak, shingle, or shake.

- Is the wood siding, soffits, and fascia in good shape? Warped? Rotting?

- Condition of painted surfaces: Is paint cracked, "alligatored," or peeling?

- Is there evidence of a modern siding such as aluminum, vinyl, or other?

FIGURE 2.18
Cast-iron columns with typical framing connections.
Source: Kidder 1904, 429.

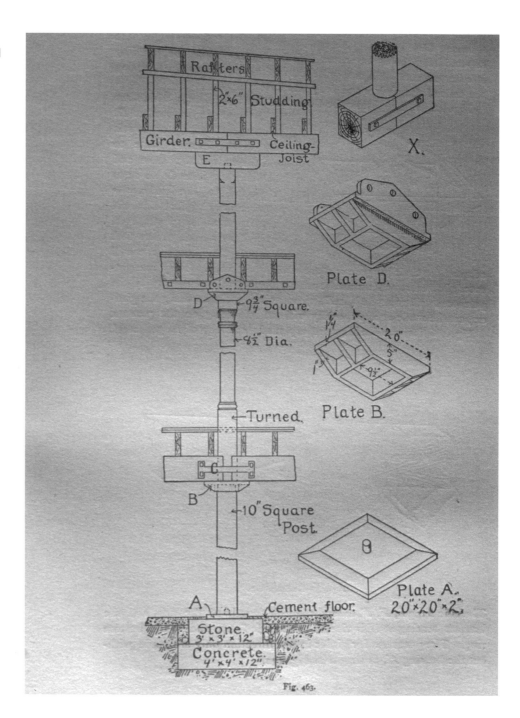

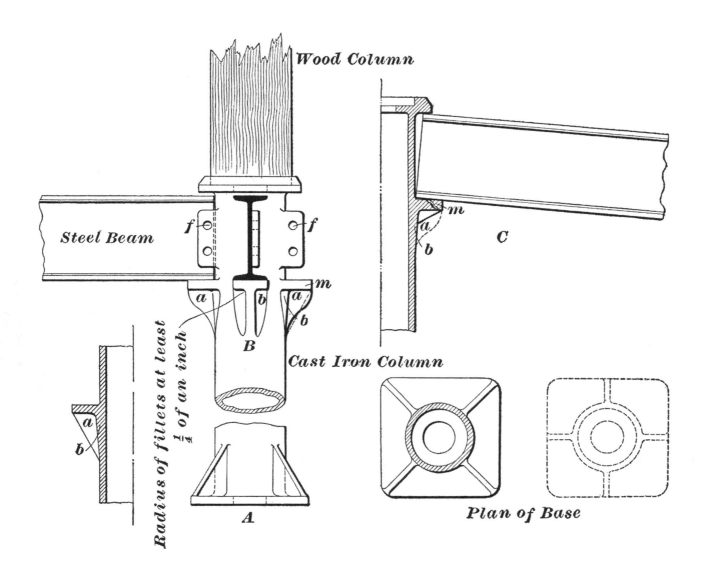

Columns

Wood Columns

Until 1860 masonry building widths were usually limited to a simple row of columns down the center of the building supporting a longitudinal wood girder. Before the pre-1860 period, columns were heavy-timber sections that normally supported the load of two to four stories and a roof (see Figure 2.16). The spans of the joists, which framed the girders supported by the columns, were approximately 25 feet maximum, that is, if the joists are spaced at 16 inches or less. The floor decking normally was 1" × plank. (At the time a 1" × would be full dimension one-inch by multiple widths.) The column in Figure 2.17 has been reinforced at some time in an effort to increase the floor capacity. The 4" × 8" members below the girder and beside the column are gusseted by the 4" × 8" knee braces. The metal cap on the wood column is allowing for the possibility of a girder joint above the column. In more important buildings, the 1" × 6" or 1" × 8" decking acted as a subfloor and a finished floor of oak, maple, pine, or hickory made a space more formal. In lesser-quality buildings, a finished pine floor was the standard.

FIGURE 2.19
Cast-iron brackets on columns for beam connections.
Source: ICS 1899B, sec. 5, p. 59.

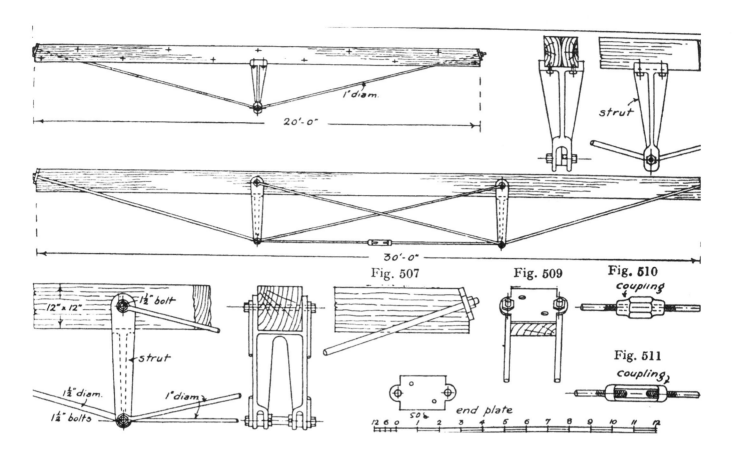

FIGURE 2.20
Details of a king-post and queen-post trussed girder.
Source: ICS 1899B, sec. 9, p. 42.

Cast-Iron Columns

Between 1850 and 1860, masonry buildings also utilized cast-iron columns. Cast iron is very good in compression and the type of construction at this time provided the columns with an axial load (see Figure 2.18). These cast-iron columns allowed additional height in the buildings. The column can be identified as cast iron by the surface, which is slightly textured. Wrought iron and steel have smooth surfaces. Edges of cast iron are rounded, and some columns have connecting lugs and brackets on them for beam connections as shown in Figure 2.19. Cast-iron columns are cast in a sand form as a molten liquid and often have connection brackets cast into the sides of the shaft as well. The connection brackets provide an eccentric load to the columns. If there are two opposing beams framing into the column and each has identical reactions, the eccentricity is eliminated. A connection of only one beam, or beams without identical reactions, the eccentricity is present. Loads on the connection brackets introduce shear and tension at point of load. When assessing cast-iron columns, make a visual inspection to determine if there are any cracks, broken edges, or decorative details. If a cast-iron column is broken and physically separated into two or more sections, it is obviously worthless and unable to function. It is practically impossible to weld cast-iron parts together.

Trussed Girders

Beginning in the 1860s, engineers began designing and utilizing trussed girders for beams and girders. The trussed girder provided itself with a single vertical strut or a double vertical strut combined with tension rods that went from the strut (or struts) to each end of the beam. The tension in the rods provided a vertical uplift at midspan while imposing compression on the beam—two kinds are shown in Figure 2.20.

Most trussed girders were single- or double-wood members. The wood girder has to be large enough in cross section to withstand the combined compression and bending stresses as produced by the loads. The gravity dead and live loads on the girder produces the tension in the rods that provides the uplift in the vertical strut. At the same time, the tension in the rods was realized at the ends of the girder as a compressive load on the girder. The trussed girder is a good solution for a heavily loaded span. It replaced the need for excessively large and deep timber members. The vertical strut, however, does not save any amount of headroom. If a trussed girder or a series of trussed girders appear in a building that is being assessed, a structural engineer experienced in rehabilitation work is needed to ascertain if new, heavier live loads on the floors increase the compressive stress on the wood girder to the point that the combined compressive stress and the flexural compressive stress exceed what is allowable.

Windows and Doors

Wood double-hung windows were normally a feature of the latter part of the pre-1860 period. The earliest colonial buildings had simpler casement or horizontal swing windows. The double-hung window gets its name from having both a movable upper and lower sash. The sash has horizontal and vertical muntin bars to divide each sash into multiple-pane panels to accommodate the glass sizes available during the period up to 1860. These decorative sash panels fall into several categories as defined by the architecture of the period. Windows could have square heads or half-round heads, depending upon the style of the building. Storefront-window compositions existed on buildings near the end of this period. There are a number of publications on the style and type of construction of windows along with dating methods. Doors from this period can be simple slab doors made of several vertical planks (styles) with horizontal planks (rails) at top, middle, and bottom on the inside to hold the planks together. Style and rail, raised panel doors, mortised joints, and the like were also introduced near the end of the pre-1860 period. Doors and windows were changed out and replaced with ease, just as they are now. Only on truly historic buildings is it necessary to date and restore or rehabilitate both doors and windows—and then only when the building is listed on the National Register of Historic Places.

Wood windows and doors are frequently changed by building owners as they wear out or become damaged. Wood frames also shrink due to dryness or rot from excessive moisture and dampness. Wood windows perform poorly at preventing air infiltration. Generations of window and door improvements in both manufacture and flashings have made replacements common. Now, double-glazed windows, with metal-clad exteriors and wood or metal interiors with thermal breaks are superior to any previous products.

Interior Finish and Details

The interior finishes of pre-1860 commercial buildings were extremely simple: Plaster on the interior sides of the masonry walls and wood partitions with wood laths and plaster finishes. The ceilings, if finished, also had wood laths and plaster. A minimum amount of trim was used, usually amounting to wood baseboards at floorline and wood door and window casings. Decorative plaster ceilings, cornices, and wall finishes might have been painted. More formal wall finishes such as *linencrusta*, wood paneling, marble paneling, and wallpapers were expected in finer buildings of this period such as government buildings, college buildings, and churches. Prior to and up to 1860, there were a number of very expensive and very formal residences in the original colonies that were very detailed. Even before the Revolutionary War, indentured servants included skilled carpenters and other craftsmen. Wealthy army officers, traders, merchants, and government officials would also import craftsmen to construct elegant houses.

Roof Assessment

Buildings of the Colonial period to 1860 predominately had gabled roofs, which were often constructed of slate. The flat roof, which had a small slope for drainage, on a few pre-1860 commercial buildings used layers of hot mopped asphalt. In either case, the roof deck would be 1" × plank wood decking laid edge to edge. In the later years of the period an asphalt impregnated paper would be laid directly on the decking to hold the hot asphalt until it solidified.

Items to observe and document when assessing the roof of a pre-1860 building include the following for gable and flat roof systems:

Gable Roof

Assess the type and condition of the roofing material.

Assess the condition of the metal flashings, valleys, ridges, and so on.

Are the gutters and scuppers functioning correctly?

Are the downspouts clear and flowing correctly?

Are there plumbing vents? How many and in what condition?

Are there skylights? Are they flashed correctly?

Condition of wood structure:
  Do any rafters appear to be sagging?
  Is the ridge level or sagging?
  Wood trusses?
  Mortise and tenon?
  Bolted heavy timber?
  Bolted steel cover plates?
  Gang nail plate trusses?
  Wrought-iron or steel plate and angle gable trusses?
  Single angles, double angles, tees?
  Wood purlins bolted to trusses, wood rafters?
  Wood 1" × plank deck?

Chimney(s):
  Is the chimney plumb, free of cracks, etc.?
  Does the chimney need to be pointed?
  Is there a flue liner in the chimney?
  Is there a damper in the flue?

Flat Roof

Assess the roofing material. Is it asphalt or built up? Has the roof been replaced a number of times? Was it a true replacement or simply a series of roofs on top of roofs?

What is the condition of the roofing material? Is it modern roofing?

Are there parapets on all sides? What is the condition of the parapet flashing?

Is there a decorative cornice on the front facade?

Is the cornice masonry or metal?

Is the cornice in good shape and counterbalanced?

What is the condition of the metal flashings?

Are there scuppers, metal boxes, and outside downspouts?

Are there roof drains? Do they work? Where are the drainage pipes within the interior of the building?

Are there roof ventilators? Are they mechanical?

Are there plumbing vents? How many and in what condition?

Is there roof access? Is it a hatch or doorway?

Is there a roof lantern? Is it a clerestory system? Is it operable or fixed? Does it open to vent?

Are there skylights? Curb type or flush? Operable or fixed? Is the flashing, glass, and other glazing in good shape?

Structure:
  Wood joist and girder with wood deck (1" $\times$ plank wood deck)?
  Wood-deck truss system or heavy wood decking?
  Wrought-iron truss system with angles, plates, and tees?
  Steel joist and girder with wood deck?

Fire Stairs

Buildings of the period prior to 1860 do not have a stair that qualifies as a fire stair under today's building codes. Typical stairs of that period would have been open, constructed from wood, and not protected or isolated in any way.

Steel exterior escape stairs that have a counterweighted pull-down ladder were often later attached to the exterior of pre-1860 buildings. These are now considered unsafe and no longer allowed by code.

New "rated" fire stairs, with appropriate "refuge space" on each floor level, have to be constructed at any rehabilitation project undertaken on a pre-1860 building. Most Model Codes and the International Building Code allow a building of 3,000 square feet or less to have only one rated fire stair. Larger buildings need additional rated fire stairs. How many depends on the number of occupants and stair locations.

Bathrooms

New, modern ADA-compliant bathrooms, with all the amenities are required for buildings of this era. These new bathroom layouts require more square footage than earlier bathrooms.

FIGURE 2.21
Béton foundation for a
masonry wall.
Source: ICS 1923B, sec. 5, p. 27.

Loads and Load Testing

Extensive changes in flooring, especially in larger areas, may alter a building's dead loads. If the existing flooring is removed for a new wood floor, and a new tile or thin-set stone floor is installed, there can be an increase in the dead load. For that reason, be aware of the weight increases. Live loads are another matter. The original use or de-sign live loads may not be known. The occupants of the building may have changed, but the use may not. Hence code officials may not have necessarily insisted on verifi-cation. Major rehabilitations in the present day, however, certainly require load veri-fication. In many cases, an engineer experienced in older building verification can certify this to the satisfaction of code officials. If there is concern about the capacity of the floors or other components, load testing is the main method of obtaining accurate confirmation. A simple, inexpensive method of load testing is to place loads on joists or beams in site (or in place) to simulate the anticipated uniform load—or a point load—that brings the member to its required bending moment. The engineer moni-tors the deflection of the member at given loads to determine the capacity of the member. The test loads can be almost anything measurable such as elevator weights, weighed and sealed sandbags, or cement bags.

Buildings from 1860 to 1950

Buildings constructed after 1860 continued in the same tradition, using load-bearing masonry and wood frame, with modifications in size, fittings, and details. During the

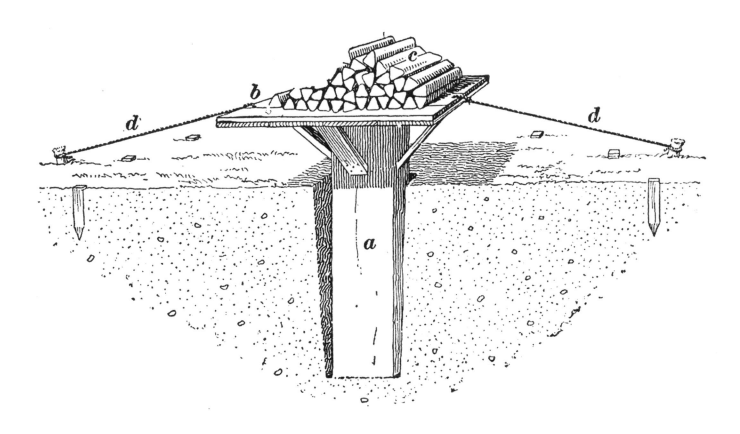

FIGURE 2.22
Twelve-inch square soil testing column with weight platform.
Source: ICS 1923B, sec. 1, p. 9.

Civil War most urban building ceased. With the end of the war in 1865 and during the Reconstruction period, building resumed, especially in the South where the destruction had been extensive, including major cities such as Atlanta, Georgia.

This period's buildings became more detailed, larger, and contained many more functional features. In many ways the entire evolution of buildings from simple enclosures to a high level of complex enclosures of multiple systems happened after 1860 and into the next century.

Foundations

Buildings constructed immediately after the Civil War as well as buildings in smaller cities in remote and rural locations continued to use early foundation laying methods. There still exists that "technology lag time"—more pronounced before 1920—between the larger urban areas of the country and the smaller cities, towns, and rural areas that lacked the professional services of engineers and architects. Stone or béton foundations were still being used in the 1870s (see Figure 2.21). Wood pilings were utilized in the coastal areas and isolated sections where marshy or poor soils existed. These were set in crude ways, usually in clusters. Pile caps consisted of wood grillages, or stone slabs, or béton at later dates, below masonry walls. This method went back to the 1840s. However, the beginnings of soil testing and understanding the capacity of piles became part of the design process in the 1870s, especially in larger cities.

Testing of and the quantitative evaluation of subsurface soils for bearing capacity began as commercial buildings, government buildings, and churches increased in size

FIGURE 2.23
Details of an underground
caisson excavation project.
*Source: Hool and Kinne 1923,
sec. 3, p. 93.*

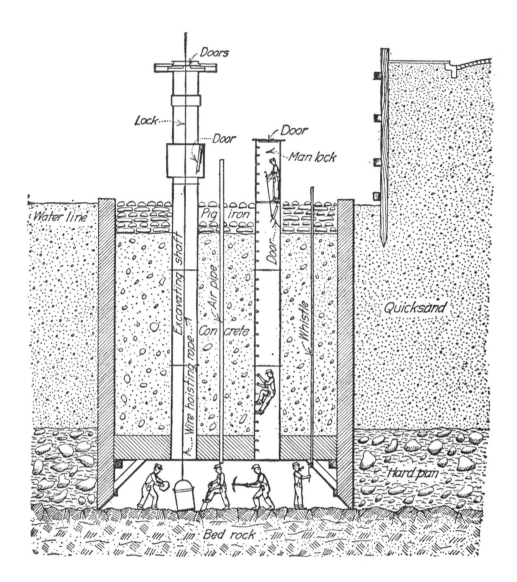

along with their corresponding increased loads on foundations. Designers of these
larger buildings even started to analyze load paths through the building and their effect
on the foundations rather than just follow traditional wall thicknesses. The early soil
tests for foundation capacity were visual inspections of the subsurface conditions at
approximately the level of the footing bearing on the soil. In the 1870s engineers and
builders used *test pits* (described earlier), a *rod test* (i.e., a steel tool driven into the
ground with soil compaction determined by the resistance or the sounds produced by
the rod while being driven), and *auger borings.* This latter method employed a helix
auger at the bottom of a manual drilling rig that was manually rotated by three to six
men to bring up samples of the subsurface strata for visual inspection. With rod exten-
sions, the drill depth could go 50 feet to make a determination.

Load tests in the 1870s consisted of a platform attached to the top of a square column exactly 12" × 12" in cross section and 2 to 3 feet long. The bottom of the column
sat on the subsurface material to be tested, and the platform would be loaded to the ex-

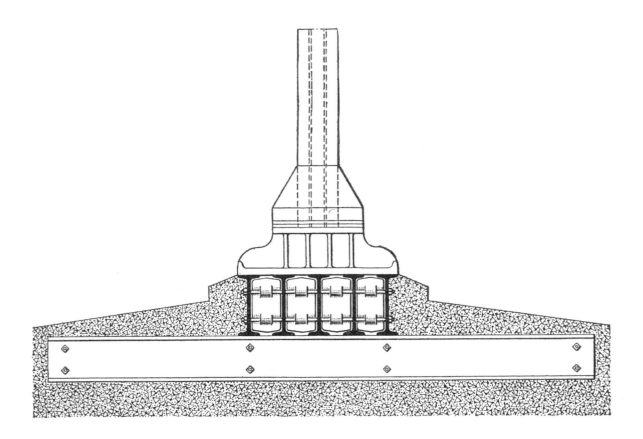

FIGURE 2.24
Early grillage foundation.
Source: Kidder 1905, 47.

pected per square foot load. The platform was tied off in a bridle mechanism to prevent contact with the side of the hole or trench. The platform was left in place for as long as seven or eight days (see Figure 2.22). The load utilized in the test would be the actual load on the footing for 48 hours with measurements made at 24 and 48 hours to determine the settlement at those intervals. Next, the load was increased by 50 percent and the platform left in place for six more days with measurements taken at 24-hour intervals.

Caissons

Beginning in the 1870s, caissons were utilized for heavy loads in areas of poor soil conditions. The caissons were hand dug by men inside the caisson, which lowered itself from its own weight. Caissons are usually taken down as far as required to reach bedrock (see Figure 2.23).

Pneumatic caissons have been used extensively on very large loads in marshy areas and in underwater locations such as bridge piers. In this period excavation under the caisson was done totally by hand with the excavated material passed out in buckets through the top of the caisson. Later advancements in the pneumatic operations included improved air flow underground and *bucket elevators* to remove the excavated debris.

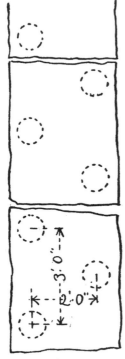

Fig. 11.

Fig. 12.

FIGURE 2.25
Early timber pile foundation with stone capping.
Source: Kidder 1905, 40.

Grillage Foundations

Grillage foundations, which appeared in larger urban areas in the late 1860s, consisted of two layers of railroad rails (or I-beams) with the top layer turned perpendicular to the lower layer and completely encased in béton. Some heavily loaded columns would have had a three-level grillage foundation. The column would have a cast base to distribute its load to the grillage. Designers realized that the best way to handle the concentrated load of a column is to distribute that load over a greater area. This led to the development of a totally new technology based on this concept. The foundation designers also realized that the grillage only needed one layer for wall foundations (see Figure 2.24).

Railroad rails came into use because they were plentiful, straight, and could carry bending loads. Rails as well as I-beams had one difficulty—staying together and remaining plumb while the béton or concrete was poured. Designers solved this problem by using spacers to tie the rails or beams together at the proper spacing. The I-beams proved superior to the railings as they could be obtained in deeper sections and could therefore carry greater loads.

Spread footings of concrete and a two-way matt of reinforcing bars, as we now know them, evolved naturally from grillage foundation. The first use of the combination of concrete and reinforcing bars took place in the 1880s. At first the use of concrete was of no special significance, we can still design massive foundations without reinforcement. The reinforcing allows thinner footings as the tension in bending of the footing is taken by the reinforcing bars. The early reinforcing steel mats were made of proprietary reinforcing bars. There were several engineers working in the concrete field dur-

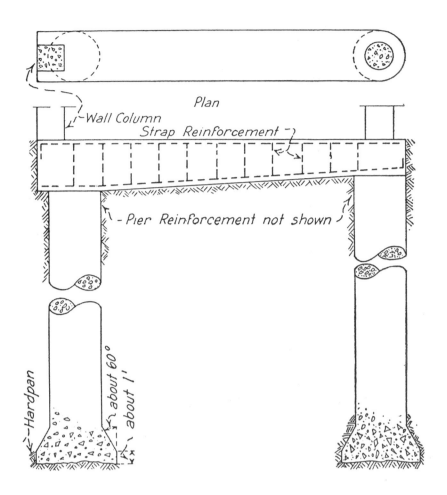

FIGURE 2.26
Drilled concrete pier founda-
tions bearing on bedrock.
Source: Huntington 1947, 164.

ing this development, and each invented and patented their own type and configuration of reinforcing for several different uses.

Piles

As noted earlier, piles were originally wood. They could only be driven about 30 feet,
which was the practical limit for the length of wood sections made for piles. Wood piles
were driven by hammers or weights that were raised and released to fall and hit the pile.
As this technology evolved, steel and concrete pilings were introduced. The number of
piles in a cluster increased as designers knew more accurately the capability of a single
pile; simple math would determine the number of piles needed to carry a building column of a specific load (see Figure 2.25).

Piers

Piers, 4 to 8 feet in diameter, have been in use for buildings throughout this period. The
pier is the correct foundation for an unstable or moist soil where the subsurface conditions have hard pan or solid bedrock 20 to 30 feet below grade. Early in the period
piers were also mainly excavated by auger type machinery. The pier would have a
columnar reinforcing bar "cage" lowered into the excavation and then the pier would
be filled with concrete. At the top of the pier, dowels for concrete columns or anchor
bolts for steel columns enabled attachment to the structure above (see Figure 2.26).

FIGURE 2.27
Early combination brick and terra-cotta block wall.
Source: Kidder and Parker 1936, 1031.

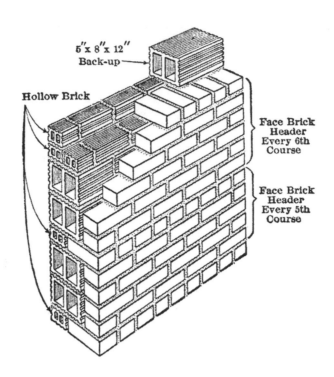

Masonry Construction

Load-Bearing Masonry

Load-bearing masonry wall systems continued into the post-1860 period that utilized lime-sand mortars and man-made brick. As previously stated, the rural areas and smaller cities lagged behind, building with earlier technologies as larger cities experienced new construction advancements and technology.

Traditionally, brick was molded and fired in kilns on-site. Mortars utilized lime slaked on-site as well. Sand came from a nearby river. Urban sites were too congested for site brick making. Instead, bricks and mortar were made in remote locations and brought to the site by horse and wagon. Historic handmade brick, laid in lime-sand mortars, have an average compressive strength of approximately 50 to 75 psi in a wall. The method of mixing the clay for the bricks (its quality, impurities, and the like), the amount of water used to make the lime putty, the air drying process, and removal of the brick from the mold—all had an effect on the quality of the final product. The kiln, however, had the largest impact on the strength of the brick. Typical kilns were spherical domes and the unfired bricks would be stacked radially around the fire in the center of the kiln, which would have an access doorway that was partially sealed. There were also openings for combustion air, feeding fuel to the fire, and exhausting the smoke from the center of the dome. The brick baked closest to the heat source was the most thoroughly fired and, correspondingly, the strongest. The bricks furthest away from the fire would get less heat and not be as thoroughly fired. These had a much lower compressive strength. These poorer-fired bricks were called *salmon brick* for their color as it was the color of smoked salmon. Salmon bricks do not hold up when exposed to weather. They absorb water, and the freeze-thaw cycle causes the face exposed to weather to shear off with each cycle. The masons of the period would keep the softer bricks and salmon bricks on the interior of walls while keeping the harder, well-fired bricks on the outside wythe of the walls. Unfortunately, even today as buildings are razed, salvage forces are cleaning the soft lime-sand mortars off the bricks and selling them to unknowing homebuilders. They in turn lay all types in the same veneer wall and many of the walls have to be replaced or heavily repaired within two to three years.

Machine-Made Brick

The 1876 Philadelphia Centennial Exposition demonstrated the first successful brick-making machine in the United States. The machine-made bricks were more uniform in dimension and denser than traditional man-made brick. The machine also allowed for specialized shapes as well as decorative shapes and sizes. The 1880s saw the introduction of colored mortars and very thin joints in the brickwork on certain notable structures as the masons demonstrated their skill. The sharp, square corners of machine-made brick allowed masons to exhibit crisper lines and more perfect-looking work. Importantly, machine-made bricks were also stronger and capable of carrying larger loads. Cement-based mortars were also developed at this time. Together with the machine-made bricks, the new mortars produced a wall that was much stronger—180 to 200 psi was common—than walls of handmade brick.

Combination Masonry Walls

The need for fireproofing building walls brought about the use of hollow clay tiles to lay in combination with brick in low height buildings and as the curtain walls of skeletal frame buildings. Hollow clay tiles came in sections or blocks that were laid with the cavities horizontal or vertical as needed. The bricks would be *face brick,* a brick of the highest quality (i.e., machine made) to act as the weather course or outside face of the wall. The bricks of the outside course (i.e., the face brick) had standard header courses to tie the wythe of brick to the tile, sometimes called *hollow brick* (see Figure 2.27).

The combination masonry walls also included concrete cinder block in the same manner as the hollow clay tiles.

Brick Cavity Wall Construction

Brick cavity wall construction was a new technique that came about after 1920 and was a predecessor of brick veneering. The *cavity wall* isolated exterior face bricks on the outside surface of the wall and lesser-cost, more imperfect brick on the inner section of the wall. The inner section of the cavity wall carried the load and was of the thickness required (i.e., one, two, or more wythes thick), depending upon the height of the wall. There were basically three types of hollow walls: *rowlock wall, bonded wall,* and *cavity wall* (see Figure 2.28).

Terra-Cotta Block Walls

Terra-cotta block shapes were manufactured in much the same manner as bricks and basically out of the same material. Brick manufacturers produced terra-cotta blocks and shapes as their efficiency in fireproof construction became known. These blocks were laid in standard masonry mortar to construct both load-bearing walls and non-load-bearing partitions, Terra-cotta blocks came in a semihollow unit, laid either with

FIGURE 2.28
Brick cavity wall construction.
Source: Huntington 1947, 164.

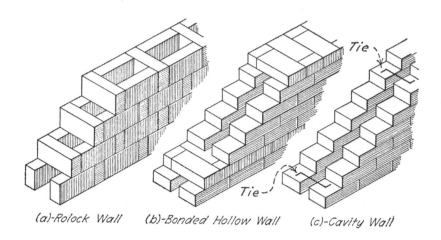

(a)-Rolock Wall   (b)-Bonded Hollow Wall   (c)-Cavity Wall

the cores arranged vertically or horizontally. The blocks also came in special shapes to form window jambs, windowsills, door jambs, and window and door heads or lintels. Lintels could be made by filling horizontal cores with concrete and reinforcing bars. These lintels would be filled with concrete while standing vertical and then placed on the two walls, as is done today. Then the next blocks would be laid normally.

The terra-cotta block would be available in several widths (sizes) to meet building needs (see Figure 2.29).

Entire buildings could be made of the new block system utilizing wood joists and floor systems, wood roof trusses, and the same technology as utilized in brick load-bearing masonry construction. These buildings would be limited to two to three stories. The exterior finishes could be cement stucco, which was troweled on easily in three courses or as best suited to the material. The smooth glazed or decorative finish could be subjected to the weather (see Figure 2.30). Most interior wall finishes were gypsum plaster applied directly to the interior face of the block. The plaster was a two- or three-coat system. This method of construction was quite suitable for house construction and small office buildings. It was suitable too for larger high-rise buildings as a curtain wall material. Also, it was very widely used for interior partitions in the larger buildings—and a glazed type was used in hallways and bathrooms especially in schools. The material had inherent value as fire-rated walls and tenant separation requirements. The real value in the terra-cotta blocks was in the construction of arched and flat-arched floor systems that were known as *fireproof construction,* which is discussed later in this chapter.

Gypsum Block Walls

Gypsum blocks were manufactured at the same time as terra-cotta blocks and were another contributor to fireproof construction. Gypsum blocks were not strong enough for load-bearing walls but were well suited for nonload-bearing bathroom walls and office partitions. The gypsum block was manufactured with one part calcium sulfate and two parts chemically combined water of crystallization. Gypsum blocks were laid with a gypsum mortar that was compatible with the block. Due to

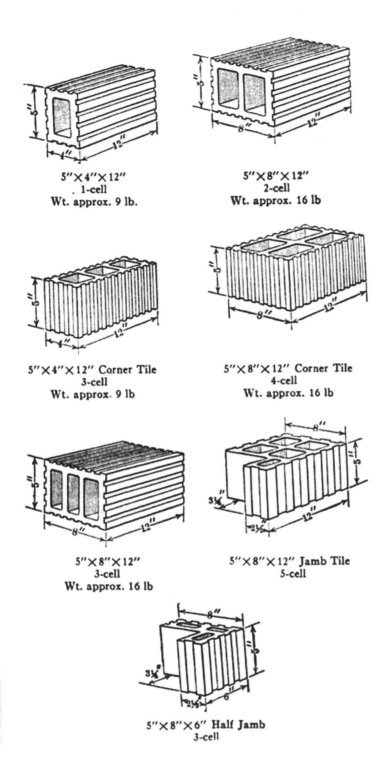

FIGURE 2.29
Terra-cotta block shapes.
*Source: Kidder and Parker 1936,
1030.*

their lack of compressive strength, gypsum blocks were never that popular with de-signers (see Figure 2.31, the color plates).

Unreinforced Cement Block Walls

Cement blocks were developed in the 1920s as a competitor to the terra-cotta block wall. These *concrete masonry units* (CMU), as they are now known, have nearly the

FIGURE 2.30
Terra-cotta construction
showing shapes for various
uses.
Source: ICS 1919, 12.

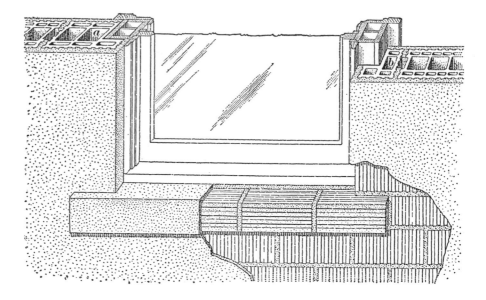

FIGURE 2.32
Early cement block wall
shapes.
Source: Huntington 1947, 280.

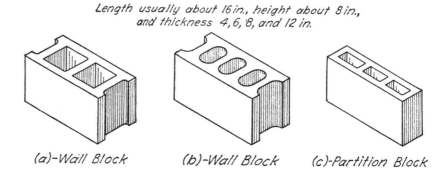

Length usually about 16 in., height about 8 in., and thickness 4, 6, 8, and 12 in.

(a)-Wall Block   *(b)-Wall Block*   *(c)-Partition Block*

same abilities as the terra-cotta blocks. They also have a rather wide footprint compared to their strength. Unreinforced block walls were utilized mainly for single-story small commercial buildings, multifamily houses, and single-family houses. They are now utilized for nonload-bearing partitions, stair enclosures, elevator enclosures, and bathroom walls (see Figure 2.32).

Reinforced Cement Block Walls

Reinforced cement block walls bear the burden of an unpredictable design methodology for reinforcing the blocks and for their concrete-filled cores. Many architects used an empirical method of design where placement of horizontal reinforcement (*dur-o-wall*) was placed at every third course and vertical reinforcing, one or two (no. 3 or 4) within concrete-filled cores at corners and 48 inches on centers. The reinforcing may or may not be embedded in the wall footing. In the late 1910s and early 1920s, the reinforcing bars were a proprietary bar from one of the concrete designers patented systems. Proper reinforcing around window and door openings as is preferred today may

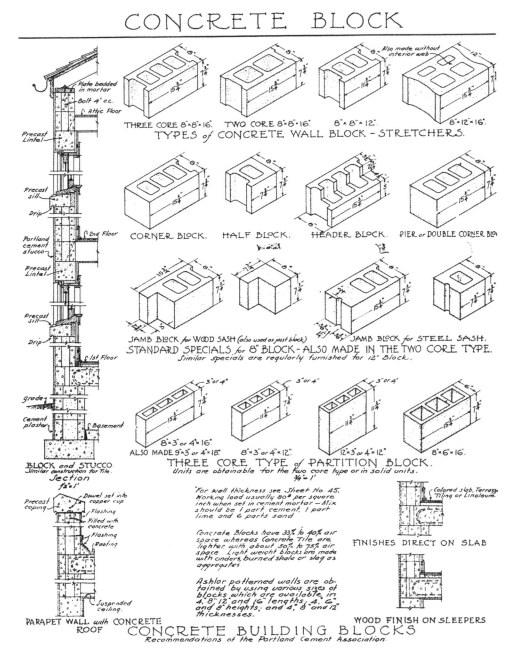

FIGURE 2.33
Reinforced cement block wall details and shapes available.
Source: Ramsey and Sleeper 1936, 52.

or may not exist on period buildings. Cement blocks were also used in walls as the back up to brick or stone exterior wall finishes (see Figure 2.33).

Fireproof Construction

The most important change in masonry happened in floor construction rather than walls. Fireproof construction came about as the need for safer fireproof buildings after many years of expensive and deadly building fires that often spread well beyond their origins. The Great Chicago Fire of 1871 was the largest loss of property ever encountered. Wood floor joists, girders, columns, and the like would not ignite as easily as

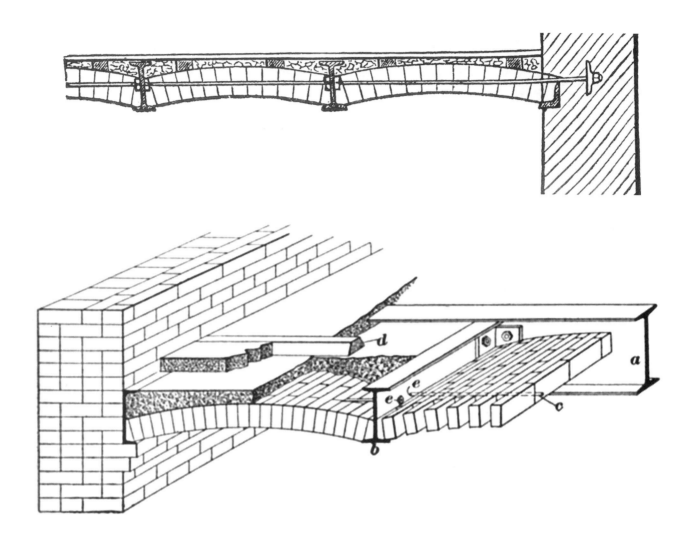

FIGURE 2.34 *(top)*
Early brick arch on wrought-iron beams for fireproof floors.
Source: Trautwine 1888, 522.

FIGURE 2.35 *(bottom)*
Fireproof floor system, brick arches with pugging and flooring nailers.
Source: ICS 1904, sec. 22, p. 15.

thinner floor decking and finished floors. But a major fire could eventually ignite all timbers and wreak havoc if not destroy the entire building. As joists and girders fell, they often destroyed masonry walls as their ends broke up their bearing pockets in the masonry. *Fire cuts* on the ends of joists provided a sloped end to the joist so as not to damage walls when joists fell—a quaint compromise that recognized that fires always cause wood joists to burn through and fall.

Brick masonry arches were developed to create support for floors by a method other than wood joists and wood-floor decking. As with any new technology, a series of steps followed in the process of developing the floor system and getting it to carry the required loads. Railroad rails or wrought-iron beams were initially used to construct the arches as shown in Figure 2.34. The flanges on the bottom of the rail worked nicely as the support for the spring points of the arches and the rail top acted as a "bulb" for strength. The rails worked for the shorter spans. Where longer spans were necessary, I-beams were required. One problem with the masonry arches was their weight and their dead loads. Another problem, common to all arches and vaults, was the outward thrust or horizontal reaction at the point of support—the spring point of the arch. Tie rods were necessary in the plane of the spring point to hold the arches together on the ends

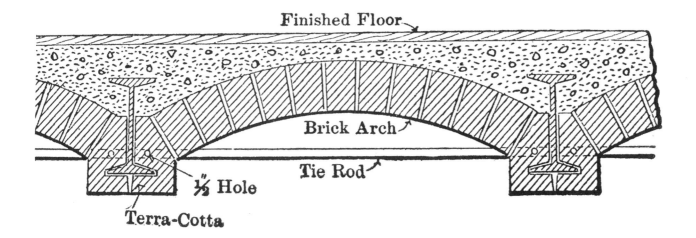

Finished Floor

Brick Arch

Tie Rod

½" Hole

Terra-Cotta

FIG. 37.—Brick Arch Construction.

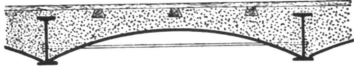

FIG. 38.—Corrugated-iron Arch.

FIGURE 2.36
Fireproof floor system showing details and special masonry shapes.
Source: Kidder and Parker 1936, 951.

FIGURE 2.37
Masonry and corrugated metal arch fireproof floor system details.
Source: Freitag 1909, 90.

where arches did not continue. (See Figure 2.35 and 2.36.) In reality, the outward thrust from one arch can be countered by an adjacent arch of the same size. The problem, as it has been through the ages, is that the end arch in the system has no counter force to equalize the horizontal outward thrust. In ancient vaults and arches, buttresses were utilized to hold the horizontal force. Tie rods have been used to hold a series of arches in place when buttresses are impractical (see Figure 2.37).

The terra-cotta was molded into many shapes to fill the required needs for fireproofing and protecting from the heat of fire. Figure 2.38 shows the typical components of the floor system—note the tile shapes that were utilized to protect the bottom flanges of the steel beams holding up the arches. The finished floor below and the furnishings could burn in a fire, but the structural elements would be protected.

As these fireproof floor systems developed and were perfected, the arches became flat. This was enabled by special terra-cotta shapes made especially for the purpose. The flat arches had the advantage of a flat ceiling for the spaces below the arches. The terra-cotta flat arch components were fluted for plaster ceilings (see Figure 2.39).

The fireproof floor systems normally had *sleepers* on top of the concrete leveling course for nailing wood flooring as the finished floor. Between the "sleepers," there was

FIGURE 2.38
Terra-cotta arches—traditional curved arch and flat arch—for fireproof floor systems.
Source: Huntington 1947, 279.

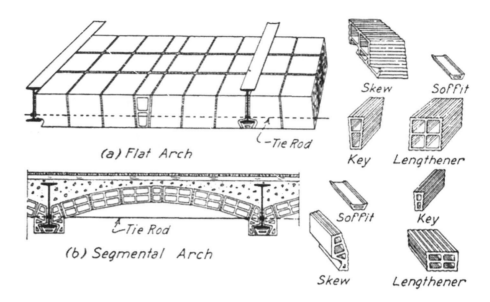

FIGURE 2.39
Terra-cotta arch details—side construction and end construction—with protection for beam sections.
Source: ICS 1905, sec. 22, p. 24.

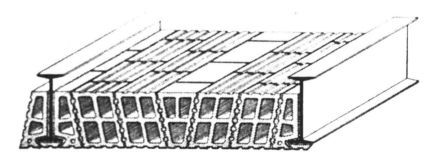

FIG. 22.—Hollow tile flat arch—side construction.

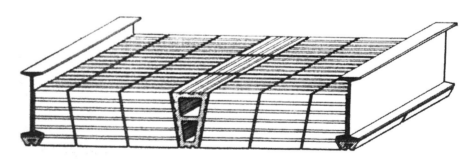

FIG. 23.—Hollow tile flat arch—end construction.

a fill of *pugging,* which is a mix of sand and dry cement powder, to give the floor a solid feel rather than a hollow, soft feel (see Figure 2.40).

Cast-Iron Columns and Building Front Facades

Cast-iron columns continued in use after 1920. Cast iron is very strong in compression and columns of cast iron can carry large loads. In a fire the cast-iron column will hold

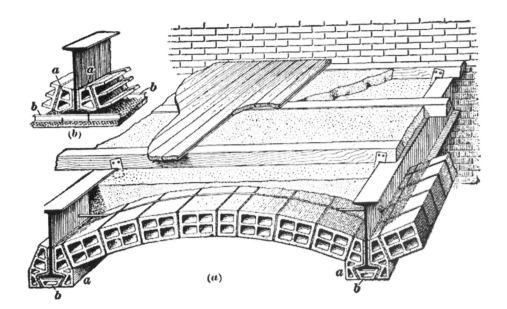

FIGURE 2.40
Fireproof floor system showing terra-cotta arch, pugging, flooring nailers, and hardwood flooring.
Source: ICS 1905, sec. 22, p. 21.

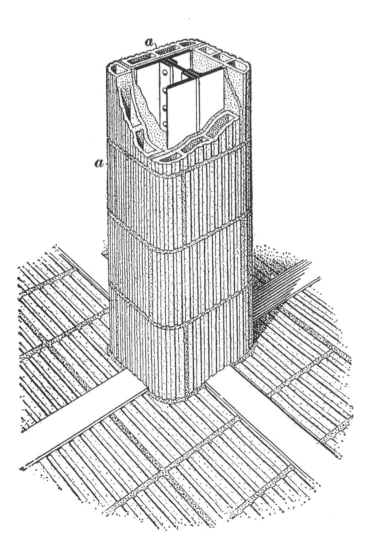

FIGURE 2.41
Terra-cotta shapes fireproofing a wrought-iron column.
Source: ICS 1919, p. 44.

its load capacity, but it cannot take the impact of falling objects or sections of floors. Bending or flexural impact loads put areas of the cast iron in tension that induces a flexural failure. Another problem with cast iron in a fire is the fact that it heats up in the presence of an intense fire, and if it is hit by water from fire hoses, it will fracture from the sudden impact of cooling. Under these conditions many columns have exploded or shattered, which destroyed their capacity to carry any load. The terra-cotta blocks that were developed as the need for fireproofing floor systems were formed in curved sections to surround round columns and other shapes capable of enclosing and protecting square column sections as shown in Figure 2.41.

Cast-iron storefronts and building fronts were developed in the 1880s to bring a semi-classical and more formal front facade to a building. It was possible to have an entire facade of cast-iron and glass as needed by the storefront. There were isolated examples of cast-iron building fronts in larger cities across the country—and in some locations there were entire blocks of this type of construction. The cast-iron building fronts were available as a catalog item, and many architects simply selected a premade design assigned with a catalog number (see Figure 2.42, the color plates). The various elements of a typical cast-iron storefront (see Figure 2.43, the color plates) included the following:

1. Dead panel below the storefront window

2. Storefront window

3. Double-entry doors

4. Transom windows

5. Cornice at second-floor level

6. Spandrels at each floor level and windows above spandrels

7. Roofline cornice

The norm for each of the remaining walls, usually three, is brick load-bearing masonry. The cast-iron building front must be inspected thoroughly and bolting brackets must be checked before the front can be certified as sound.

Balloon Frame

The balloon frame was the first wood construction method of this era that evolved in response to the new industrialized production of nominal-sized wood members. The balloon frame did not require the use of mortise and tenon joints. The development of nails and nail technology coincided with the production of modular-sized boards for standardized wood framing and both were necessary for the balloon frame to work. The first nails in use to assemble the framing were *cut nails* (nails that were cut in a tapered section from a malleable-iron plate). By 1875, wire nails became dominant for framing. The Great Chicago Fire of 1871 solidified the place of the balloon frame in construction, as there was a dramatic need for a faster form of construction. The identifying characteristic of balloon-frame construction is the studs, which are two stories tall. The studs actually go from the sill plate at foundation level to the top plate at the ceiling of the second floor (see Figure 2.44). Joists for the second floor are nailed to the studs at the proper height and then the floor decking is nailed to the joists. There is blocking between studs below joists to reinforce their support. At midheight, between

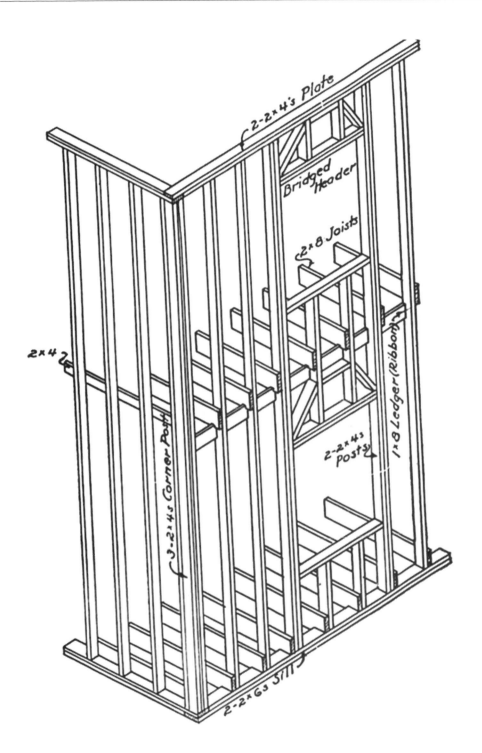

FIGURE 2.44
Balloon-frame construction showing continuous studs.
Source: Voss and Varney 1926A, 75.

floors, there is blocking for fire stops. The balloon-framed building would have to be braced for lateral loads from wind—that would be done with *let-in bracing*, usually a 2" × 4"–diagonal member, fitted into two-inch slots in the framing (studs and plates) so that the outside faces of the diagonal member and the framing were in one plane to receive the sheathing (usually 1" × 6", on the diagonal for strength) that would completely cover the exterior with the exception of the window and door openings (see Figure 2.45).

FIGURE 2.45
Balloon-frame construction showing continuous studs and different window header designs.
Source: Kidder and Parker 1936, 722.

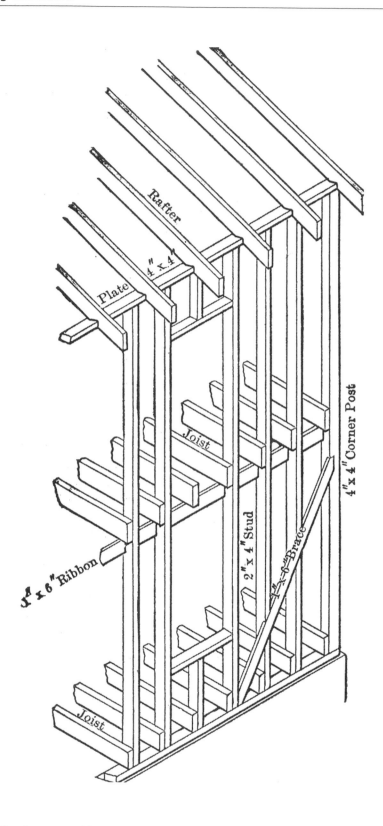

Platform or Western Construction

Platform—or Western— construction was developed on the West Coast in the 1850s. It took about 50 years, however, for designers and builders to employ it throughout the rest of the United States. Balloon framing required studs as long as 20 feet and required

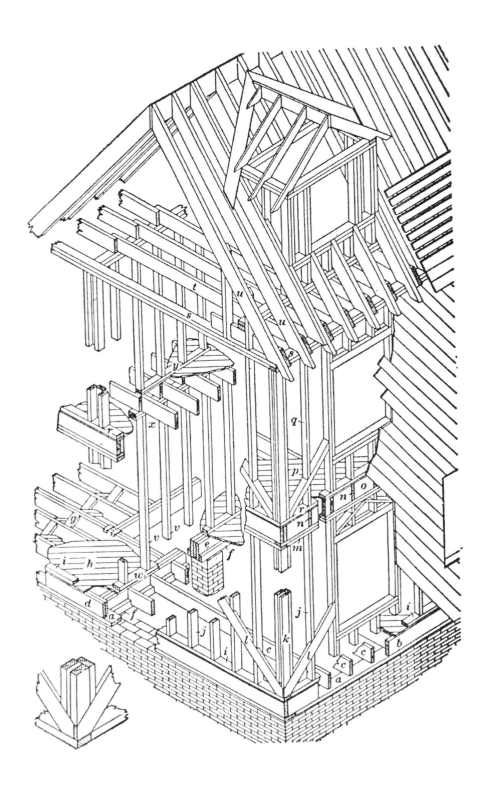

FIGURE 2.46
Western or platform construction showing platforms at each floor level.
Source: Kidder and Parker 1936, 745.

some rather tedious detailing, especially in the field. The platform frame was adopted by the rest of the country as the 20-foot plus studs were always a problem because they could warp and make inconsistent walls—and it required a lot of manpower to get the walls erected. The platform frame required only 8- to 10-foot studs, and equally

FIGURE 2.47
Skeletal frame construction showing steel and wrought-iron framing.
Source: Freitag 1909, 71.

important, the speed and ease of construction made it popular. On the top of each wall (the level of each floor) was a platform, the next floor, which served as a working platform for the erection of new walls above and to the next floor above or the deck for the roof or roof trusses. The method also made it much easier to construct window and door headers. They could now be constructed by doubling studs on the outside edges and placing either deep members across the opening or a simple trussed header with the diagonal members reaching up to the two wall top plates. Wire nails also came into mass production at about the time that the platform frame became popular. This added to the versatility of the system as the wire nails could be obtained in several sizes.

In the early period of the platform construction, the use of let-in bracing and 1" × 6"– diagonal sheathing would be needed (see Figure 2.46). As plywood became widely used in the 1950s, it was learned that its inherent stiffness made it perfect for exterior wall sheathing.

Skeletal Frame Construction

The skeletal frame developed in parallel with certain other building features that complemented the new method. The need for high-rise buildings to contain the spread of urban centers required technical changes. Brick load-bearing construction had its limits as the walls at the ground floor had to be several feet thick to get to heights of 10 stories. The ground floor walls were seven feet thick on the Monadnock Building in Chicago, the last of the great load-bearing masonry buildings.

Elevators were under development during the post-1860 era. However, it took many attempts to find the best form of lift and control. Water-powered cylinder-type elevators, which operated on city water systems, used the water pressure to raise the elevator cab and discharged water to lower it. The development of the electric rheostat allowed the electrically powered cable elevators to operate smoothly, and this gave architects the opportunity to design and develop the skyscraper of the late 1880s and 1890s. The emergence of the wrought-iron beams, columns, and built-up girders of plates and angles allowed the skeletal frame to achieve the heights required (see Figure 2.47).

The skeletal frame revolutionized office building construction. The desired new heights were achieved and the total square footage per land footprint was dramatically increased. One advantage was the speed of construction. With the use of massive amounts of manpower, many of the early skeletal frame buildings were completed in less than a year. It took an average of 25 working hours to set the steelwork for a complete story during the construction of the New York Life Building in Chicago.

Wrought-Iron and Early Skeletal Frame Building

Early skyscrapers of skeletal frame construction were made with wrought-iron columns and beams with many of these members made up of multiple plates and angles or other sections. Wrought-iron sections and structural components began production in the late 1870s and early 1880s and ended production in the late 1880s, as structural steel took over due to its advantages. The production of wrought-iron shapes for building members lasted approximately 10 years before structural steel came into wide usage. All major wrought-iron members and structural steel members were built-up or compound assemblies of multiple shapes. Their connections were riveted at the site as frames were erected (see Figure 2.48 and 2.49). This lasted even into the years after World War II. Eventually, on-site riveting was halted by the introduction of noise ordinances in urban areas.

Wrought-iron columns were made up of plates and angles and Z-shapes to obtain many custom sizes. Designers created larger columns, beams, and girders of multiple plate and angle combinations. Smaller beams and floor joists would be chosen from standard sizes. Producers of wrought-iron and steel shapes issued complete catalogs containing detailed information about the sizes, and capacities of their products. Plates and angles came in several sizes, and designers made custom combinations. Also,

FIGURE 2.48
Wrought-iron construction showing a riveted knee joint, beam to column.
Source: ICS 1905B, sec. 31, p. 5.

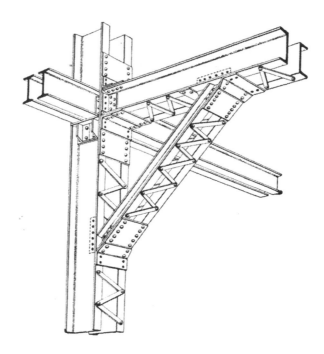

FIGURE 2.49
Wrought-iron construction showing a riveted moment connection between beam and column.
Source: ICS 1905B, sec. 16, p. 45.

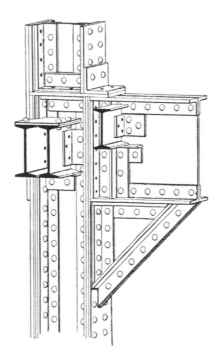

engineers affiliated with wrought-iron and steel producers designed special shapes and sizes that were available to independent architects and engineers through catalogue specifications (see Figure 2.50).

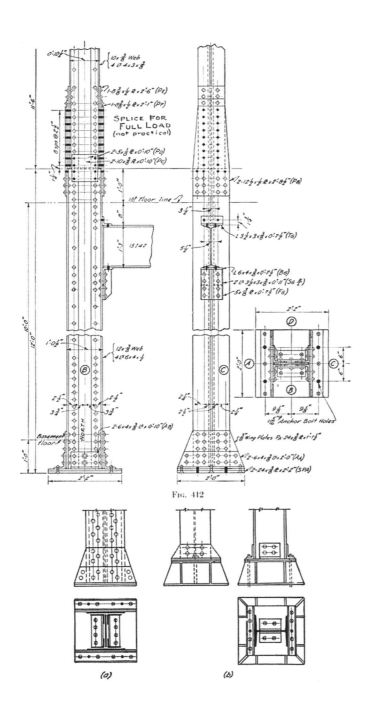

FIGURE 2.50
Wrought-iron column built
up of several riveted shapes.
*Source: Voss and Varney
1926B, 388.*

Fig. 412

Fireproofing of Steel Frames

During the period 1900–1930, some steel beams and columns were encased in concrete to fireproof them. However, it is nearly impossible to tell if a structure under assessment is this type. Usually careful determination of the original construction date can support the theory that concrete encasement exists (see Figure 2.51).

One can only assume that the steel framing for a building was designed to carry the additional dead loads from its concrete encasement. If the additional loads were not considered, the beam surely would show excessive deflection immediately after the formwork was removed. As a part of any assessment, and even more so on a building

FIGURE 2.51
Concrete-encased wrought-iron or steel beam section.
Source: ICS 1919, 64.

FIGURE 2.52
Wrought-iron or steel beam section encased in metal lathe and plaster.
Source: ICS 1919, 67.

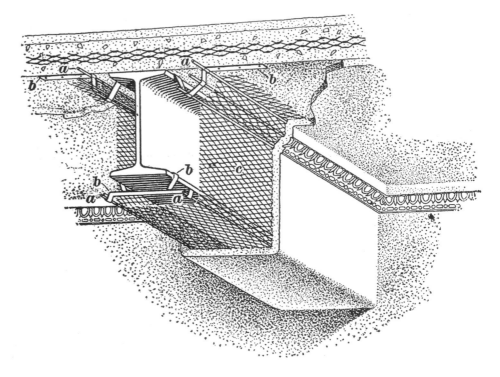

that one thinks might use concrete encasement, cracks in the concrete could be an indication of an encased beam. The encasement process did not include any reinforcing bars in addition to the steel beam. Therefore, more cracks and larger cracks in the tension zone of the beam are expected. The cover on the bottom and sides of the beam are thicker on an encasement because it is intended for fireproofing. This additional thickness magnifies the cracks, and this indication can be used in identifying the encase-

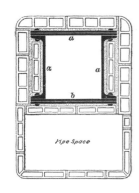
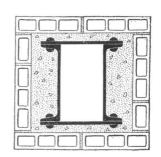

FIGURE 2.53
Terra-cotta shapes and plaster for column fireproofing.
Source: ICS 1919, 44, 45.

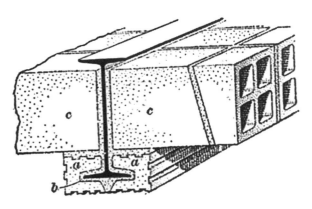

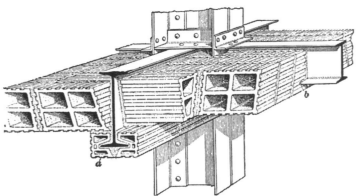

ment rather than a reinforced concrete beam. To identify steel beams within the encasement and obtain enough detail to get approximate dimensions x-ray photography is used (see Chapter 8, "Testing"). Load testing is another method of obtaining the original design loads and also allows one to evaluate the members with an addition to the original design live load.

Some beams may be protected by plaster on expanded metal mesh. The word *protected* here means that the beam was "invisibly" protected from moisture and other contaminants and heat from fire (see Figure 2.52).

FIGURE 2.54
Terra-cotta shapes for flat arch and beam protection.
Source: ICS 1919, 14, 15.

Terra-Cotta Fireproofing Shapes

Fireproof floors were not the only system where terra-cotta blocks were needed for fireproofing beams and columns. The material could be produced in countless shapes for fitting around columns as well, while providing fire ratings of as high as four hours with proper thickness and plaster covering (see Figure 2.53 and 2.54).

As seen in Figure 2.53 and 2.54, there were a number of ways to fireproof wrought-iron and structural steel members. The column could be left relatively close to the size of the member with tight-fitting, constant thickness terra-cotta shapes, or the column could have an additional dead space for vertical pipe chases and electrical and communication wires. Wrought-iron and steel members when fireproofed can provide

FIGURE 2.55
A 1938 building law showing fire resistance for protection of steel beams and columns.
Source: Huntington 1947, 433.

THICKNESS OF FIRE-RESISTIVE MATERIALS

(For Protection of Structural-Steel Members for Various Fire Ratings, According to the 1938 " Building " Code of New York City)

Fire-Resistive Materials	Inches Required for Rating			
	4 hr.	3 hr.	2 hr.	1 hr.
Brick, burned clay or shale	$3\frac{3}{4}$	$3\frac{3}{4}$	$2\frac{1}{4}$	$2\frac{1}{4}$
Brick, sand lime	"	"	"	"
Concrete brick, block, or tile, except cinder-concrete units	"	"	"	"
Hollow or solid cinder-concrete block and tile having a compressive strength of at least 700 lb. per sq. in. of gross area	$2\frac{1}{2}$	2	2	$1\frac{1}{2}$
Solid gypsum block (to obtain 4-hr. rating must be plastered with $\frac{1}{2}$ in. of gypsum plaster)	2	2	$1\frac{1}{2}$	1
Gypsum poured in place and reinforced	2	$1\frac{1}{2}$	$1\frac{1}{2}$	1
Hollow or solid burned clay tile or combinations of tile and concrete	$2\frac{1}{2}$	2	2	$1\frac{1}{2}$
Metal lath and gypsum plaster	$2\frac{1}{2}$	2	$1\frac{1}{2}$	$\frac{7}{8}$
Cement concrete, Grade I*	2	2	$1\frac{1}{2}$	1
Cement concrete, Grade II†	4	3	2	$1\frac{1}{2}$
Cement concrete, Grade II with wire mesh	3	2	2	$1\frac{1}{2}$
Hollow gypsum block (to obtain 4-hr. rating must be plastered with $\frac{1}{2}$ in. of gypsum plaster)	3	3	3	3

* Grade I concrete has aggregate consisting of limestone, traprock, blast-furnace slag, cinders, calcareous gravel.
† Grade II concrete has aggregate consisting of granite or siliceous gravel.

FIGURE 2.56
Portal frame showing the portal, beam at top, and eye-bar bracing for floor above.
Source: ICS 1905B, sec. 31, p. 65.

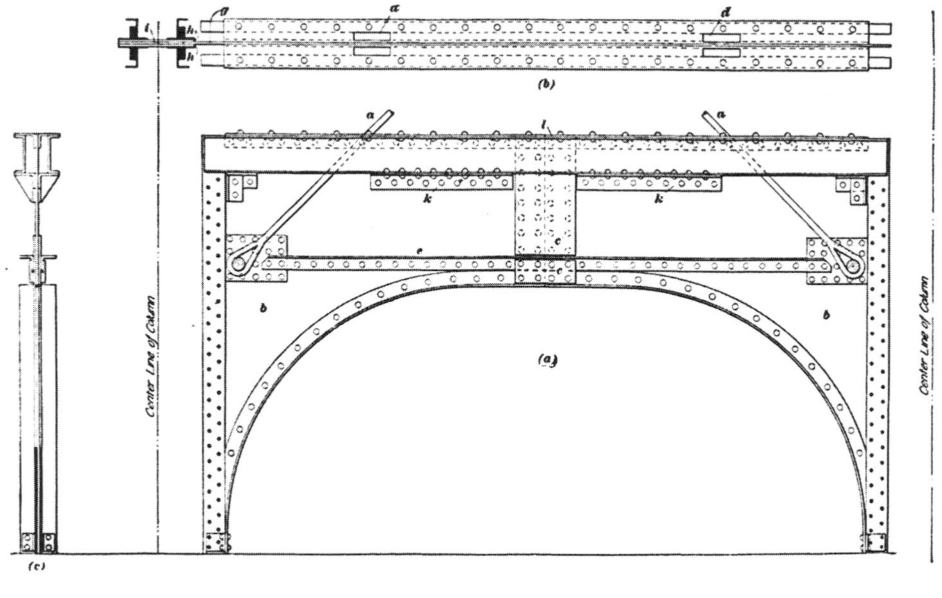

adequate protection to the building frame to allow people inside time to exit safely, as shown in Figure 2.55. The fireproofed beams also protect the frame and its structural integrity for fires of normal duration and intensity.

Portal Frames

Designers realized very early that for the new skyscrapers resisting wind loads was crucial. They understood the concept of moment-resisting connections, diagonal bracing, K-bracing, knee bracing, and portal frames. The portal frame is a rigid assembly of two columns and a beam that produces a piece of a frame that has the appearance of a "portal" as shown in Figure 2. 56. The portal frame could be and was stacked (via field riv-

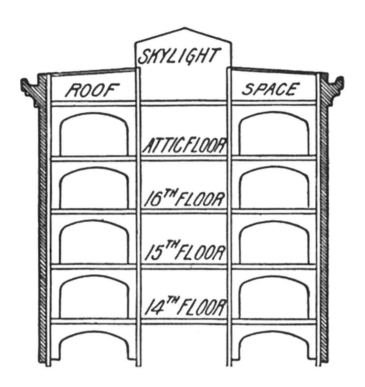

FIGURE 2.57
Portal frame wind bracing
layout for a building.
Source: Freitag 1909, 271.

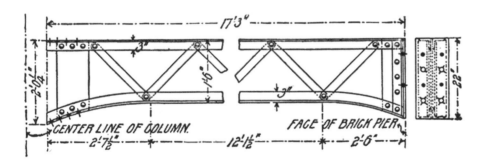

FIGURE 2.58
Open-trussed portal frame.
Source: Freitag 1909, 271.

eted or bolted connections) vertically one over the other for 20-plus story building frames.

The connections, as shown in Figure 2.57 and 2.58, would provide knee braces and act as a portion of the wind-load bracing for a tall building of the era. The portal frame was the preferred method utilized by many designers, as the portal provided a rigid frame between two columns. A multifloor building would contain a series of portal frames vertically and in several structural bays to negate the wind loads that could come from any direction (see Figures 2.59, 2.60, and 2.61).

Early Structural Steel Frames

Structural steels began to be produced in the mid to late 1880s. As soon as this material proved metallurgically superior, structural steel was adopted and produced in practically every shape previously made with wrought iron. Skeletal frames of structural steel were, for all practical purposes, almost identical with wrought-iron frames.

FIGURE 2.59
Portal frame wind-
bracing layout for an
1890s skyscraper.
Source: Birkmire 1894, 196.

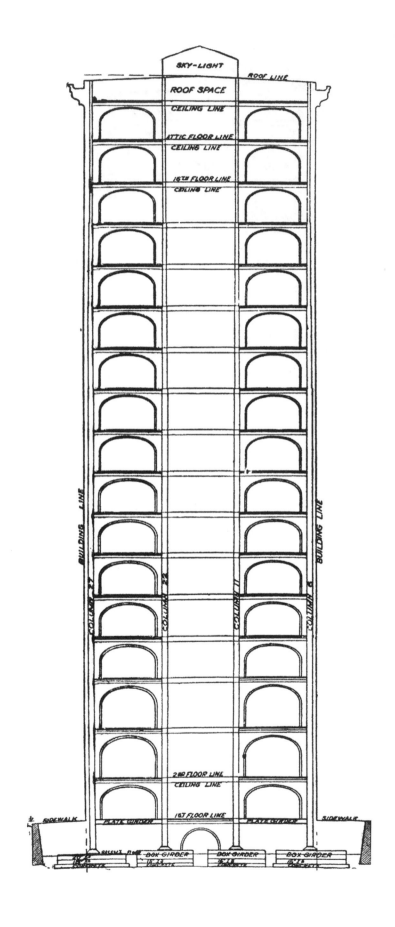

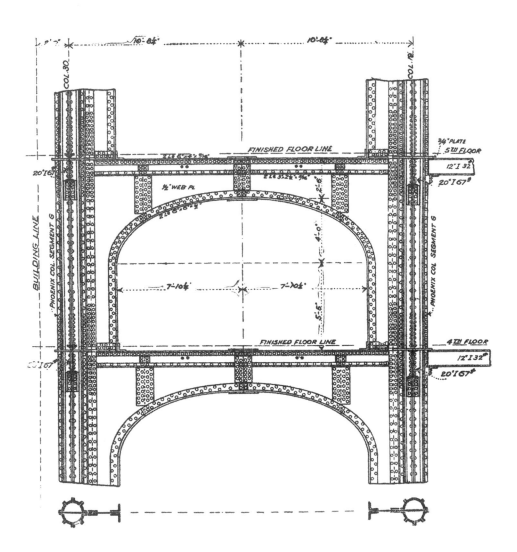

FIGURE 2.60
Portal frame showing the column relation to a portal frame.
Source: Birkmire 1894, 199.

Fairly soon after production began, plates, angles, and beams continued to be hot rolled and larger beam and column sections would be added. In 1900 ASTM A9 steel was produced with a minimum yield stress of 30,000 psi—the allowable working stress at this time was 18,000 psi. By 1948 ASTM A7 was in production with an allowable working stress of 20,000 psi. Beams, columns, plates, and smaller component shapes, such as angles, were produced in these aforementioned steels. Rivets, plates, and shapes were all produced in these and other grades of steel as well.

One problem with assessing structural steel building frames and associated parts is that it is usually not known which grade or specification of steel one is looking at. Accurately dating original components of the building provides some answer. However, later additions or modifications may have a different grade of steel in keeping with the period or possibly of the earlier production. Steels can be tested if a sample is available. A *tensile test* can determine the strength of the sample and verify if the sample is steel; knowing the strength helps determine the grade (see Figure 2.62, 2.63, and 2.64).

FIGURE 2.61
Shape combinations required
to construct a portal frame.
Source: Birkmire 1894, 200.

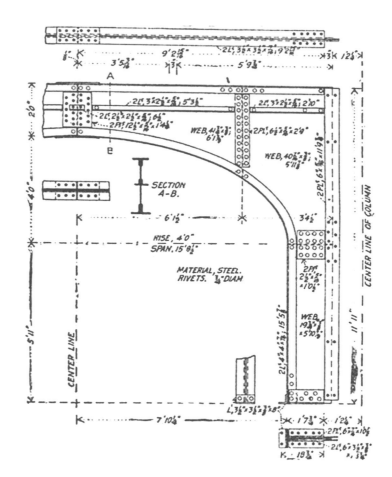

FIGURE 2.62
Engineer C. H. Becker
inspecting steel framing
at the Chicago Civic Opera.

FIGURE 2.63
Adler & Sullivan's Guaranty Building framing showing the new innovation of finishing exterior walls via a curtain wall system before ground level walls are completed.
Source: Birkmire 1898, 107.

Reinforced Concrete Construction

Reinforced concrete building frames (cast in place) had their true beginning in 1914 with the Ingalls Building in Cincinnati, Ohio. In the usual manner, a few years transpired before these structures became widely used. The near halt of construction during World War II provided a period in which concrete technology developed.

A number of engineers researched and developed reinforced concrete theory through testing full-scale models. The raw cement was also the subject of experiments, but mainly with additives and usually in a pure laboratory environment. The full-scale testing included casting and curing beams and columns with reinforcing sizes and

arrangements very closely controlled. These members were then loaded to failure and monitored throughout the process. As a consequence, and out of necessity, researchers developed and patented their own reinforcing bars, sizes, and patterns. No standardized method or coordination existed between researchers, and they produced their own design and detail specifications (see Figure 2.65 and 2.66).

In 1928 a joint committee, formed to standardize design requirements, adopted the Reinforced Concrete Building Regulations. This code lasted approximately 10 years with revisions and updates. On slab systems, use of drop panels at the top of columns—to prevent *punching shear*—is a standard way to identify the date and type

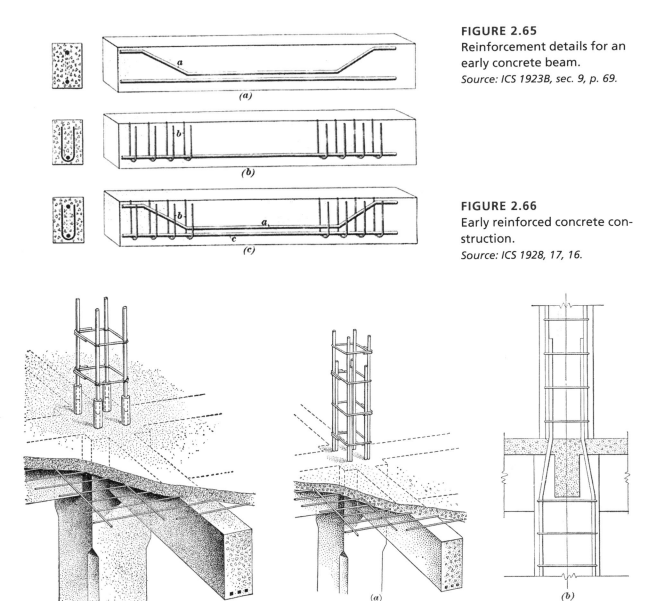

FIGURE 2.65
Reinforcement details for an early concrete beam.
Source: ICS 1923B, sec. 9, p. 69.

FIGURE 2.66
Early reinforced concrete construction.
Source: ICS 1928, 17, 16.

of construction (see Figure 2.67 and 2.68). The code of today grew out of these regulations in 1937. Reinforcement was standardized with the acceptance of the ACI Building Code Requirements for Reinforced Concrete, ACI 318, which also brought about uniform design requirements.

Early in the period of reinforced concrete construction, a number of terra-cotta shapes were used as spacers or fillers between uniquely shaped reinforced concrete beams. This was before cast-in-place reinforced beams and slabs became common and when terra-cotta was being used in fireproofing (see Figure 2.69 through 2.71). Also during this time, concrete engineers developed their own patented systems that were mainly the size and configuration of the reinforcing. They marketed their systems through catalogues and load tables (see Figure 2.72 through 2.74).

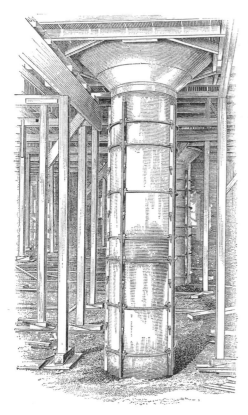

FIGURE 2.67 (left)
Reinforced concrete column shear capital for a floor slab.
Source: ICS 1923B, sec. 9, p. 79.

FIGURE 2.68 (right)
Reinforced concrete column shear capital and a shear block for a floor slab.
Source: ICS 1928, 13.

The assessment of a reinforced concrete building structure is highly dependent upon the date of the original construction, which helps to ascertain a possible design methodology. In the absence of any specific date, an approximate date can be assumed. If the occupant use of the building is not changing, it may be acceptable to the local authority to consider the reinforced concrete frame as adequate. If further analysis is necessary to satisfy local authorities, certification may be possible through load testing under the direction of a licensed engineer.

Fire Stairs

Reinforced concrete buildings of this era would exist mainly from about 1920 to 1950. Many had properly enclosed stairways that may qualify as fire stairs today. In some instances, the discharge at the ground floor may not be on an exterior wall. Even if this is the case, the codes allow a rated corridor to a door on an exterior wall. If additional fire stairs are required by code, it is relatively easy on a reinforced concrete structure to add one by sawing the required openings in the slabs. A licensed engineer can then certify the cutting position and necessary repairs can be made to the structure if needed. Usually the cinderblock construction of the enclosure walls will suffice to be built up to the bottom of the slab at the line of the saw cut. If code officials require the refuge areas for wheelchairs, they can be included in the design of any new fire stairs. Space has to be found to add refuge areas at the entrance ends of any existing stairs if needed to conform.

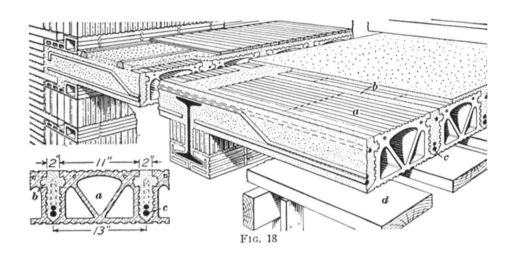

FIGURE 2.69
Combined concrete floor system with terra-cotta shapes acting in combination with reinforced concrete shapes to create one-way floor systems.
Source: ICS 1919, 35.

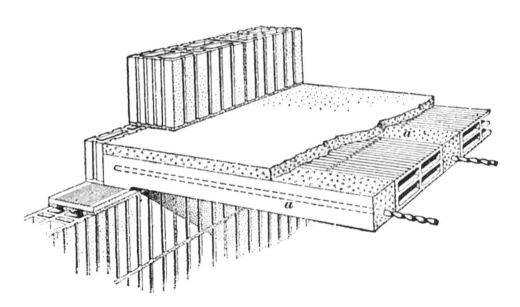

FIGURE 2.70
Composite Concrete Floor System utilizing a hollow flat terra-cotta shape as filler between cast in place concrete floor sections (almost like beams, but dependent upon each other to comprise a floor).
Source: ICS 1919, 39.

Buildings from 1950 to the Present

Modern Structural Steel Construction

Modern steel construction after 1950 has taken on a slightly different appearance than the previous period. The steel shapes have not changed, however, modern designers use the *W-shape* predominantly and basically in singular use (not doubled at the outside edge of building). The use of bolts rather than rivets during this period eliminated riveting and that noise entirely. Also, *shop welding* of connection assemblies, with bolts used during erection, is a post-1950 design and construction mechanism (see Figures 2.75 through 2.78, the color plates).

Curtain wall systems became lighter and employed a new range of materials as heavy stone, marbles, granites, and cast stone became too expensive on all but some

FIGURE 2.71
Combined concrete floor system with terra-cotta shapes acting as spacers and infill spaces with a topping slab.
Source: ICS 1919, 40.

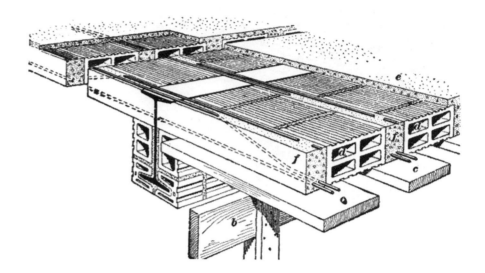

FIGURE 2.72
Longitudinal and shear reinforcing for a simple span concrete beam.
Source: Reid 1907, 247.

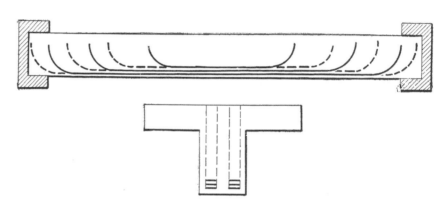

FIGURE 2.73
Patented reinforcing system for a concrete beam.
Source: ICS 1905B, sec. 13, p. 71

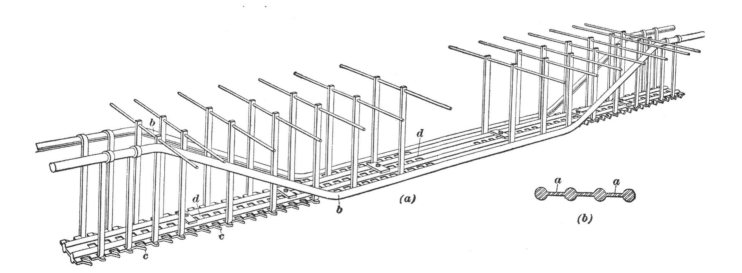

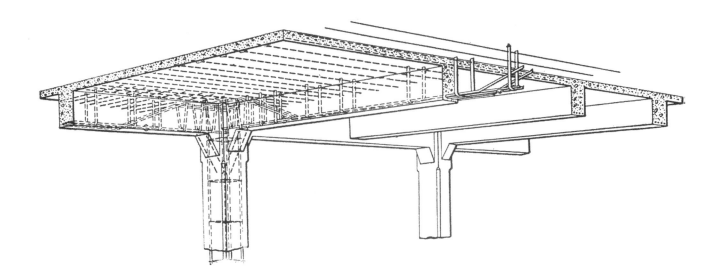

FIGURE 2.74
Reinforced concrete column, beam, and slab intersection
Source: Reid 1907, 512.

institutional buildings. Lighter panels of synthetic materials and glass curtain walls became popular.

Field welding and rigid-frame steel construction were design innovations that brought about a generally lighter frame. Columns would almost always be hot-rolled sections rather than built-up sections. And Z-sections were discontinued not long into this period.

Lightweight, cold-formed steel studs were developed and came into general use for nonload-bearing partitions as shown in Figure 2.79 (see the color plates). They have advantages in fire ratings for tennant separation. Gypsum board (Sheetrock) is the product of choice for the entire period for interior wall finishes. Acoustical ceiling tiles are dominant for this period, as they are mounted within tracks suspended from the bottom of joists, beams, girders, and corrugated metal decking (for floor slab above). The tracks are a lightweight special-formed grid that enables the ceiling tiles to be removed and replaced as needed to make modifications to any system between the ceiling tiles and the structure above.

Fireproofing can now be achieved with a spray-on application of fibrous material, water-based, with a primer adhesive as required and a final coat sealer. Modern spray-on fireproofing to protect structural steels is easily identifiable if access to this basic element of the structure is possible.

Synthetic stucco is very popular at present. It is normally applied on exterior surfaces as a weatherproof final enclosure. It has had a multitude of problems, but if used properly on commercial applications, it has a viable place in the market. The application of the synthetic stucco is troweled by hand in successive coats. It is placed over a plastic or metal mesh similar to the expanded metals that were used on cement stucco in the period from 1900 to 1950. The material is attached to an insulating fiberboard that is semistructural. The fiberboard is attached to metal studs with screws. In residential uses, the mesh is applied to a vapor barrier on the particle board sheathing. If the enclosure is too tight, the system is not allowed to breathe and condensation is trapped at the face of the particle board, which then causes deterioration and damp rot that attracts termites when the stucco is taken to ground level.

Preengineered Steel Buildings

Preengineered steel buildings are unique to this period and are used on long-span, open-warehouse-type structures that must be kept free of columns. Most are gable-type roof structures that feature a *haunch* at the connection between the column and rafter. On these buildings, the preengineered frame is actually of three-hinged, arch-type construction. Roof pitch would normally be plus or minus 5 to 12 feet. However, the type is adaptable for churches when a higher pitch provides a more acceptable design. The preengineered steel building normally serves a use that requires storage space as well as an office layout for self-contained business use; larger ones accommodate a second floor within the structure, as the roof slope would provide adequate height in the vicinity of the ridge.

Modern Reinforced Concrete Construction

Modern reinforced concrete construction utilizes a standard type *deformed rebar* that comes in size numbers from 3 to 11, 14, and 18 with the size numbers corresponding to one-eighth of an inch in diameter. Modern concretes are tightly controlled by ASTM and ACI provisions, and mixes can be proportioned to result in a range of ultimate strengths from 2,000 to 10,000 psi and greater. Most of the very high strength concretes are for specialty uses. Building construction utilizes 3,000 to 5,000 psi concrete. Additives are common, with the most common ones being air entrainment (for several reasons including workability) and a high early strength additive (to provide an accelerated cure). In many modern structures (typically concrete slab on metal deck), the roof slab is of a lightweight insulating concrete.

Cast-in-Place Reinforced Concrete

Cast-in-place reinforced concrete, as the name implies, is cast in forms and in sequence through the building until the frame is completed. This construction is fairly labor intense and has a curing time requirement that is not always desirable for the construction schedule. Standard concrete requires a 28-day curing time before loads can be attained. Unless additives are used, most designers will not allow formwork to be removed until 24 to 28 days after a pour or when test cylinders show sufficient strength.

As can be easily envisioned, the cast-in-place reinforced concrete structure requires a longer construction period than other types of modern construction (see Figure 2.80; Figure 2.81 in the color plates).

Prestressed Concrete Construction

Prestressed concrete construction utilizes beams (standard beams, single tees, and double tees), girders, and floor planks cast in controlled plant conditions and utilizing prestressed cables as reinforcing. The cables are normally prestressed to 270 ksi (kilo pounds per square inch) tension in forms, and the concrete is cast. Most prestressing yards actually cast long sections (as long as 500 to 600 feet)—whatever is required by the job. The sections are cut to length, which includes cutting the cables, while the tension is still on the cables, and the cables compress the concrete. This stresses the concrete in compression and creates the prestressed condition.

The design concept is that gravity loading removes part of the compression in the tension zone of the flexural member. The compression in the compression zone should

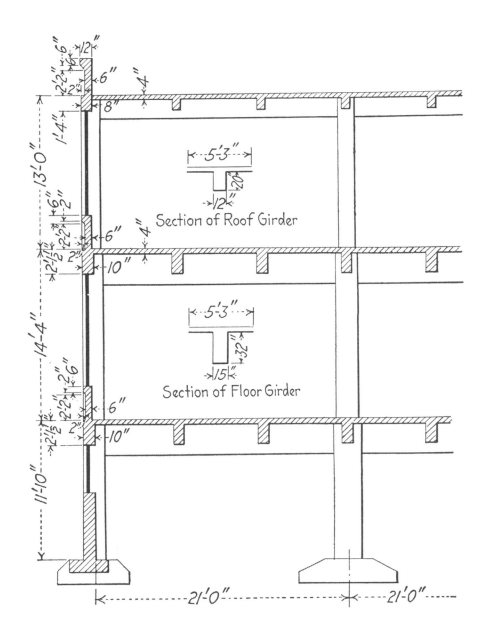

FIGURE 2.80
Reinforced concrete
construction.
*Source: Urquhart and O'Rourke
1926, 220.*

not exceed the maximum allowable. Prestressed concrete is limited and designs that utilize the method are kept in the simple frame concept that does not utilize continuity or "negative moments" at supports. Figure 2.82 (the color plates) presents two photographs of a building of block construction with prestressed concrete planks as its floor system. The next floor of block is laid directly on top of the prestressed concrete planks. The blocks supporting the planks are filled with concrete and two rebar in each core. Lintels over doors and windows are plain precast concrete.

Posttensioned Concrete Construction:

Posttensioned concrete construction is as slow as cast-in-place construction and is actually a modified form of that kind of construction. It takes formwork as detailed as the cast-in-place construction, and the beams, girders, and slabs are cast with conduits in the locations where reinforcement is required. After a curing period, cables are inserted in the conduits, and the stressing takes place in this postperiod and only after this step can the forms be removed. Cables are stressed to 270 ksi, one by one. When stressed, wedges are driven manually into the conduit (encased in concrete) to hold the cables as the tensioning is released. This method is more usable for certain requirements than the prestressed method. Continuity (i.e., continuous members, beam-to-column connections, etc.) can be achieved, as conduits and cables can be located in both the lower and upper zones of the members (see Figure 2.83 and Figure 2.84 in the color plates). A popular form of this construction is the use of slabs-only-type floor construction, rather than slabs with beams and the like. Two-way slabs of adequate thickness can replace the need for beams between slabs.

Electrical Systems: CHAPTER 3
Background

Historical Review of Electrical Systems

Understanding the existing electrical system is essential for safety, occupant comfort, productivity, and satisfaction when considering a building for adaptive reuse. In new buildings it typically composes 10 to 15 percent of the construction cost. In existing buildings, it can be even larger. When possible, the existing system should be maintained. However, it is not unusual to find electric supplies and wiring to be obsolete, inadequate, or even hazardous for modern usages.

In this section we look at the three phases of building electrification. This survey covers the original systems and includes discussions of lighting, signal, and vertical transportation systems.

Pre–Civil War Buildings

Prior to late 1800s no building was wired for electricity. For this reason, obviously, structures in their original condition do not have electrical systems. If any of these early structures have electricity, it would have been installed after its original construction—often with some degree of change to the original character of the structure because pre–Civil War buildings were not built with accessible cavity spaces in which to hide conduit and wiring. For these reasons, the character and functionality of pre–Civil War buildings should be evaluated based on the date of electrification and the feasibility, aesthetics, and cost of installing new or upgraded electrical systems.

Buildings 1860 to 1950

If one discounts the use of candles and lanterns, the first lighting systems in buildings constructed before the availability of electric power were lit by gas. Structures built after the Civil War and up until about the 1890s had pipes and fittings that supplied gas from a central utility. When these buildings were electrified, the gas lighting system was often removed or capped. These structures, too, had to be retrofitted with electric wires and supplies in the late 1800s when utility companies made electricity available. Electricity was very much in demand for commercial and institutional structures, especially those in which vertical transportation systems—elevators and escalators—required electricity to operate. Thus, in a matter of years, electricity use became virtually universal.

The electrical systems installed during this era are very likely obsolete by today's standards and needs. Conduits can be reused if their location and size are suitable. But in general a completely new electrical system is necessary.

Post-1950 Buildings

During the postwar years following World War II, electrical power systems developed into their current form. Components such as transformers, switchboards and panels, overcurrent protection, and modern wire insulation materials were installed during this time. More often than not, if their capacity is adequate, the electrical systems in most postwar structures are generally suitable for continued use. Air-conditioning, often the largest end-use of electricity, became common in residential, commercial and institutional buildings. The introduction of electronics such as communications systems, computers, security systems, and the like have also greatly changed the distribution of electric power end use. But the increased energy use has been partially offset by introduction of many new energy-saving technologies.

Identification and Evaluation

The next sections describe how to identify the types of electrical systems found in existing buildings under consideration for adaptive reuse. Guidance is also provided for making the right decisions about upgrade and replacement.

Determining the Type of System

A simple walk-through and visual observation are helpful in identifying the system. Tools to have include flashlights, camera, pen and paper or recorder, and measuring tape. Simple voltmeters are helpful but not essential. Identification can begin in the occupied space or the electrical room. Concentrate on the things one sees in every building but probably do not think about consciously: light fixtures, daylight coming through windows, building orientation, electrical receptacles, fire alarms, emergency lighting, and electrical panels. Compare your observations with the clues below. Look for closed doors that may lead to electrical spaces. Observe conduits, wiring, panels, and motors where visible. In electrical rooms, observe the external appearance of equipment. The external appearance usually indicates the age and even internal condition. Record the nameplate information for major items such as motors, transformers, and panels. This helps date and identify the equipment. Look for labels, service logs, schematic drawings, and other important paper documentation pasted on electric service boxes.

Electrical Power Systems

Most commercial and institutional buildings are supplied with three-phase electrical power systems at 208 volts. If the utility power is from an overhead supply on poles, the transformers are often hung on the nearest pole. Figure 3.1 shows a pole-mounted transformer. A set of three transformers (Figure 3.2) indicates a three-phase system as contrasted with the single transformer of a single-phase system. If the building transformers are in a single steel enclosure at ground level or inside, as shown in Figure 3.3,

FIGURE 3.1
A single pole-mounted transformer indicates a single-phase electric service for a residence or small commercial building. The capacity for large motors is limited.

the nameplate should describe the type of system. The three-phase system is preferable, because it allows more durable, more efficient, and larger motors. Very large buildings—100,000 square feet and larger —and industrial buildings may have three–phase systems at 480 volts. This higher voltage system allows smaller and thus less expensive wiring. The nameplate on the switchboard (Figure 3.4), the large electrical panel where the electrical service comes into the building, identifies the type of system. A rough estimate of the installed electrical capacity of the building can be made by multiplying the ampere rating of the service switch or circuit breaker by the voltage. The answer will be in watts and when this is divided by the gross area of the building, the power density in watts per square feet (W/sf) is obtained. For three-phase systems, multiply the result by the square root of three: 1.732.

Power density *W/sf* = Amperes × Volts [single phase]

Power density *W/sf* = Amperes × Volts × 1.732 [three phase]

Estimating electrical capacity in this way helps us understand whether the existing electrical system has the capacity for the new use. Typical new commercial building power densities range from about 8 W/sf to 15 W/sf.

FIGURE 3.2
Three pole-mounted transformers indicate a three-phase electric service for a commercial building. This system is more capable and flexible than a single-phase system.

FIGURE 3.3
A pad-mounted transformer for a commercial building indicates an underground electric service that is more aesthetically pleasing than an overhead service.

FIGURE 3.4
The switchboard is the entry and main distribution point for electrical power. The photograph shows a relatively new electrical switchboard and branch circuit panels for a small commercial building.

FIGURE 3.5
Surface-mounted fluorescent lighting installed in a previous renovation has high contrast between the bright lens and the darker ceiling around the luminaire. The exposed surface raceway is unattractive.

Residential and small commercial buildings are normally supplied with single-phase 240-volt systems. Motors up to about five horsepower can be obtained in single-phase so this system is satisfactory for buildings with approximately five tons of air-conditioning or multiples of systems of this size or smaller. Air-cooled unitary air-conditioners develop about one ton of cooling per horsepower.

Lighting Systems

Since the 1940s, interior lighting has been dominated by fluorescent light sources. These are readily identified by their familiar tubular shapes. The standard lamps for many years have been the 1.5" diameter T-12 lamps, which come in four- and eight-

FIGURE 3.6
New semidirect fluorescent luminaires reduce the contrast between the luminaire and the adjacent ceiling by directing some light onto the ceiling. This reduces glare and improves comfort.

FIGURE 3.7
Electrical room in a remodeled building showing meters, panels, and conduits (identified by arrows)

foot lengths. These lamps were commonly used in fixtures with plastic prismatic lenses (see Figure 3.5). While existing fluorescent systems continue in service, it may be more economical to replace them with newer lamp types discussed in this chapter. In general, new fluorescent or *high-intensity discharge* (HID) lamps cannot simply be inserted into existing sockets. They must have matching ballasts to function properly. Current office and school-lighting designs utilize indirect or semi-indirect fixtures like those in Figure 3.6 to minimize glare, so it may be preferable to convert the lighting to this style instead of simply replacing sockets and ballasts to use high-efficiency T-8 or T-5 lamps in existing fixtures.

For lighting systems—and electrical outlet supplies—the components associated with these systems should be evaluated for reuse. Concealed raceways, conduit tubing, panel boxes, and the like (see Figure 3.7) can be very expensive to replace. Thus every effort should be made to incorporate them into the new use. Nameplate information from components, as mentioned previously, can help identify system age and type in subsequent discussions with electrical engineers, manufacturers, and the like.

Communication Systems

Communication systems include telephone, computer network cable (e.g., CAT5, CAT6), cable television, time clock systems, public address systems—and building automation (discussed at the end of this chapter). The suitability of some of these systems specific to some previous use (school, factory, etc.) may not always fit with adaptive reuse plans. Often the decision making comes down to disconnecting them, leaving them in place, salvaging them, or removing and disposing them.

Fire and Security Alarm Systems

Like communication systems, fire and security alarms are probably not usable in adaptive reuse. Sometimes fire alarm systems can be used in part. Again, such "infrastructure" as raceways (conduit), pull stations, sprinkler plumbing, alarms, horns, annunciator panels, and main panels can be used again. Here nameplate information helps identify system age and type for obtaining service and parts.

Vertical Transportation Systems

Early elevator systems were powered by novel means with steam, hydraulic pressure, and electricity. By the 1920s electric motor-driven traction elevators had emerged as the dominant technology for mid- and high-rise buildings and other structures in which elevators had been installed or retrofit. Direct current motors allowed satisfactory speed control for passenger elevators as shown in Figure 3.8. Less-expensive, geared alternating current motors were used for freight elevator service as shown in Figure 3.9 and for simple passenger elevators in buildings with fewer floors as shown in Figure 3.10.

Clues to System Type

A major difference in electrical systems is that between residential and commercial wiring. Commercial building and high-rise residential wiring must be in conduit as shown in Figure 3.11. Low-rise residential wiring may be installed with nonmetallic (see Figure 3.12) or armored cable (see Figure 3.13). Such differences should be observed.

Three-phase power systems for commercial uses have three power wires and a neutral (in white insulation) wire in the service. (This is the main wiring connecting the

FIGURE 3.8
Gearless traction elevators have long been the standard for passenger service. This figure depicts the entire system of a 1920s gearless traction passenger elevator with the motor in the penthouse.
Source: Gay 1947, Copyright © 1947 John Wiley & Sons. Reprinted with permission of John Wiley & Sons.

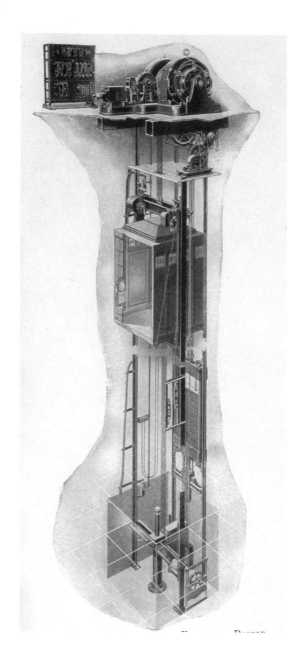

utility power to the building.) Single-phase power systems for small commercial and residential systems have two power wires and a grounded neutral (white insulation) wire. Electrical panels typically have nameplates identifying their type and capacity.

Elevator motors, motors for garage door openers, heating and air-conditioning equipment, and the like will also have nameplates giving electrical characteristics, manufacturer's data, and other information for determining if they can be retrofit into a new use. Record this information when inspecting the building's electric and related systems.

Figure 3.14 shows a gearless traction machine in a 20-story former office building being converted to residential condominiums. Geared machines have a distinctive second axle at 90 degrees to the motor axis.

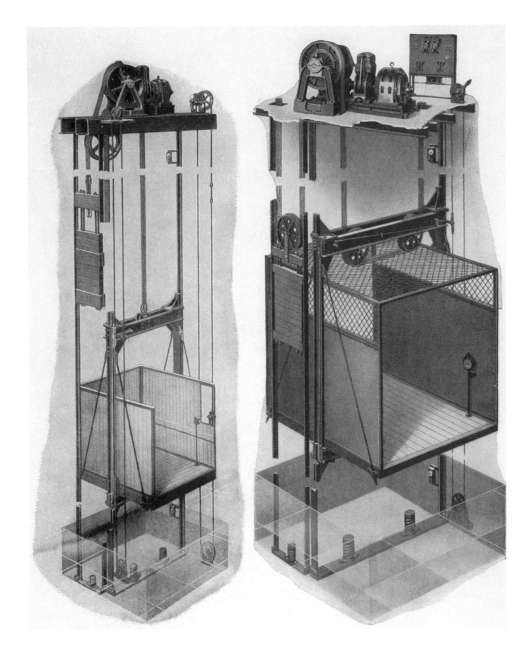

FIGURE 3.9
Freight elevators do not require the speed and smooth operation of passenger elevators, so they commonly are lower-cost geared type. Those shown in this figure have the motor in the penthouse at the top of the hoistway.
Source: Gay 1947, Copyright © 1947 John Wiley & Sons. Reprinted with permission of John Wiley & Sons.

Operating Condition

Visual inspection of electrical devices and panels provides useful information about their current and past condition as well as the systems of which they are a part. Electrical faults almost always result in heating and sometimes fire. If an electrical device or panel has scorched or blackened areas, this is a sure sign of a previous or even ongoing problem such as loose connections. Here the connection is not forcing good electrical continuity between the conductor and the terminal, so additional resistance is introduced and this resistance generates heat. The consequence is discoloration and deterioration of the area, arcing and sparking, and even smoke or fire at the terminal. Connections covered with plastic electrical tape may be indicative of poor workmanship.

FIGURE 3.10
Low-rise buildings sometimes have geared passenger elevators such as the one shown here. They are slower than the gearless type. Here the motor is on the lowest floor served.
Source: Gay 1947, Copyright © 1947 John Wiley & Sons. Reprinted with permission of John Wiley & Sons.

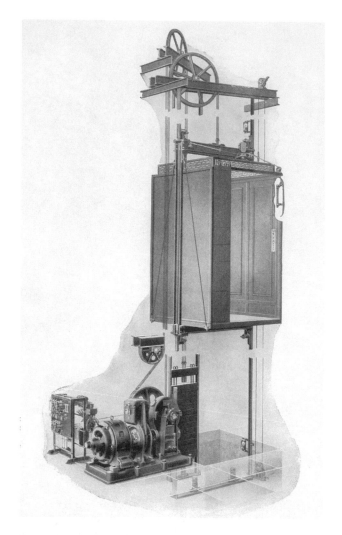

FIGURE 3.11
Electrical wiring in commercial buildings must be installed in conduit. Here an exposed box ready for a duplex receptacle with the wiring already pulled through the exposed conduit.

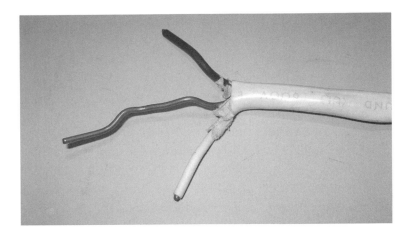

FIGURE 3.12
Electrical wiring in residential buildings can be nonmetallic cable, an assembly of insulated wires in a plastic jacket also known as Type NM and colloquially by the brand name *Romex*.

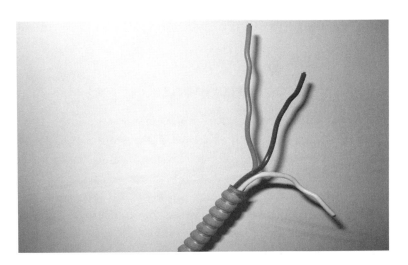

FIGURE 3.13
Electrical wiring in residential buildings can also be armored cable. This is a manufactured assembly of insulated wires identified as *Type AC*.

FIGURE 3.14
A gearless traction elevator machine at the top of a hoistway in a high-rise office being converted to residential condominiums. It will continue in service.

Cracked insulation on wires is often a sign of other problems or neglect. Receptacles with only the two slots and no third hole for an equipment ground conductor often indicate an obsolete system that must be replaced. Aluminum branch circuit wires at receptacles or switches indicate a need for new copper wires. Aluminum wire in small sizes has not proven safe and is no longer permitted.

The cost of copper has historically been quite volatile. At the time of this writing, because of the increased commodity values of copper and other metals, theft of these materials from buildings has become an all-too-common problem. Such theft, which is typically visible and usually comes with collateral damage of walls, ceilings, panel boxes, and the like, can often be detected during a visual inspection. Such thefts can add considerably to the cost of adaptive reuse.

Chapter 8, "Testing," has more specific information on the operating condition of motors and equipment, performing amperage tests under load, infrared thermometer scans, and high-potential insulation testing in order to determine defects in electrical systems.

Evaluation of Performance

Lighting is undergoing dramatic improvements at the time of this writing. Fluorescent lighting is available in highly efficient T-5 lamps and convenient compact lamps. *Light-emitting diode* (LED) lamps are quickly approaching commercial use. It is now possible to adequately illuminate office and classroom spaces with power densities of about 1 watt per square foot. Therefore, in general, it is feasible to replace existing lighting with the newer sources unless historical appearance is paramount. Since these sources are more efficient and use less power, the existing wiring and panels may be suitable for reuse if the locations of fixtures are satisfactory. Observe the existing lighting as it relates to new room configurations, illumination of surfaces, and conformity in appearance with the new interior.

FIGURE 3.15
Surface raceways may be necessary when new wiring cannot be installed in cavities. This concrete block construction does not lend itself to concealed rewiring.

Evaluation of Suitability for New Application

Existing electrical systems can sometimes continue in service when a building is adapted to a new use. Obviously, if the system meets the needs of the new use, retaining it is the least expensive option. Once the existing system type is identified and its condition and performance evaluated, and results indicate potential for continued use, several issues must be addressed. These issues are discussed next.

Available Space

In building electrical systems, space is a concern mainly for panel locations and routing wires. When existing panel locations are not suitable for the new use, that the new panels will usually be smaller than older panels must be factored in. If new locations

FIGURE 3.16
Electrical communication wiring may have to be installed on an exterior wall during an adaptive reuse project if the construction does not permit access to cavities inside.

FIGURE 3.17
Surface-mounted panels and raceways can mar the appearance of historic structures when concealed wiring is not feasible.

are necessary, space for electrical closets must be allocated. In brick construction, it is impossible to run new wiring unless furred spaces on the face of the masonry are provided. In hollow-concrete-block construction, it may be possible to "fish" new cables through the cavities if permitted. Hollow-wall construction, using wood or metal studs, makes the installation of new cable or raceways easy, although patching of existing finish material may be required after installation. If other options fail, several types of surface raceways, such as the kind shown in Figure 3.15, are available. In some cases wiring in conduits must be exposed outside the building as shown in Figure 3.16.

Conformance with Character of the Building

Electrical systems are usually not part of historic buildings, so minimizing the visual impact of equipment and wiring is necessary. Visual conformity rules out surface raceways and panels as shown in Figure 3.17. Such rules dictate that existing light fixtures must be preserved or that new fixtures must be carefully chosen to conform. It may be possible to substitute compact fluorescent lamps for the incandescent lamps that were originally used in the fixtures.

Electrical Code

Across the United States, electrical work in buildings must conform to the local electrical code. In most cases, it is the National Electrical Code, NFPA 70. If the cost of the work is half or more of the value of the building, existing electrical systems must be also brought up to current code requirements.

Energy Efficiency

The electrical power distribution system consumes very little electrical energy. It is electrical devices, such as lighting and motors, that consume energy and whose efficiency is important. Lighting in particular is a major power user. However, as noted in the section "Evaluation of Performance" (page 106), major improvements in efficiency are being made. This is doubly important for air-conditioned buildings, because the energy used by the lights must then be removed by the cooling system in warm weather. (Conversely, in winter, heat from lighting is beneficial for spaces on the building perimeter.)

A second major electrical user is the air-conditioning system. In most of the United States, it rivals lighting as the greatest electrical load. Though to a lesser degree than lighting, efficiency improvements are taking place in cooling technology also. While it is probably not cost effective to remove a functioning air-conditioning system just to replace it with a more efficient one, if the existing system does not meet new control-zone needs or is approaching the end of its useful life, then efficiency should be part of the consideration of a replacement decision.

Life-Cycle Cost

Investments in new or replacement electrical systems and equipment are often decided on code or capacity need issues rather than discretion. However, some choices in electrical systems may be made based on return on investment. In these cases the use of life-cycle cost analysis provides the best information, a topic that is discussed in detail in Chapter 6.

Sustainability

The electrical distribution system is designed to supply power to devices—not to the panels and conductors—whose efficiency is important. Newer devices are almost always more efficient than older devices. High-efficiency transformers and fan and pump motors usually are more expensive, but cost savings and reductions in electrical power and attendant air pollutants and greenhouse gases can be significant. This is one area where life-cycle cost analysis between choices of efficiency levels may be justified.

On the other hand, continuing to use existing equipment is sustainable in the sense that no new resources are required. However, the LEED® (Leadership in Energy and Environmental Design) Green Building Rating System gives credits for reuse or continuing to use existing building components while specifically excluding mechanical, plumbing, and electrical systems.

Electrical Power Systems

If the project is conversion to residential, existing raceways may be used for new wiring. If the conversion is from residential to commercial, it will probably be necessary to rewire the building to provide wire in conduit, except on a very small scale. The power density (watts per square foot) in commercial buildings is usually considerably higher than in residential buildings, so larger panels and conductors and more receptacles are indicated.

Lighting Systems

In buildings with relatively new lighting systems, it may be feasible to continue the systems in use. Criteria on which to base this decision include the efficacy (lumens per watt) of the sources, the density of light (foot-candles) on the work plane, and the glare conditions produced by the fixtures. New fixtures and lamps will almost always require less power than existing systems, so existing conductors should be adequate.

Light from the sun—*daylighting*—was essential in buildings before fluorescent lighting was widely available. However, during the latter part of the twentieth century, building designers chose to use electrical lighting instead of natural light. The idea was to minimize summer solar heat gain by minimizing window area since available conventional window glass transmitted much of the solar spectrum into the space. This transition was also facilitated by powerful cooling systems that were now affordable and the cost of electricity was low. Earlier, daylighting often resulted in undesirable glare as well.

FIGURE 3.18
Window glass available today can be selected to minimize solar heat gain through windows. The solar spectral performance of some coated window glasses shows high visible light transmittance and low infrared transmittance.

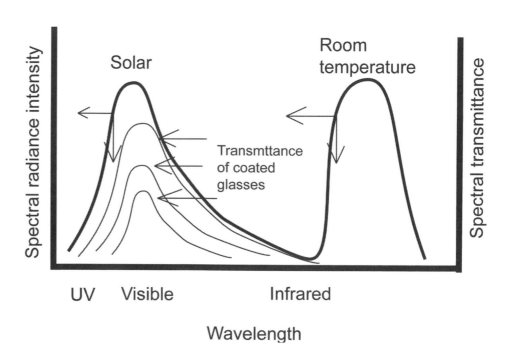

Buildings designed to use daylight usually had windows in most or all rooms, or skylights or clerestory windows overhead. It is now recognized that in spite of the rapid improvements in electrical light sources, daylighting is still desirable from the standpoint of occupant satisfaction as well as energy efficiency. The most efficient watt of electricity is still the one not used. If the building under consideration was designed so many of its spaces have access to daylight, it is prudent to consider taking advantage of this in the reuse. Studies have shown that occupant satisfaction and productivity can be improved by utilizing natural lighting.

Many advances have been made in the technology and techniques of daylighting. Optimal use of these daylighting improvements makes it feasible to incorporate these into a reuse project. For example, window glass that blocks most of the infrared and ultraviolet portions of the solar spectrum while transmitting much of the visible portion is now available at affordable prices. Figure 3.18 shows the spectral performance of such a glass with a low-e coating. The measure of thermal performance is the *solar heat gain coefficient* (SHGC) or sometimes the *shading coefficient* (SC). The SHGC is defined as the fraction of incident solar heat that penetrates through the glass to the interior. The SC is defined as the amount of solar heat penetrating the glass divided by the amount of that heat that would penetrate a sheet of one-eighth-inch thick clear glass. Thus smaller is better in both cases. The two measures can be approximately equated by SC equals 1.15 SHGC. The best glass is one that has the highest ratio of visible light transmittance to radiant heat transmittance. Insulating glass cuts the conductive heat loss in the winter and the conductive gain in the summer in half.

FIGURE 3.19
Designing or redesigning for the use of daylight is usually effective if electric lights are controlled to dim or turn off when daylight is sufficient. Light shelves such as these near the top of a window can enhance the distribution of natural light.

Designers now usually strive to eliminate direct beam radiation and optimize indirect or reflected daylight. External movable shades or internal adjustable shades can control that direct beam sunlight and glare. External overhangs effectively shade south-facing windows while vertical fins work best on east- and west-facing windows.

Light shelves can be added to existing windows to improve daylighting performance as shown in Figure 3.19. The shelf is inserted one-half to three-quarters the window height, but above eye level. The top surface of the light shelf acts to reflect the light entering through the glass above the shelf toward the back of the room. The shelf also is a shade that reduces the direct solar radiation on the floor area near the window. Its relative position vertically in the window and horizontally inside and outside must be determined by graphic analysis or experimentally. It can be constructed of lightweight materials to minimize new support requirements.

Light tubes or light pipes are also being used for daylighting. In some buildings where preservation of the roof's appearance is not an issue, light tubes are a solution in transporting or distributing natural or artificial light.

Communication Systems

As discussed earlier in the chapter, it is not likely that existing communications systems will be reusable under adaptive reuse conditions. Even the most common system, the telephone, has undergone major changes in recent years and existing internal components such as wiring are probably obsolete.

FIGURE 3.20
When multiple tenants occupy a reused building, it is economical to provide an electrical meter for each tenant. Multiple electrical meters installed during adaptive reuse to an office or condo project makes occupants responsible for their use of electrical power.

FIGURE 2.7
Rising damp at floor level:
Church building with water
against foundations and
basement walls.

FIGURE 2.8
Rising damp showing efflorescent salts above floor level.

FIGURE 2.9
Building exterior with liquid membrane injection holes just above sidewalk.

FIGURE 2.10
Building with descending damp coming from water getting into the parapet wall above.

FIGURE 2.31
Gypsum block partition.

FIGURE 2.42
Cast-iron building facade
in unrestored condition,
Memphis, Tennessee.

FIGURE 2.43
Cast-iron building facades in unrestored condition in Louisville, Kentucky's Cast-Iron District.

FIGURE 2.75
Sixty-foot steel truss supported by latticed steel columns.

FIGURE 2.76
Structural steel frame
showing diagonal bracing.

FIGURE 2.78
Diagonal bracing for lateral
loads on a mid-rise building.

FIGURE 2.77
Rigid-frame structural steel
building under construction.

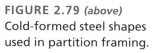

FIGURE 2.79 *(above)*
Cold-formed steel shapes used in partition framing.

FIGURE 2.81 *(top right)*
Reinforced concrete building frame in Austin, Texas.

FIGURE 2.83
Posttensioned concrete mid-rise building frame, girders, and slabs without beams.

FIGURE 2-85
Tendons of a posttensioned concrete, after posttensioning, but before tendons are cut off.

FIGURE 2.82 *(both photos at left)*
Construction of motel units using cement block and prestressed concrete plank.

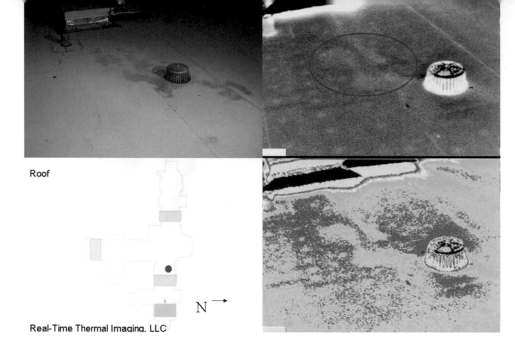

FIGURE 8.4
This photograph depicts a roof with a leak. The upper left corner contains a standard image of the roof, the upper right a black and white infrared image of the roof with the leak identified by the circle, and the lower right is a color infrared image. In this view the bright colors of the roof drain and the roof curbs indicate the heat loss through these components.
Source: Bob Melia and Barbara Melia Morris, Real Time Thermal Imaging, Mandeville, LA.

Roof

N →

Real-Time Thermal Imaging, LLC

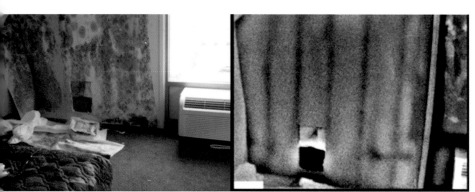

FIGURE 8.3
Three views of a wood stud construction exterior wall. On the top left is a standard photograph, on the top right is a black and white infrared photograph, and on the bottom is a colored infrared photograph. Surface temperatures result in variations in infrared radiation that can be detected. The temperature differences are caused by heat flowing through materials at varying rates.
Source: Bob Melia and Barbara Melia Morris, Real Time Thermal Imaging, Mandeville, LA.

al-Time Thermal Imaging LLC

FIGURE 8.8
On the upper right is a standard photograph of the intersection of the ceiling and two walls. On the upper left is a black and white thermal image showing two very dark areas. On the lower left is a color thermal image—the dark areas are bright yellow (cooler in the color-temperature scale). The lower right image was taken in the attic space above the lobby. Two spaces between ceiling joists, corresponding to the yellow rectangles, have no insulation.
Source: Bob Melia and Barbara Melia Morris, Real Time Thermal Imaging, Mandeville, LA.

Thermal image

Normal

Color thermal image

57.2

F

44.4

EMISS=1.00   GAIN=12   RNG=1   50.1

Real-Time Thermal Imaging, LLC

Missing insul

Fire and Security Alarm Systems

Sometimes components such as the fire and smoke alarm components listed above are suitable, but not often. It is highly likely that completely new systems will be required.

Vertical Transportation Systems

Elevator and escalator systems often can be upgraded and continued in use. New electronic controls and finish materials often make them suitable for the new occupancy. The elevator machine shown in Figure 3.14 will continue to be used in the new occupancy.

Selection of New Systems

Electrical Power Systems

Standard utility power in the 208 volt, three-phase, four-wire wye system is the choice for most projects converting to commercial use. In conversions from commercial or industrial to residential use, it is frequently desirable to give each residence or apartment its own electrical meter as shown in Figure 3.20. This may allow the continued reuse of the existing three-phase system if the utility rules permit submetering of tenant property—or if the utility wishes to own and distribute through the three-phase system and give each residence its individual single-phase metered system.

With the current interest in sustainable electrical power, many owners are considering on-site generation using *photovoltaic* (PV) panels installed on the building. These panels can be mounted on the ground or upon or integral with the roof itself or on the south facade of the building. Improvements in panel technology have boosted efficiencies to the 16 percent level and, at the same time, lowered costs. At this writing the installed cost of a residential-scale PV system such as that shown in Figure 3.21 is about $8 per watt and PV-generated electrical power costs more than $0.33 per kilowatt-hour (kWh) as compared with utility power at $0.05 to $0.10 per kWh. Photovolataic power cost should continue to decline. The PV panels generate *direct current* (DC) electrical power, which is usually converted to *alternating current* (AC) via an inverter so it can be used by the conventional building system. In this form, excess power can be resold to the utility at a premium. In DC form excess power can be stored in batteries for later use. Note that in the cost comparison above, sunlight is still free, but the amortized cost of the installation is used to estimate the cost of electricity from PV systems.

Lighting Systems

New lighting for school, retail, or office spaces is almost universally fluorescent and uses the highly efficient T-5 lamps. Power densities are decreasing to 1 watt per square foot (W/sf) or less from previous levels of 3 to 4 W/sf. Luminaires are selected for indirect or semi-indirect distribution of light to minimize glare. In spaces with higher ceilings, metal halide lamps are competitive with fluorescents. In residential spaces,

FIGURE 3.21
Direct conversion of sunlight to electricity with photovoltaic panels is achieved with a residential scale photovoltaic electric power system. Systems such as this are becoming more efficient and cost-effective.

FIGURE 3.22
In some older buildings, ceiling space is limited. Computer cabling, too extensive to conceal above a new ceiling, may have to be exposed where structural beams cross the space.

compact fluorescent lamps give the traditional look and color of incandescent lamps at one-quarter the energy and ten times the life. They can be used in traditional fixtures with screw bases and integral ballasts or in newly designed fixtures with permanent ballasts.

Communication, Fire, and Security Systems

The electronics revolution of the last half of the twentieth century has continued and is providing new and expanded communication abilities in buildings. Some of them were listed above. Integrated control systems include *building automation systems* (BAS) as well as many of the traditional communication and signal systems and new data recording and management functions to operate the building. Occupancy sensing, lighting, and heating, ventilating, and air-conditioning (HVAC) control, remote monitoring and internet communications may also be incorporated. Extensive communications such as the computer cables shown in Figure 3.22 may be difficult to fit in older buildings with low floor-to-floor heights.

Mechanical Systems CHAPTER 4

Understanding the existing *heating, ventilating, and air-conditioning* (HVAC) system is essential when evaluating a building for adaptive reuse. Like the electrical systems described in the previous chapter, the HVAC system consists of expensive components and is one of the most important systems of any building occupied by people. The HVAC system is necessary for their comfort, productivity, and satisfaction.

Heating, Ventilating, and Air-Conditioning Systems: Background

In new buildings the HVAC system is typically 20 to 30 percent of the construction cost. In existing buildings, it can consume even a larger fraction of the budget if a complete replacement is required. Careful planning for reusing or replacing the HVAC System can pay dividends in these areas. For the majority of older buildings, unless they have already had some renovations, the HVAC system should probably be replaced.

Pre–Civil War Buildings

Prior to the American Civil War (1860–1865), almost all buildings of the size typically under consideration for reuse here were heated by open masonry fireplaces with chimneys. The fireplaces gave a characteristic appearance to the interior while the chimneys were dominant exterior features. It may be desirable to retain these features in the adaptive reuse to give continuity and the warmth they signify.

Continued use of the fireplaces will likely necessitate the installation of a liner within the flue and a damper in each chimney to reduce air loss up the chimney when not in use. The many air passages of the chimneys causes the building to have significantly higher rates of infiltration than other buildings and may require added heating and cooling capacity and energy use. In these cases, owners can close off or remove the fireplaces.

Comfort in warm weather was attainable by natural ventilation in buildings of this era. Consequently, operable windows, high ceilings, transoms over corridor doors, and "finger" plans of one or two rooms deep were typical. Such features can be advantageous in certain climates today. However, buildings today especially have an excess of internal heat that can be only removed by air-conditioning in warm weather. Their balance point, the outdoor temperature at which neither heating nor cooling is required, is typically in the 30°F–50°F range as charted in Figure 4.1.

Natural ventilation can often remove sufficient heat to provide comfort between this temperature and about 60°F without running the cooling system. Ventilation through open windows offers occupants a degree of thermal control that they find satisfactory and pleasing in contrast to the remote and impersonal thermostat. Many of

FIGURE 4.1
A balance-point chart reveals the building's need for heating or cooling at different outdoor temperatures. Most offices need cooling at outdoor temperatures well below room temperature. Such buildings can make use of natural ventilation or economizer cycles for energy-efficient comfort cooling. This balance-point chart for an office building shows a change from heating to cooling at 63°F.

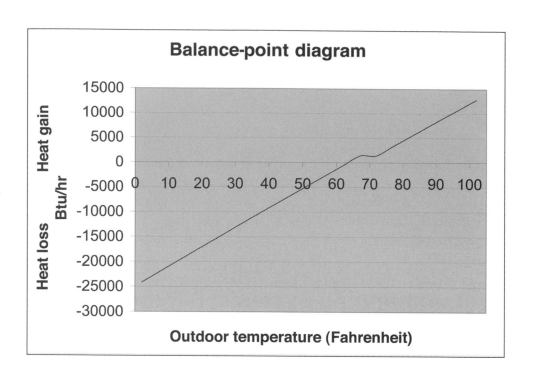

the natural ventilation features also enhance the distribution of daylight (discussed in Chapter 3). Hence it is often most efficient and sustainable to retain natural ventilation in the reuse plan.

Operable windows have disadvantages in commercial buildings. For example, windows can be inadvertently left open to admit rain, insects, excessively hot or cold air, and human intruders. A sophisticated HVAC-control system can be compromised by uncontrolled leakage. These drawbacks must be weighed against the potential advantages in making a decision on natural ventilation.

Buildings 1860 to 1950

In the middle of the nineteenth century, the steam boiler, which had been developed for pumps, rail engines, steamboats, and other machines requiring motive power, started seeing use in heating buildings. This application allowed the combustion process to be remote from the occupied area and eliminated the mess and inconvenience of carrying fuel to each fireplace. It also improved the efficiency and control of space heating. Over the last half-century, the central heating system became the norm in medium and large buildings. In large cities, such as New York and on some college campuses, district-heating systems to serve many buildings were developed. Natural ventilation, however, remained the only hope for warm weather comfort during this time.

Central Steam Heat with Radiators

Heat was typically delivered in the form of steam piped from the boiler to the radiators in occupied spaces. The cast-iron tubular radiator was the most common form (see Figure 4.2) and is familiar to most people. Steam and condensate pipes were usually

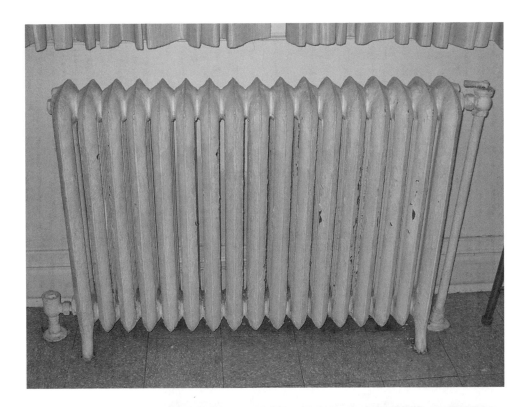

FIGURE 4.2
Cast-iron radiators were the standard way of delivering heat to multiple individual spaces until forced-air became common. This radiator uses steam as evidenced by the trap (enlarged fitting at the outlet – bottom left) and the air vent on the right end.

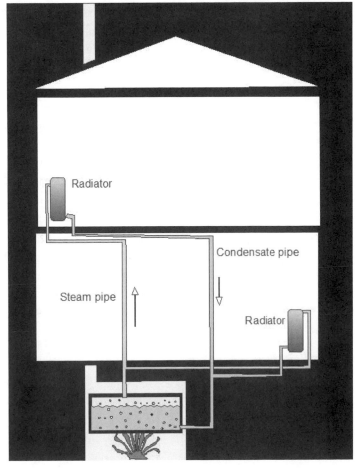

FIGURE 4.3
A complete steam-heating system with radiators in spaces. The boiler in the basement generates steam that flows by pressure to the radiators and returns as condensate by gravity.

FIGURE 4.4
The Scotch marine fire tube boiler is, and was, a common type of boiler for both steam and hot water systems in buildings. It can be fired with oil, propane, or natural gas.

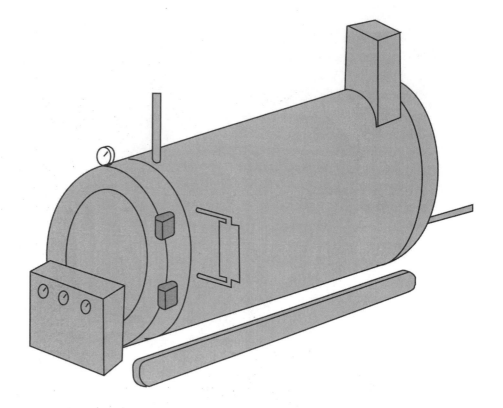

steel with screwed connections. Steam systems can be distinguished from hot water systems by the following features: traps on the outlet (lower) pipe of the radiator, air vents near the top of the radiator, water level gauges on the boiler, and large supply and small return pipes. (A schematic diagram of a steam-heating system is shown in Figure 4.3.) The most common fuel for these systems was coal, which cannot be used today without extensive air pollution controls. Many boilers were converted to oil or natural gas and may continue in operation; but they have the disadvantage of low efficiency. A typical fire-tube boiler is shown in Figure 4.4.

Steam is an efficient transport medium for heat. However, because of the high temperature—212°F at atmospheric pressure and hotter at higher temperatures—and concentrated energy, it is difficult to control the temperature in steam-heated spaces. The condensate, formed when steam gives up its heat, often has air dissolved in it, and the resulting liquid is corrosive to steel pipe. Consequently, the piping that returns condensate may be seriously corroded and need replacement. Screwed pipe connections also corrode at the threads and may not be reusable. When corroded pipes are subject to the force of unscrewing the connections, they often spring leaks. For this reason many pipefitters recommend not repairing old screwed steel pipe and, instead, removing and replacing the entire system.

Central Hot Water Systems with Radiators or Convectors

Hot water heating followed the development of steam heating and used many of the same components. Early systems used gravity to circulate lower-density hot water upward to radiators while higher-density return flows sank through return pipes back to the boiler. Pipes were large to facilitate flow driven by small density differences. The availability of small electric motors to power pumps in the early twentieth century

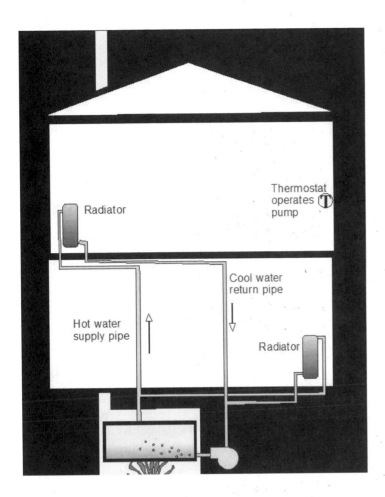

FIGURE 4.5
The technology that followed the steam system, the hot water system is more easily controlled and more flexible than steam. This schematic diagram of a forced circulation, hot water heating system shows its similarity to steam, but with a pump for water circulation.

made forced-circulation hot water possible, and these systems became very popular. Hot water systems are less susceptible to dissolved air and subsequent pipe corrosion than is steam, although the problems of screwed connections may be still present. It is quite possible to reuse all or part of such a hot water heating system such as the one in Figure 4.5 if its condition is acceptable upon inspection and it fits with other aspects of the adaptive reuse.

Gravity Warm Air Systems

Beginning in the late 1800s, gravity warm air systems were installed in upscale residences. Gravity air circulation required large ducts and large grilles in floors as shown in Figure 4.6 and would not be compatible with air-conditioning. Continued use of such a system is probably not economical when much higher-efficiency furnaces compatible with cooling are available.

Early Forced-Air Heating and Cooling Systems

In the early part of the twentieth century, larger buildings had steam-heating systems and natural, or a combination of natural and forced, ventilation. Figure 4.7 shows forced-air ventilation ducts terminating in a classroom. Since these ducts were usually formed by cavities in the structure and were not insulated, they are not usable in today's all-air heating and cooling systems.

FIGURE 4.6
Gravity warm air heating systems were popular for residences during the early part of the twentieth century. They distributed warm air from central coal, oil, or gas furnaces. The availability of electric motors for fans, and the smaller ducts of fan-powered systems, led to their decline.

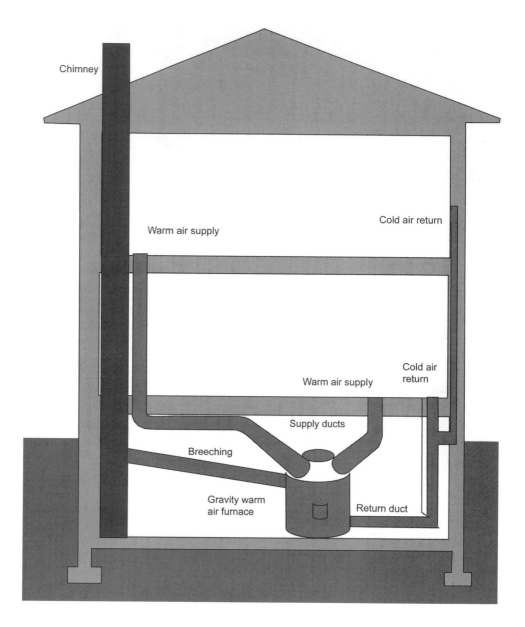

The development and commercialization of refrigeration and air-conditioning in the early 1900s made it feasible to provide fan-driven, ducted, air heating and cooling systems in larger buildings. Among the earliest users were theaters, churches, hotels, hospitals, offices, and public buildings. Industries with special humidity control requirements, such as printing and textiles, were leaders in this advancement. Reuse of components of these systems is often feasible. In particular, the ducts may be serviceable after cleaning and inspecting for leaks. Heating and cooling coils possibly can be retained if capacity is suitable and corrosion is not a problem. Boilers, as discussed earlier, may be obsolete in terms of efficiency. And refrigeration systems will be older than their expected service lives and are almost certainly not reusable.

District steam-heating systems have been in use in large cities, industrial complexes, and college campuses for a century or more. A building that has a central steam plant

FIGURE 4.7
Large buildings, before the general use of air-conditioning, depended on natural or fan-powered ventilation for summer cooling. Here room terminations of forced-air ventilation shafts in a 1920s-era building. These passages are not suitable for air-conditioning use.

available should, in most cases, continue to make use of this source. The central plant can be more efficient and sustainable than individual building boilers and can provide heat at lower cost.

Post-1950 Buildings

As U.S. industry returned to peacetime production after World War II, the availability of electric motors and the tooling to make other components for air-conditioning systems for most commercial and institutional buildings made them more affordable for their owners. A wide variety of systems evolved and many are suitable for use today. The HVAC systems in buildings of this era should be carefully analyzed for continued use.

Air Systems

Most small- and medium-sized buildings constructed after 1950 are served by systems that deliver heating and cooling through ducted air from central units. The central units may be located on roofs or in mechanical rooms with outdoor condensing units. Heating is generally provided by indirect fuel-fired furnaces or heat pumps. Air is commonly distributed at a constant flow rate and the temperature is controlled by

FIGURE 4.8
A unitary-packaged heating and cooling unit of the 1960s. Similar units are in common use today.
Source: 1967 ASHRAE Guide and Databook, Figure 3, p. 519.

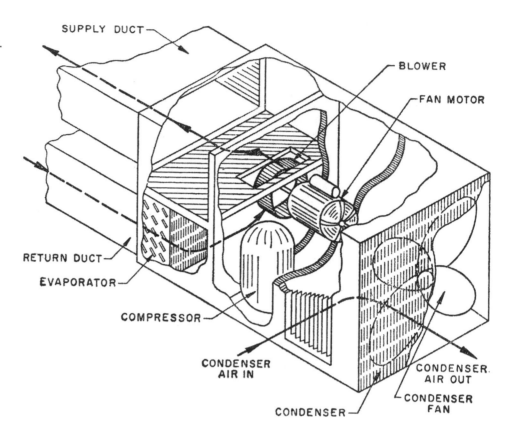

thermostats. Such a system may serve a residence or a building, or a portion of either. Most systems are single zone—that is, they have a single thermostat, no matter how many rooms are served by the same system. This may present a problem, and the issue is discussed below. A representative small air system is shown in Figure 4.8.

Small systems with self-contained refrigeration and heating systems such as the one in Figure 4.9 are sometimes identified as "unitary" systems. They are also available in a two-component configuration called a *split system*. The indoor component usually consists of a furnace and a direct-expansion refrigerant cooling coil, while the outdoor component houses the refrigeration compressor and air-cooled condenser. Such a system is depicted in Figures 4.10 and 4.11. They can have cooling capacities up to 25 tons or so. They are shipped assembled from the manufacturer with most of the necessary accessories for installation. Replacement parts are usually available from the manufacturer for at least 10 years after the date of manufacture and from third-party manufacturers for longer times. It is often quite possible to continue these systems in service with some refurbishing or to replace them with newer versions of the same units utilizing the same ducts. Note that these are single-zone systems operating under the control of a single thermostat. Such configurations may not be acceptable if several rooms are served by one system. Expectations have changed since the days when it was sufficient to merely be cooler than the hot conditions outdoors.

Larger buildings built in the modern period can also have all-air systems. These take the form of central air-handling units (fans, coils, filters, and dampers) with hot water piped from boilers and cold water piped from refrigeration systems called *water*

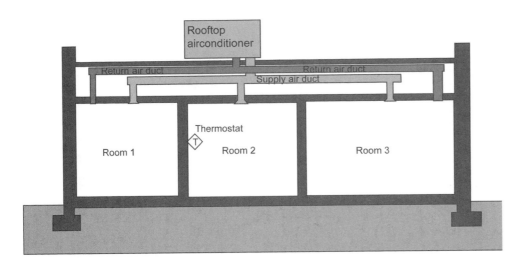

FIGURE 4.9
A small single-zone air-conditioning system that is common in small commercial buildings. It is often mounted on the roof with ducts above a dropped ceiling.

FIGURE 4.10
Another common arrangement for small-building heating and cooling is a unitary split system. Here is the indoor component of such a system using a gas furnace.

FIGURE 4.11
The outdoor components of unitary split systems are condensing units such as these, which house compressors, condensing coils, and fans.

FIGURE 4.12
The most popular large-building HVAC system in North America is the *variable air volume* (VAV) system. This schematic shows the heart of the system—the central air-handling unit with its fan, coils, and dampers. Note that heating is accomplished by hot water convectors.

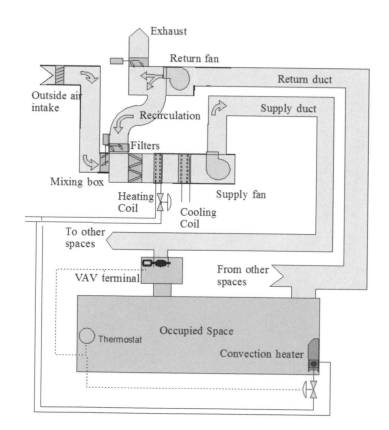

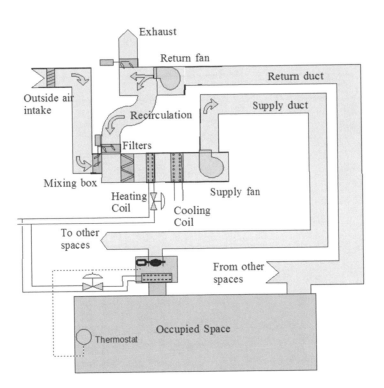

FIGURE 4.13
A popular system before the oil crisis of the 1970s, the all-air terminal reheat system differs from the VAV system in delivering air at a constant flow but variable temperature. It functions well, but it is not energy efficient.

chillers. Local zone control can have several forms. The most common is a damper regulated by a room thermostat that varies the air supply in proportion to the heat gain. Heating may be supplied through the same duct system or through a separate perimeter hot water convection system. All-air systems can provide adequate ventilation air with good filtration, quiet operation, flexibility, and sophisticated controls. They are considered the most desirable building systems and will almost always be continued in service with some replacement components as necessary and, perhaps, updated controls. A simple diagram of a *variable air volume (VAV)* or *variable flow-rate system* is shown in Figure 4.12.

Another common large-building, all-air heating and cooling system is a *reheat system* (see Figure 4.13). In this system, cooled air is delivered, usually at constant flow, from an air-handling unit through a duct system to the occupied spaces. At each space, the air passes through a heating coil controlled by the space thermostat. This coil usually is supplied with hot water, but it can also be electric resistance heat. If the space needed less than full cooling, the thermostat added heat until the temperature of the supply air matched the heat gain or, in the winter, the heat loss. The name—reheat system—derives from this reheating of air that has already been cooled. This system is capable of good control of space temperature and humidity. However, energy codes now prohibit its use except in special circumstances, and the cost of energy makes it too expensive to operate. Sometimes it is possible to add airflow control dampers and fan-speed controls to convert it to a hybrid VAV reheat system and thus reduce the amount of air being reheated. If it is necessary to have the supply duct flowing cold air to cool some spaces all year, reheating to heat other spaces is still very costly.

Another all-air system, used in large buildings from the 1950s to the 1980s, used two parallel supply ducts to deliver air around the building. The systems' name, *dual duct*

FIGURE 4.14
Another large-building system is the all-air double-duct system. It utilizes a dual pathway for supply air through either a hot or cold duct. The two streams are mixed for temperature control, so it is relatively energy inefficient, and the extra supply duct is costly. However, the system provides good control.

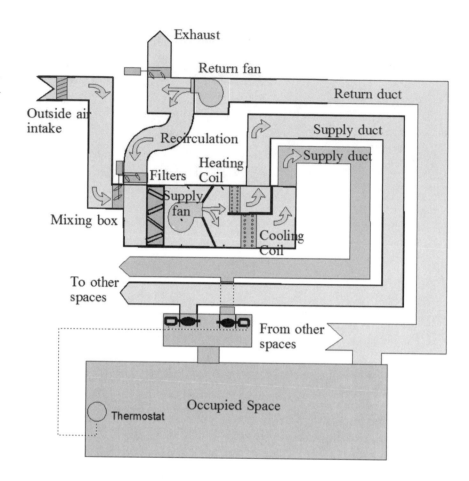

or *double duct*, describes this arrangement (see Figure 4.14). One duct carried cold air and the other hot air. At each space branch ducts connected these main supply ducts to "mixing boxes" or terminals that housed dampers controlled by the space thermostat. When a space needed cooling the damper moved to close the hot air duct and open the cold air duct. When the space needed heat, the damper to the duct opened. The largest problem occurred when the space needed neither heating nor cooling. In this case both dampers partially opened to mix hot with cold to supply neutral air to the room. As with the reheat system, it is sometimes possible to continue a dual-duct system's life by adding terminal controls to reduce airflow rates at partial load instead of mixing two air streams. Fan speed controls can be added to reduce fan energy consumption and noise issues.

The multizone system, similar to the dual-duct system (see Figure 4.15), has two parallel paths for the supply air. A heating and a cooling coil are mounted one above the other in the air-handling unit. A single fan is positioned to blow air through both coils. Downstream from the coils are sets of dampers controlled by thermostats in the spaces served. The dampers are arranged to control the supply airflow so it passes through the heating or the cooling coil, or partially through both, to achieve a mixed-air temperature suitable for the space needs. The mixed air for each room, after passing through the dampers, flows through a dedicated duct to each space. This system operates like the dual-duct system, but the dampers are in the air-handling unit instead of in or near the space served. This system is less costly than a dual-duct system for

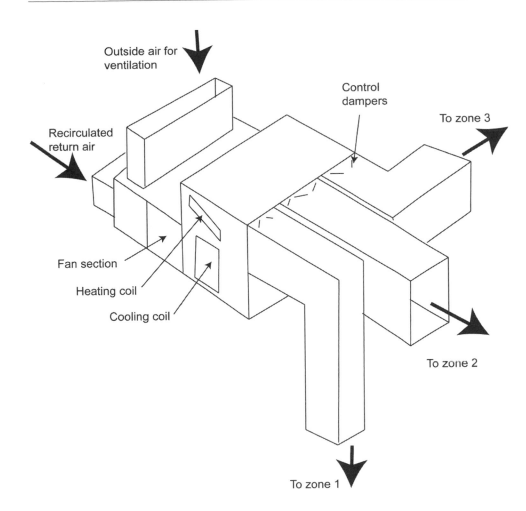

Outside air for ventilation

Recirculated return air

Control dampers

To zone 3

Fan section

Heating coil

Cooling coil

To zone 2

To zone 1

FIGURE 4.15
For medium-sized commercial buildings, an all-air multizone system has been a common choice in the 1950–1990 time frame. Its operation is similar to the double-duct system, but with the mixing dampers in the air-handling unit.

small sizes up to 12 to 14 control zones. Its major disadvantage is that, because each room has a dedicated supply duct, it is difficult to find space for the many small ducts to run from mechanical room to occupied rooms. The heat source is typically a hot water system with fuel-fired boiler and the cooling may be via a direct-expansion refrigeration cycle or a chilled water coil supplied by a water chiller.

Water Systems

Larger buildings, with many small spaces such as private offices or classrooms, may be equipped with all-water systems. These have individual cabinet units in the rooms with hot and chilled water coils and fans. Central boilers and chillers provide the sources of hot and chilled water. If the reuse also involves multiple small spaces, this system may serve quite well. Replacement of components as indicated by inspection while reusing piping is often all that is required. Changes in ventilation codes that took place beginning in the 1990s may require installation of a separate ventilation system since all-water systems often had only openings in the back of the cabinet to admit outdoor air. A fan-coil system as shown in Figure 4.16 is representative of such systems.

Air-Water Systems

Other systems found in larger buildings constructed recently are classified as *air-water*. One popular system has a central circulating water loop with a boiler and an evaporative

FIGURE 4.16
An all-water HVAC system, such as the fan-coil system, transports heat in water, a more compact form of heat, and thus requires less space than an air system. The small cabinets in each space do the heating or cooling as needed.

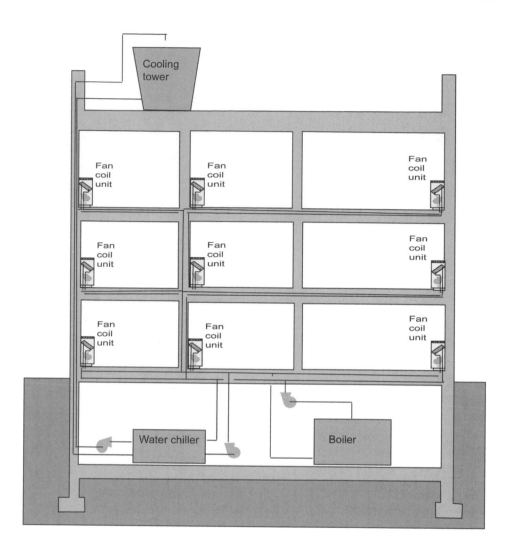

cooler. Connected to the water loop are closed-loop, water-to-air heat pumps for individual spaces as shown diagrammatically in Figure 4.17. These heat pumps condition the spaces under control of local thermostats and extract heat from, or reject heat into, the circulating water. Systems of this type can be quite efficient and satisfactory. The ventilation code changes mentioned previously can also affect this type of system.

Other Systems

Some buildings have systems that do not fit neatly into the above categories. One such system is the packaged terminal air-conditioner (PTAC) system frequently found in hotels, motels, and dormitories. This system is completely self-contained within a package set in a hole through the wall (Figure 4.18). Each room is independent of the others. It has the advantage of low first cost and easy replacement, but the disadvantages of noise, short life, low efficiency, and poor humidity control. Unless the reuse of the building has goals similar to the above uses, it may be advantageous to consider replacement of the system.

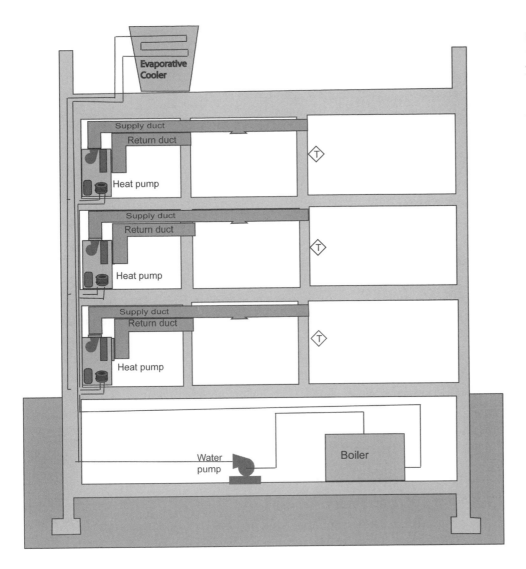

FIGURE 4.17
Developed over the past 30 years, the water-source heat-pump system uses a circulating water stream as a heat source or sink for the heat pumps connected. Each unit can heat or cool as its space demands. A boiler provides heat if all units are heating, and a closed-circuit cooler discharges heat if all units are cooling.

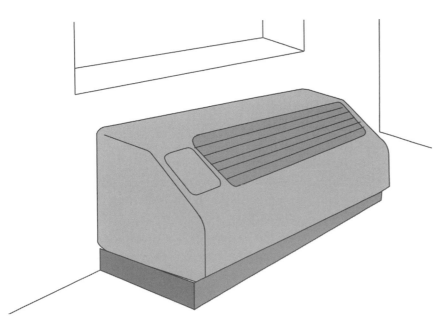

FIGURE 4.18
Small individual room units called packaged terminal air-conditioners (PTAC) are low first-cost selections for spaces needing individual controls such as motels or apartments.

Identification and Evaluation

The previous survey describes the types of HVAC systems that can be found in existing buildings under consideration for adaptive reuse. This section helps identify the system and provides guidance for evaluating it.

Determining the Type of System

Observation

A simple walk-through and visual observation is all that is needed to identify the system. Useful tools include flashlights, camera, pen and paper or recorder, and measuring tape. Identification can begin immediately inside—or even outside—the building wherever components of the system are visible or where the center of the system exists, such as the mechanical room, furnace room, basement, rooftop, and the like. Concentrate on the things a person sees in every building but probably does not think about consciously such as radiators, convectors, grilles, registers and diffusers, thermostats and control panels, and units in cabinets. Compare observations with the clues discussed in the following subsection. Look for closed doors that may lead to mechanical spaces. Observe pipes and ducts where visible. In mechanical rooms, observe the external appearance of equipment. External appearance is often an indicator of internal condition. Record the nameplate information for major items such as boilers, chillers, cooling towers, and pumps. This will help find their age and may be useful in system identification.

Clues to System Type

In the occupied space of the building, look for familiar components such as radiators or convectors. If present, it can be either a steam or hot water system. If the radiator has a larger pipe at one end and a smaller pipe at the bottom on the other end with a fitting larger than the pipe, it is probably a steam system. If not, it is probably a hot water system.

If none of these are observed, look for cabinets that may house fan-coil or *package terminal air conditioner* units. Both are usually on outside walls. Fan-coil units have grilles on top and toe space returns and are about nine inches thick. The PTAC units have grilles for both supply and return and are more likely to be constructed of plastics. They have an air-cooled condenser that extends through the wall and is exposed on the exterior behind the unit. Figure 4.19 shows an exterior view of a building that has had PTAC units installed during an earlier renovation.

Unfortunately, a PTAC unit, when removed, leaves a sizable hole in the building wall that must be carefully closed. Figure 4.20 shows the cavity formed by a PTAC sleeve after removal of the unit.

If neither radiators or convectors nor fan-coil or PTAC units are observed in the spaces, look for air inlets (grilles or diffusers) in the ceiling or walls. These are indicators of all-air type systems, air-conditioning, and a fairly modern system. Next look for ducts and control damper boxes that may indicate variable flow controls. Follow the ducts to mechanical rooms, if possible, to observe the air-handling units. These are

FIGURE 4.19
An aesthetic consideration for PTAC units is the appearance of the grilles from the exterior.

physically large metal enclosures that house, in order of airflow direction, mixing boxes, filters, heating and cooling coils, and fans. Look for pipes carrying hot or chilled water connected through the sides of the cabinet to coils inside.

A central system has a primary mechanical room with boilers and chillers. This space is typically in the basement or on the roof. Boilers are large objects with water pipes connected on top. Coal, oil, and gas boilers have connections to chimneys or stacks that extend above the roof. Coal boilers are supplied with coal through a stoker from a coal bunker. The stoker connection is at the front of the boiler. Oil-fired boilers have a burner on the front of the boiler with a blower and supply pipes connecting it to an oil storage tank. Gas boilers have much simpler piping with a series of valves in the piping at the boiler.

Water chillers are also physically imposing objects with large water pipe connections. Two of these chillers are connected to pumps and circulate chilled water to the air-handling units and other parts of the building, and two are connected to pumps that circulate water to a cooling tower located outside.

Operating Condition

While using the clues above to identify the type of HVAC system, observe the external condition of the components. Dirt, corrosion, and accumulations of debris and trash are indications of careless maintenance and point to a need for a more in-depth examination of the systems. Air-handling units with panels removed and not replaced, or not properly replaced, and duct or pipe insulation that has been removed or left hanging are further causes for more investigation into the system. Electric motors with exposed wiring are dangerous and reflect careless workmanship, as are unrepaired pipe leaks. Welded steel pipe and copper pipe are considered to have very long service lives as contrasted with screwed steel or plastic (except underground), but leaks can occur at fittings in any pipe material. Figure 4.21 shows steel steam pipes with leaks detected by rust stains. External corrosion is usually accompanied by internal corrosion and is a cause for concern if the pipe, duct, or equipment is to be retained in service. Further examination is indicated.

As mentioned in Chapter 3, copper has a history of volatile prices. When the price is high, as it is at this writing, copper is a target for thieves. Copper water pipes, coils, and refrigerant piping can disappear from unoccupied or unsecured buildings. When copper pipe or equipment is visible outside, it may be important to cover it or at least fence it to impede potential thieves. Buildings that have been vacant for some time should be checked to identify missing components.

FIGURE 4.21
When inspecting a project for adaptive reuse, it is important to observe piping for leaks. Leaking steam pipes usually leave rust stains such as this one.

Performance

If it appears feasible to continue using a preexisting HVAC system, the next step is to test it at the limits of its operating envelope—that is, a *functional performance test*. This test requires extensive HVAC experience and precise instrumentation. The original design documents, if available, are helpful. Obviously, if the test could be performed with the outdoor temperature at winter and summer design conditions, it would be desirable albeit rarely possible.

Large central HVAC systems have the advantage of sophisticated controls that can be used in conducting and documenting performance tests. For an all-air system, the system is operated in open-loop control with the heating and cooling off but the fan running and all control dampers open. All temperature and flow measurements should be in agreement and the airflow should conform to design flow. Outside and return air dampers should be opened and closed and the resulting flows measured. The heating and cooling control valves are then individually cycled open in turn and left until a steady state is reached. The water flow rates and the discharge temperatures should agree with design conditions or with a proportional ratio of design based on the ambient weather at the time of the test. The instrumentation can be used to test for control valve leaks with the control valves closed. In closed-loop control mode, the control system should be observed for instability. Chillers and boilers should be tested for full load capacity and control stability. Control terminal tests include full cooling airflow rates and control accuracy. Tests for air-water systems would be similar to these.

Testing unitary systems for performance is much simpler but gives proportionally less information. For one thing, the control systems are usually not capable of doing much more than starting and stopping the equipment. To test the heating mode, the thermostat is set for a high temperature; after the system has had time to reach a reasonably steady state, the temperature difference between supply and return air is measured and compared with nominal ranges. Cooling is tested in a similar manner.

Suitability Evaluation for New Application

Existing HVAC systems can sometimes be continued in service when a building is being adapted to a new use. Obviously, if the system meets the needs of the new use, retaining it is the least expensive option. Once the type of existing system has been identified and its condition and performance evaluated, and the results indicate potential for continued use, several issues must be addressed, which are described in the following subsections.

Zone Control

Occupant comfort and satisfaction are linked to productivity, so it is of first importance to maximize the individual's ability to control his or her local environment and especially the air temperature. Maximum zone control is to give each person a thermostat and a temperature-control device, but this is rarely possible. Minimum zone control, on the other hand, is a single thermostat for an entire building. For this to work satisfactorily, all occupants have to agree on one temperature—a rare circumstance. Some systems, such as all-air VAV systems, are often quite flexible and can easily have new zones added or existing zones combined into a new zone. The PTAC and some air-water systems provide control zones for each room. A building designer, manager, or owner must balance the economics of the existing HVAC zone control capabilities with the desires and expectations of the occupants when deciding on retaining the system. Ignoring the individual comfort issue is a perilous course.

Air Quality

Building codes now include requirements for ventilation of occupied spaces (see Figure 4.22) to assure good *indoor air quality* (IAQ). The HVAC systems not only provide heating and cooling, but they control air quality by diluting indoor contaminants with outdoor air or by removing contaminants with filters. The system's ability to deliver satisfactory air quality must be a part of the evaluation for continued use. All-air systems can deliver large ventialation air flow rates and can usually be equipped with high efficiency filters. However, they commonly return air from large sections—entire

FIGURE 4.22
Today the ventilation rates for buildings are established by building codes typically based on ASHRAE (American Society of Heating, Refrigerating and Air-Conditioning Engineers) Ventilation Standard 62.

floors or even the entire building—condition it and redistribute it to the same areas. Mixing air from some spaces may not be recommended. Air, for example, from kitchens, laboratories, and swimming pools should not be returned to classrooms or office spaces. Return air from one apartment should not be mixed with that of another.

Steam and hot water heating systems have no capability for ventilation or filtration, so this function must be performed by a supplementary system. Air-water systems and PTAC systems have limited capabilities and may need supplementary ventilation, depending on the density of occupants and the sources of contaminants. In the southern parts of the United States, humidity control of ventilation air requires special care in design. In all areas ventilation air uses large amounts of energy—especially in the cold northern parts of North America—thus using as little outside air as possible consistent with good IAQ and including heat recovery where feasible are good practices. If new point sources of air pollutants such as kitchens or copy machines are to be installed, local exhaust systems should also be added.

Fire Codes

Fire codes historically have become more stringent as knowledge and technology advanced. It is likely that an HVAC system more than a few years old will not meet current codes. Among the areas that may require investigation are protection of penetrations through rated construction elements, pressurization and ventilation of high-rise stairwells, smoke and fire detection, and smoke evacuation.

Acoustics

In many adaptive reuse projects, new acoustical requirements will have to be reconciled. New acoustic barriers between offices or apartments may be penetrated by existing air ducts or pipes and such penetrations must be carefully sealed. Air ducts, and especially those with air outlets on both sides of the barrier, may require sound traps to limit

FIGURE 4.23
If there is space for an existing boiler, there is certainly space for a replacement. This drawing shows the volume occupied by a typical scotch marine boiler compared with the space required by a modern high efficiency boiler of the same heating capacity.

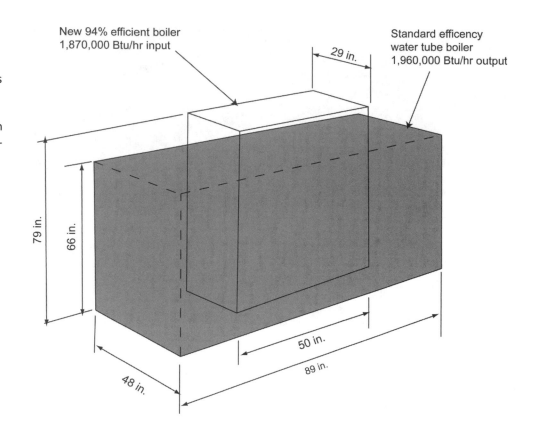

New 94% efficient boiler
1,870,000 Btu/hr input

Standard efficency
water tube boiler
1,960,000 Btu/hr output

29 in.

79 in.

66 in.

50 in.

89 in.

48 in.

transmission. Existing air ducts may carry air at a velocity that causes noise from turbulent flow. The solution may be to enlarge the ducts, install sound traps on the outlets, or enclose the ducts in a sound enclosure. Noise from existing mechanical rooms may be a nuisance in the reuse situation and new walls with higher transmission losses may be the answer. Steam heat was notoriously prone to "water hammer" and clanging as the steam flow started or stopped. Elimination of dips in the pipe and installation of drip traps often removed the accumulated pools of condensate that caused the noise.

Rotating equipment in mechanical rooms can transfer vibrations to the structure that can cause annoying noise at a great distance from the source, thus making the source difficult to identify. The answer to vibrations is to decouple the rotating equipment from the structure by isolation mountings. Pipes and ducts connected to such equipment may also have to have isolation supports.

Energy Efficiency

Though continued use of existing equipment can be economically disadvantageous, there can be a natural resistance to replacing equipment that appears to be running well. Operating efficiency of HVAC equipment has increased dramatically over time. Boilers from the early half of the twentieth century had combustion efficiencies in the 60 to 70 percent range. Now boilers are advertised at 95 percent efficiency. The physical size of these boilers has decreased at the same time. Figure 4.23 shows a comparison of two boilers of approximately the same capacity. Older boilers are even larger than the standard water tube boiler depicted. The new high-efficiency boiler will easily fit in the standard boiler's space and will pass though a 30-inch door.

Centrifugal water chillers built during that time were rated at about 1.2 kilowatt per ton (kW/ton) and now chillers can be purchased at 0.7 kW/ton or less. Unitary cooling equipment from the same period had *energy-efficiency ratios* (EERs) in the range of 8 British thermal units per kilowatt (Btu/kW) and new equipment can now be purchased with EERs of 14 or more. Electric motor efficiencies have improved from about 85 to 90 percent or more. A decision regarding replacement on the basis of efficiency improvement requires a careful analysis of operating costs. Records of utility costs and fuel consumption for the building can be used to make projections of costs with new equipment. Expected remaining service life of the equipment is a factor and this is discussed in the next section. Reduction of emissions and consumption of fossil fuels is also a factor.

The most accurate comparison of economic alternatives can be accomplished by using a *life-cycle-cost analysis*. This procedure is as follows: A specific time period is selected. This is often the expected life of a piece of equipment or a building. First costs for each alternative (obviously, the first cost of an existing system is zero) are amortized over this period, including replacements or salvage value, if any. Operating costs, including predicted inflation, are estimated along with maintenance costs. All of these costs are added together to get the complete cost of owning the alternative over its life. All alternatives are compared, and the one whose total cost is lowest is normally chosen. A detailed description of this analytical technique is presented in Chapter 7.

Expected Service Life

It is difficult to predict with certainty when a piece of equipment or system will cease to function or become economically infeasible to repair. The American Society of Heating, Refrigerating and Air-Conditioning Engineers (ASHRAE) has published a table, "Estimated Service Lives of Various System Components," in its 2003 *Applications Handbook* that is the best source of information on the subject. This table is reproduced in Figure 4.24. The reader is cautioned to use this information only in a general sense to compare alternative components, perform the life-cycle analysis, or evaluate continued use versus replacement. The ASHRAE organization has also established a freely available online database of HVAC equipment service experience that is detailed and dynamic in the sense that users continuously update and expand the data (www.ashrae.org).

Unitary equipment, such as residential or small commercial split or packaged air-conditioning equipment, has an estimated service life of 15 years. The typical failure that leads to replacement instead of repair is a failure of the compressor. This component is the most complicated and expensive part of a unitary system and the one subject to the most stressful operating conditions. A failure of a fan or a leak in a coil can often be economically repaired, but after a few years a compressor replacement may be almost as expensive as a new unit and so a decision to replace is made.

Air-handling units are key component in any all-air system. These large metal boxes contain fans, coils (liquid-to-air heat exchangers), filters, and dampers. The useful life of an air-handling unit as an assembly is not listed in Figure 4.24. This is probably because the cabinet can be used for a very long time while replacing the internal components as necessary. As long as the heating and cooling capacity of the unit is satisfactory for the spaces served the existing ducts, air distribution devices, and air-handling units

Equipment Item	Median Years	Equipment Item	Median Years	Equipment Item	Median Years
Air conditioners		Air terminals		Air-cooled condensers	20
Window unit	10	Diffusers, grilles, and registers	27	Evaporative condensers	20
Residential single or split package	15	Induction and fan-coil units	20	Insulation	
Commercial through-the-wall	15	VAV and double-duct boxes	20	Molded	20
Water-cooled package	15	Air washers	17	Blanket	24
Heat pumps		Ductwork	30	Pumps	
Residential air-to-air	15[b]	Dampers	20	Base-mounted	20
Commercial air-to-air	15	Fans		Pipe-mounted	10
Commercial water-to-air	19	Centrifugal	25	Sump and well	10
Roof-top air conditioners		Axial	20	Condensate	15
Single-zone	15	Propeller	15	Reciprocating engines	20
Multizone	15	Ventilating roof-mounted	20	Steam turbines	30
Boilers, hot water (steam)		Coils		Electric motors	18
Steel water-tube	24 (30)	DX, water, or steam	20	Motor starters	17
Steel fire-tube	25 (25)	Electric	15	Electric transformers	30
Cast iron	35 (30)	Heat exchangers		Controls	
Electric	15	Shell-and-tube	24	Pneumatic	20
Burners	21	Reciprocating compressors	20	Electric	16
Furnaces		Package chillers		Electronic	15
Gas- or oil-fired	18	Reciprocating	20	Valve actuators	
Unit heaters		Centrifugal	23	Hydraulic	15
Gas or electric	13	Absorption	23	Pneumatic	20
Hot water or steam	20	Cooling towers		Self-contained	10
Radiant heaters		Galvanized metal	20		
Electric	10	Wood	20		
Hot water or steam	25	Ceramic	34		

Notes: 1. ASHRAE makes no claims as to the *statistical* validity of any of the data presented in this table.

2. Table lists base values that should be adjusted for local conditions (see the section on Service Life).

Source: Data obtained from a survey of the United States by ASHRAE Technical Committee TC 1.8 (Akalin 1978).

[a] See Lovvorn and Hiller (1985) and Easton Consultants (1986) for further information.

[b] Data updated by TC 1.8 in 1986.

FIGURE 4.24

Estimated Service Lives of Various System Components

Source: American Society of Heating, Refrigerating and Air-Conditioning Engineers, Applications Handbook (Atlanta: ASHRAE 2003), Table 3, p. 36.3.

can remain in use. If capacity is okay, the fan and coils can also be used. Insufficient capacity, clogged internal tubing, or leaks are signals that coil replacement may be required. Centrifugal fan bearings must be serviced and probably changed at intervals but the fan shaft, wheel, and scroll should not deteriorate unless there has been rusting from water carryover from coil to fan.

Ducts are listed at 30 years. The insulation needed for hot or cold ducts will probably have to be replaced before that time, because it is listed at 20 to 24 years. Check for asbestos in the insulation. Pipes are not listed. The life of copper pipes is very long. Steel pipes used in closed-loop systems should not have dangerous corrosion either inside or out unless water treatment has been neglected or condensation on the outside has been very serious. Their service life is very long as well. If the system has both copper and steel, look for possible electrolytic corrosion in the steel. Pipe insulation frequently contained carcinogenic asbestos before this insulating and fireproofing material was banned. Any inspection that involves disturbing potentially asbestos-containing insulation should be performed by trained inspectors wearing protective masks and clothing. If such material is suspected to be present, a full-scale asbestos inspection is advisable. It can sometimes be left in place and encapsulated but is usually removed by qualified contractors under controlled conditions.

Pumps can fail at the shaft seal or bearings, but this is usually easily repaired. Shaft corrosion or rotor erosion can also be rectified by repair or replacement. Electric motors are likely to fail before the pump itself has to be replaced. Their service life is estimated at 18 years as compared with 20 for a base-mounted pump. Alignment of base-mounted pumps must be regularly checked to assure long life.

Boilers are inspected at regular intervals by local or state inspectors. Their reports can give very good information on the condition of boilers and hence the expected useful life can be assessed. The typical manner of failure is internal corrosion or movement and leakage due to thermal expansion. If boilers are well maintained they can be very durable. Service lives range from 24 to 35 years, depending on type and material.

Refrigeration equipment life is partially a function of its type. Small reciprocating compressors used with direct-expansion coils have relatively short lives of 10 to 15 years. However, large centrifugal and rotary compressors may be still functioning after 25 years. Failures in these type compressors are usually electric motor or bearing faults. If failure occurs near the end of the expected service life, it may not be economical to repair. Recently, ecological concern about some chlorinated fluorocarbon refrigerants has lead to their discontinuance, and this usually means removing the compressor as well. Poorly maintained water-cooled condensers may fail due to internal clogging or corrosion.

Cooling towers have somewhat shorter lives of 20 years, because they are exposed to water during normal operation. In metal towers rust and corrosion are the normal failure modes. In wood towers, it is deterioration of the wood itself.

Simple on-off electric thermostats in unitary HVAC systems can operate satisfactorily for many years. But controls are one of the more troublesome and short-lived parts of a large HVAC system. Figure 4.24 shows controls having service lives of 10 to 20 years. Diligent maintenance and replacement of deteriorating components can extend the life toward the longer end of this range, but replacement with upgraded newer equipment will be recommended at about 20 years. Advancements in capabilities make it feasible to replace and upgrade controls when major troubles occur in the later stages of the estimated life.

Selection of New Systems

If the existing HVAC system is not suitable for continued use in the building, a decision about the new system must be made. This is a major decision in the adaptive reuse project. The HVAC system is the most expensive single system in the building and has a major role in the occupant's satisfaction with the building. Several variables must be considered in the decision.

Available Space

A major constraint in existing buildings is the interior space available for new equipment. Many older buildings had minimal floor-to-floor heights. Horizontal air distribution through ducts above ceilings typically requires at least 24 to 30 inches of vertical space from ceiling to structure. It may be possible to furr down parts of the ceiling for the ducts and leave the remainder at a higher level to give a less cramped feeling. Figure 4.25 shows a furred ceiling space for ductwork where there was no space for ducts above the original ceiling. The height of the door head determined the vertical dimen-

sion of the ducts. The height of doors and windows establishes a nearly absolute minimum ceiling elevation. Building codes require 7.5 feet or more of headroom. If duct space for horizontal distribution above the ceiling is not available, an all-air system is probably not the best choice. Heat can be transported in a stream of water much more compactly, so some type of air-water system is indicated in that case.

If space for horizontal ducts is available, the next question is the space for air-handling units. Air-handling units supply conditioned air through the ducts and can be located on each floor if space for a mechanical room is available. Mechanical rooms for central station air-handling units range from a minimum of about 150 square feet to 1,000 square feet or more. The room should be adjacent to an outside wall for access to outside air for ventilation. If space is not available on every floor of a multistory building, air-handling units can be located where convenient to serve several stories through vertical ducts.

Central equipment such as boilers and chillers can be located in basement, ground level, or rooftop mechanical rooms. This equipment is heavy, and structural support becomes very important if the floor is not on grade. Access for service and movement of equipment and supplies is critical for central mechanical rooms. Boilers must have chimneys or stacks to vent combustion gases and chillers must have cooling towers that are located outdoors. In addition to the fuel savings offered by new higher efficiency boilers, many have the added advantage of smaller gas vents that can be run horizontally to the exterior.

One-story buildings with "flat" (low-slope) roofs can be effectively served with heating and cooling from roof-mounted unitary equipment. This is a relatively low-cost system that needs no inside space except for ducts. The rooftop equipment is exposed to view and may detract from the historic appearance of the building, if that is important. It is also heavy, and the roof structure should be carefully analyzed for adequacy. Rooftop systems can even be extended to two or three stories, but the cost and space advantages decline sharply.

Water-to-air heat pump systems are often good choices where duct space is limited. The heat pump itself can be located in a closet near the space served or even overhead. These units can serve areas of 100 to 1,000 square feet so that ducts are relatively small and short. The units are looped together with recirculating water lines and some central mechanical room space is necessary for pumps and boilers.

In extreme cases with no internal space available, the PTAC system mentioned earlier can be utilized. These units serve individual spaces and are located in the perimeter walls. They have inherent zone control in the space served and are relatively low in initial cost, but the disadvantages are major. The external appearance of the condenser grilles is usually considered to detract from the building's appearance. The units are noisy in operation and relatively inefficient and short-lived.

Thermal Resistance of Walls and Roof

Planning a new HVAC system in a building requires estimating the rate of heat flow into and out of the building in order to select the capacity of the system. Working with an existing building carries the disadvantage of not knowing the insulation value of the roof and walls with the same degree of certainty as a new building. On the other hand, it gives the advantage of being able to measure the building's performance in various ways. If the walls and roof can be opened for visual inspection of the interior, the probable thermal resistance can be estimated from the materials observed. If not, or if the number of openings is limited, several techniques can be applied to estimate the resistance. Utility bills provide historical fuel and electrical consumption information that can be used with weather records to estimate how the building performed with the previous occupancy. While not exact, this gives a good estimate of whole-building performance.

Thermal imaging with an infrared camera can reveal the thermal and moisture conditions in walls and roofs by showing differences in temperature. (This is discussed and illustrated in Chapter 8.) Infrared thermometers (also covered in Chapter 8) give a more limited indication of surface temperatures.

FIGURE 4.26
When considering an existing building for adaptive reuse, its relative airtightness is important is planning for an energy-efficient and sustainable new use. A leaky building uses more energy and can be very uncomfortable. A blower door for measuring air leakage is illustrated here.

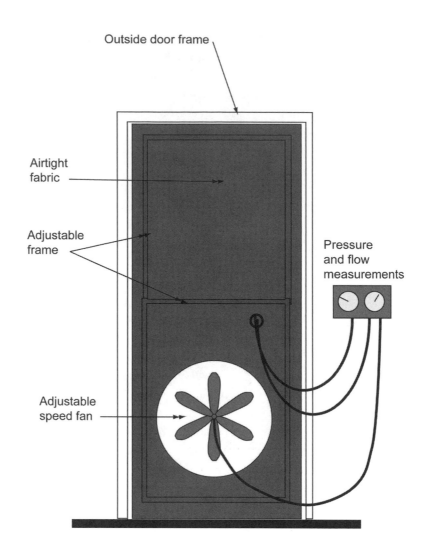

One major factor in heat flow is the rate of air leakage through the building envelope called *infiltration*. For small buildings, this can be measured by a *blower door*. This device is a panel containing a fan and an airflow measuring instrument that can be installed to cover an open doorway. It pressurizes the building and measures the resulting leak rate. Figure 4.26 shows a simple diagram of a blower door.

Information on overall building performance can also be gained by heating the building to a temperature above comfortable, when the outdoor air is cool, skies overcast, and the temperature relatively stable. The heating system is then turned off, and the temperature indoors is recorded as it decays. The resulting curve can be related to the time constant of the building, which is a measure of thermal mass. The key here is to measure the indoor temperature in a location that gives the best representation of the whole building. This test can be done in the cooling season also. However, outdoor temperature swings are more rapid and solar radiation complicates the issue. Another technique for estimating thermal resistance is by using an insulated enclosure that can be adhered to the inside of an exterior wall or roof. Input to an electric heater, in the box, controlled by a precise thermostat gives an indication of the rate of heat loss through the wall area covered by the box.

Zone Control

The importance of zone control and the ability of various existing systems to meet the need is now discussed. Given the previous discussion, the choice of a new HVAC system must be based on its ability to provide satisfactory zone control.

Conforming with the Character of the Building

If the building being adaptively reused has architectural character, the HVAC system should be selected so that it does not detract from that character. For example, in the authors' opinion, cutting through the facade of an early-twentieth-century building for PTAC grilles is to be avoided. In some cases carefully designed new ductwork can be exposed in the building to enhance the esthetics of the space. In small buildings, especially residential buildings constructed prior to the 1930s, it may be desirable to install a unitary heating and cooling system that has concealed ducts. At least one manufacturer produces a unitary system with two-inch diameter flexible ducts that can be hidden inside walls. The supply air duct outlets, two-inch diameter holes, are unobtrusively located in the floor or ceiling corners. In the special case of a residence with a gravity warm air heating system, the existing ducts can probably be replaced with new insulated ducts for cooling as well as heating. The existing cast-iron grilles can be reused.

If the new HVAC system in a medium to large building is to be concealed as much as possible, this is generally best accomplished using an air-water system. Water pipes can be concealed in relatively small wall and ceiling spaces and fan-coil units can be enclosed in furred ceiling or wall cabinets or closets. Air inlet and outlet grilles can be designed to appear in character with the rest of the interior.

Central equipment such as boilers, chillers, and pumps require a mechanical room. If the building had a boiler originally, the boiler room should be large enough to serve this purpose. New gas-fired boilers are much smaller than old steel or cast-iron boilers (see Figure 4.23). Some can be vented through small vents and even through walls without a chimney. The heat rejection equipment for the cooling system usually must be outdoors and may be difficult to conceal. Air-cooled condensers and cooling towers are bulky and need large amounts of air to operate. Surrounding them in walled enclosures is usually the most economical solution. Cooling towers can be located at some distance from the mechanical room, but air-cooled condensers must be close.

Building Codes

Building codes continually become more stringent as society becomes more concerned with safety and protection of property and as technology advances. Most buildings under consideration for adaptive reuse will not meet current codes whether the HVAC system is to be retained or replaced. An example of code issues to be expected includes enclosure of mechanical rooms in rated construction. This may mean new walls, floors, and ceilings must be constructed to provide the necessary rating.

Energy codes are in effect in most of the United States and Canada. The International Existing Building Code does not dictate that an existing building must meet the new building energy code requirements, but that new systems installed in it do so. System minimum efficiencies are thereby established. Another kind of code, which is relatively new, are ventilation codes. Such codes require outdoor air for ventilation that will not have been a requirement in older buildings and are discussed later in this chapter.

Acoustics

Selection and design of a replacement HVAC system must be sensitive to acoustical needs of the occupied spaces. Annoying noise can be a factor in occupant satisfaction and productivity. The noise concerns of PTAC systems have already been noted. Air-water systems can have noise problems that usually originate in the fan-coil unit. If these are carefully selected to have low noise levels, these systems should not cause complaints. All-air systems have the potential for the lowest noise of the alternative choices. With these systems, air-handling unit noise emanating from the mechanical rooms is the most likely trouble source. Good low-transmission partitions should control this. Similarly, central-station boilers, pumps, and chillers must be separated from occupied spaces by adequate barriers. Outdoor condensers or cooling towers are quite noisy and should be located away from occupants or have sufficient barriers.

Unitary systems also can present noise problems. Rooftop units directly above occupied spaces can transmit annoying structural vibrations and airborne noise. The vibration is greatest if the units are located in the center of beams or joists and smallest if the units are located over columns. The indoor section of unitary split systems are usually quiet enough to be acceptable if enclosed in gypsum board and stud closets but not if suspended above acoustic tile ceilings.

Air noise originating in grilles and diffusers can be avoided by careful selection for low noise, while air noise from ducts can be avoided by keeping velocities low. Fan noise can be absorbed by turns, acoustic lining material, or longer runs of duct or by sound absorbers if necessary.

Energy Efficiency

The 2006 International Existing Building Code requires that, in the case of alterations, the alterations must conform to the International Energy Conservation Code. The entire building, however, does not have to comply. Thus a new HVAC system should be designed to the standards for a new building. Even though other aspects of the building such as insulation do not have to be improved, it is possible that upgrades in thermal resistance will reduce heat loss and gain and, consequently, reduce the required capacity of HVAC equipment sufficiently to offset the costs of the improvements. Specifically, new windows, roof insulation, efficient lighting, and reductions in air leakage should be considered even if not required by code.

In many adaptive reuse projects, the most efficient way to deliver occupant comfort and satisfaction is with a hybrid passive and active HVAC system. Many existing buildings were built before air-conditioning and have architectural features for passive ventilation cooling. This natural ventilation can be utilized during mild weather and the active system can manually or automatically take over during cold or hot weather.

Among the many types of HVAC systems discussed thus far, one of the most energy

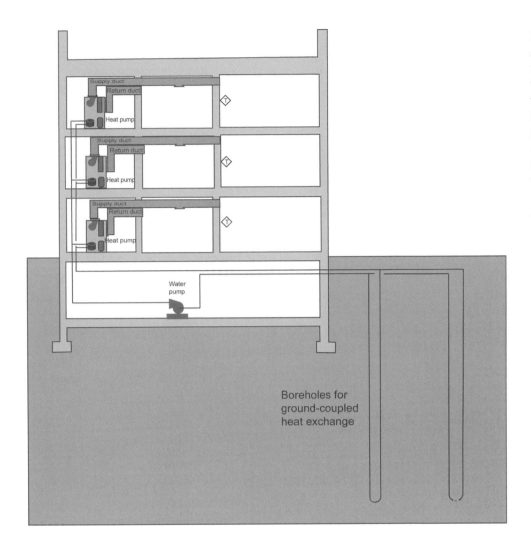

FIGURE 4.27
A highly efficient development of the closed-loop water source heat pump system is the ground-coupled heat pump system. Buried pipe shown here forms a heat exchanger that discharges heat to or absorbs heat from the ground. An EER as high as 15 or 20 can be obtained, but at the additional cost of the buried pipe field.

efficient is the ground-coupled heat pump shown in Figure 4.27. While this system costs more than others because of its buried piping, the extra cost is often returned in five years or less. If this system is not feasible, another efficient system is the recirculating loop heat-pump system (see Figure 4.17). In the order of probable decreasing efficiency, other standard systems to consider are all-air, air-water, all-water, unitary, and PTAC.

Life-Cycle Cost

This is one of many sophisticated cost comparison methods that evaluate capital investment and ongoing operations and maintenance costs over the life of an HVAC system for purposes of making a choice among alternatives. It requires estimates of future costs or inflation rates of fuel, energy, equipment, and service life for equipment as well. (This method of comparing alternatives is detailed in Chapter 7.) The National Institute for Standards and Technology (NIST) publishes *Handbook 135* with an annual supplement and the Building Life-Cycle Cost (BLCC) computer program that gives details about the procedure.

Air Quality

The ability to deliver sufficient outdoor air, or filter recirculated air to keep airborne contaminants below a threshold, is an essential attribute of an HVAC system. During the 1980s and 1990s, partly as a consequence of reduced ventilation air in the face of the energy crisis of the 1970s, a new phenomenon called *sick building syndrome* appeared. While the syndrome was never widespread, the dangers of poor air quality became apparent to all and ventilation codes were rewritten to improve the situation. An older building may have no ventilation system at all, or an inadequate one, and this would be sufficient reason to elect to install a new system.

The ventilation performance of the various systems discussed in this chapter varies greatly. The all-air system is best able to offer large flow rates of outdoor air or almost any level of filtration, and air-water systems are somewhat less able. All-water systems can supply small amounts of ventilation air by intake openings in the back of the cabinet; but this is uncontrolled and subject to external wind and interior pressure forces. Only coarse filters can be accommodated in most of these systems. The optimal solution is a separate ducted ventilation system that can deliver conditioned air at or below room temperature in summer, and at or above in winter. This is also true of unitary and PTAC systems, except where only minimal ventilation is required.

Sustainable Adaptive Reuse

Sustainable reuse for mechanical systems embodies maximizing the retention and continued use of components and materials already in the building. This concept is about choosing new materials and systems to be the most efficient and environmentally friendly available. The rates of heat gain and loss are most dependent on the thermal resistance provided by insulation in the roof, windows, and walls and the minimization of solar gains. Chapter 6, Sustainability, covers this topic in more detail.

Plumbing, Bathrooms, Accessibility, and Fire Systems

Without indoor plumbing, buildings are not habitable. For that reason understanding the existing plumbing system in a building being considered for adaptive reuse is essential. This may be difficult because pipes, and especially drain pipes, are often buried in the structure. In new buildings this system typically constitutes about 10 percent of the construction cost. In existing buildings it can consume even a larger fraction of the budget if a complete replacement is required. The plumbing system is very important in occupant health, safety, and comfort. To meet these needs, and to be cost effective, reusing and replacing the plumbing system should be carefully planned. For the majority of buildings under consideration for reuse, most of the plumbing system can be retained. For many older buildings, however, partial or complete replacement is needed.

Historical Review of Plumbing Systems

Pre–Civil War Buildings

Few working plumbing systems, as originally installed, exist in buildings from this period. Some buildings had water piped in and some had sanitary drains. Primitive fire-suppression water systems have been reported in some industrial buildings. Gutters and downspouts are the systems most likely to be encountered. Some buildings of this period and into the 1920s had rainwater-collection systems and storage cisterns to supply drinking water. Although this is usually a feature found in residences, it may also be found in nonresidential buildings as well. It may be preserved as a historic artifact rather than a working system. It also could be used to supply water for irrigation or flushing toilets. If other plumbing is found, it is probably of more recent vintage.

Buildings 1860 to 1950

With the development of sanitary drainage and the water seal trap, indoor plumbing gradually became the norm during the late 1800s. Interior storm drain systems made low-slope roofs feasible. Cast-iron pipe dominated the market and still remains a premium pipe material for drain lines. An example of a cast-iron rain leader is shown in Figure 5.1. Water supply lines under utility or elevated tank pressure carried water throughout buildings in steel pipe with threaded joints.

FIGURE 5.1
Iron pipe rain leaders are common in existing buildings built prior to about 1980. They have extremely long service lives.

Copper tubing was gradually introduced and became widespread following the interruption of World War II. Since then it has become the standard material for supply pipe sizes of two and three inches in diameter. Vitrified china lavatories and water closets, along with enameled cast-iron sinks and tubs, also became the standard fixtures throughout this period. As discussed in Chapters 3 and 4, copper is currently very attractive to thieves and should be protected.

Post-1950 Buildings

Plumbing matured as an engineering practice during this period. The primary change is in materials (fiberglass and other synthetics). Assuming the number and location of fixtures is suitable for the reuse; piping systems will probably meet current codes and be satisfactory to remain in service. Storm-drain systems should be satisfactory with perhaps some insulation to prevent condensation and dripping. Fire-suppression systems probably have large enough pipe, although the sprinklers themselves may have to be replaced. Gas pipe is likely to be similar to that installed today.

Identification and Evaluation

The above sections describe the plumbing systems to be expected in existing buildings under consideration for adaptive reuse. This section will help identify the system and give guidance for evaluating it. In this book, the rooms containing plumbing fixtures are termed toilets. The china fixtures for human waste are termed water closets.

Determining the Types of Systems

A simple walk-through and visual observation are enough to identify the system. Useful tools include flashlights, camera, pen and paper, recorder, and measuring tape. The various rooms in the occupied space, wherever water is used or dispelled, should reveal enough information. Basements, mechanical room, and the like also can *type* the system. Look for those things many take for granted: plumbing fixtures, water heaters, drinking fountains, exposed piping, roof drains, floor drains, and cleanouts. Note the condition and appearance of the fixtures. Observe the locations of toilets relative to each other. Are they stacked or randomly arranged? This provides clues to the location and routing of piping. Note the nameplate information on the water heater for future research into heating capacity and the approximate age. Count the number of lavatories, water closets, and drinking fountains on each floor for comparison with current code fixture requirements.

For factory buildings, lofts, and the like, there are other considerations. Industrial plants often used water in large quantities so adapting a former factory to residential or commercial use should not require additional water service capacity. The industrial distribution system within the building probably will need replacement.

Storm Drainage Systems

If the building has a sloping roof it is almost certain to have external gutters and downspouts. These will be easily observed and evaluated from the outside. If the roof is a low-slope ("flat") roof, the rain is probably collected in roof drains that are found in the lowest places on the roof. From the roof drains, water is carried in interior rain leaders down to the lowest parts of the building and to the municipal storm drains at the street. Combined sanitary and storm systems such as the one shown in Figure 5.2 are no longer allowed. The rain leaders are large pipes and their location is inflexible, so they will have to be "worked around." Horizontal portions of rain leaders may prevent air ducts from being located where desired and may determine ceiling heights on the top floor.

Potable Water Supply Systems

A very important issue is the source of potable water. Utility water is clean and dependable, but well water must be tested and maintained. Well sources are only likely in rural

FIGURE 5.2
In the past cities had combined sanitary and storm sewer systems. These are no longer permitted and buildings with the two joined together must be retrofitted for separate sewers.

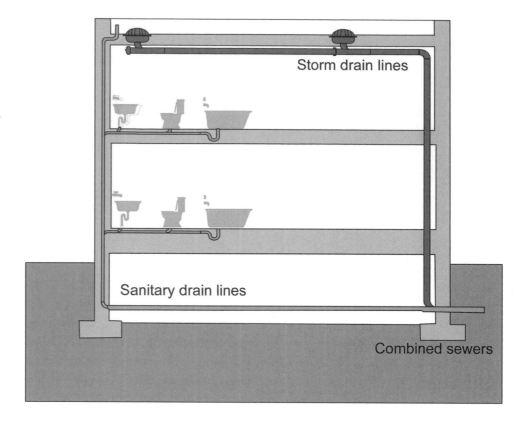

areas. A water meter pit near the street is a sure indicator of a utility source. Water pressure must be adequate—that is, a minimum of 60 psig (pound-force per square inch gauge) at the service entrance when operating—but not too high; 100 psig or so is probably too high for comfortable use. Pressure-regulating valves can manage high pressures. Tall buildings are more likely to have low-pressure problems on upper floors. Scaling, layers of precipitated minerals that were originally dissolved in the water, reduces the internal diameter of the pipe and affects flow rates. Figure 5.3 shows a section of steel pipe whose internal area is severely reduced (to one-quarter) by scaling.

Pipe material is important. Steel pipe, even galvanized, is subject to rust corrosion and to internal scaling in hard water areas (i.e., with high concentrations of dissolved minerals). Copper pipe is the premium material but can also be subject to scaling in hard water areas. Plastic pipe, such as polyvinyl chloride (PVC) and chlorinated polyvinyl chloride (CPVC), is satisfactory, but other types, such as polybutylene, have given problems. All plastic pipe materials are softened by high temperatures and should be supported at close intervals.

Tall buildings may not have enough utility pressure to deliver water to the upper floors. Utility pressure of 100 psig can lift water about 150 feet, or 10 stories. Buildings built before the 1970s often had a large storage tank on an upper floor or the roof. Water was pumped up to this tank and then distributed by gravity downward through the building. Figure 5.4 shows a schematic diagram of such a system. The presence of a large tank on an upper floor or the roof is a sure indicator of such a system. Some of the water in the tank may have been reserved for fire-suppression systems.

FIGURE 5.3
In some areas, potable water can be *hard*, that is, have high concentrations of dissolved minerals. When this water is heated, the minerals can precipitate and deposit *scale* on the pipe walls. This section of steel pipe is severely restricted by scale.

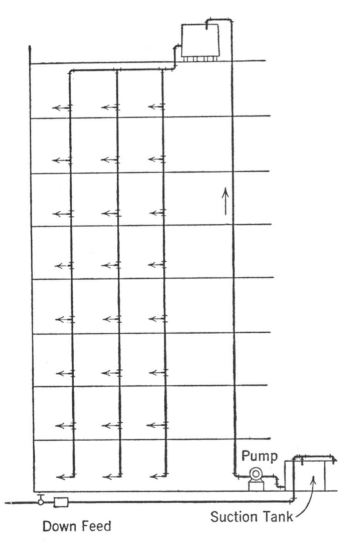

Down Feed

Pump

Suction Tank

FIGURE 5.4
Utility water systems do not have sufficient pressure to lift water to the upper floors of high-rise buildings. Prior to the availability of variable-speed pump motors in the 1990s, a down-feed potable water supply system was a good solution to the need for delivery of potable water at high elevations.
Source: 1967 ASHRAE Guide and Databook, Figure 1, p. 743.

FIGURE 5.5
Plumbing practices acceptable in the past may not be so today. This S-trap lavatory is illegal in most plumbing codes and would have to be replaced.

Sanitary Drainage Systems

Disposal of wastewater is an important issue. Utility sanitary sewers are dependable and require little maintenance by the building owner. On-site disposal of septic tanks and subsurface drain fields, or packaged aeration plants, may be limited in capacity and require extensive maintenance. Sanitary drain, waste, and vent (DWV) systems have larger pipe sizes than supply systems, and drainage is by gravity. For this reason they are less flexible in location than supply pipes. Some fittings and materials used in older systems are no longer allowed: the S-trap in Figure 5.5, for example. Other fittings, such as the house trap" shown in Figure 5.6, are unnecessary and undesirable.

Gas Piping Systems

Natural or propane gas piping may be confined to mechanical rooms, such as the pipe serving the boiler in Figure 5.7. They can also run around a building to serve rooftop heating, ventilating, and air-conditioning (HVAC) units. While it should not be a serious concern, gas pipe should be pressure tested before placing in operation.

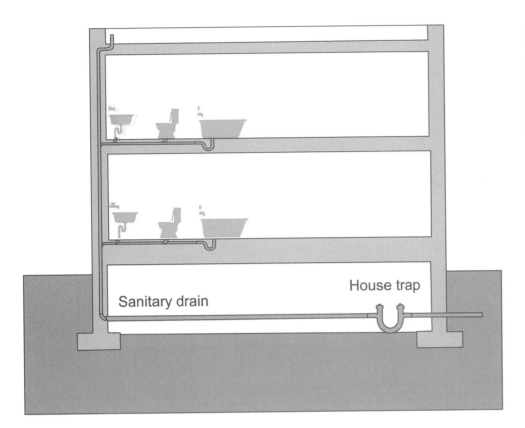

FIGURE 5.6
The house trap, a fitting from the early days of indoor plumbing, is obsolete. Frequently the source of stoppages, such traps should be removed.

FIGURE 5.7
Natural gas usually has no corrosive constituents and its piping should last a long time. This gas pipe at the boiler is probably suitable for continued use.

FIGURE 5.8
This building, being converted from bank offices to residential condominiums, has sprinkler piping from a 1980s renovation that will have to be changed.

FIGURE 5.9
Adaptive reuses often have a new suspended ceiling installed. In this case the existing upright fire protection sprinklers had to be converted to pendant sprinklers located below a new ceiling.

Fire-Suppression Systems

Fire-suppression sprinkler systems can be found in older warehouse, manufacturing buildings, and the like, as well as newer buildings. They must be checked for suitability for a new occupancy classification as well as inspected and tested by the fire service authorities. Steel pipe is subject to corrosion, and frequently when old pipe is disturbed by removing some part of it, other joints, and especially screwed joints, may develop leaks. Figure 5.8 shows sprinkler piping from a 1980s remodeling with some threaded joints and some grooved coupling joints. The temperature rating of sprinkler heads may be incorrect for a new occupancy, or upright heads such as those in Figure 5.8 may need to be replaced by pendent heads in a new ceiling. Figure 5.9 shows sprinkler piping with pendant sprinklers ready for a new suspended ceiling. Note the limited ceiling space.

Operating Condition

The water supply should be visually inspected where accessible and tested for adequate pressure and for water quality. Pressure tests may be performed with simple gauges attached to hose connections. Test pressure should be one and a half times the working pressure or 50 psig, whichever is greater. Water quality tests are usually done by the water utility or a chemistry laboratory.

Sanitary and storm drainage systems should be tested for leakage with water, air or pressurized smoke. Before testing, close all openings in the section to be tested. Isolate sections if desired by inserting inflatable bladders into the pipe at cleanout openings or at branches where fixtures have been removed. To test with water, fill the system with water at the highest opening and observe for leaks for at least 15 minutes. To test with air, pressurize the system to 5 psig and leave under pressure for at least 15 minutes. A loss in pressure indicates a leak, which can be located by sound, but the leak may be difficult to identify. To test with smoke, fill the system with smoke from machines, pressurize the system to one inch of water column and leave under pressure for at least 15 minutes. The location of a leak can be readily observed by the smoke issuing through it. Testing is further discussed in Chapter 8.

Suitability Evaluation for New Application

Available Space

For commercial buildings plumbing codes generally require lavatory facilities for both genders on each floor. Access to these facilities must be reasonable, from the travel distances to special considerations for the physically challenged. Today's codes require more fixtures than older codes did. If a building considered for reuse did not have a similar occupancy to what is planned, it may be necessary to add toilets. This can add to construction costs. Additional runs of pipe to reach the new toilets may require channeling through existing concrete floors or creating new vertical chases. If the new occupancy is residential, then it is likely to require many new bathrooms and kitchen facilities. The introduction of low-water consumption closets has reduced drainage flow rates, so existing pipes should have adequate capacity for some additional fixtures.

FIGURE 5.10
Here the height of a new ceiling is determined by the horizontal portion of a rain leader.

FIGURE 5.11
Pipe penetrations through existing fire-rated construction must have protection to preserve the integrity of the rating. In this case each new pipe penetration has a listed collar to protect its hole.

Plumbing systems are less bulky than mechanical systems, but they still require some space. The most common space conflict is room for horizontal drain lines because they slope downward. Figure 5.10 shows the vertical space limitations often encountered between window heads and rain leaders. It is critical for the lines to have adequate slope to provide flow and keep solid materials in suspension, so ceiling heights may have to be lowered rather than change pipe slope.

Conformance with the Character of the Building

If a building is to retain its original character, replacement plumbing fixtures must be selected to match the period as much as possible. Many manufacturers now make fixtures that appear to be from earlier eras but meet today's codes.

Fire Code

Penetrations through fire-rated construction, both existing and new, must maintain the integrity of the rating. This involves selection of UL(Underwriters Labs) approved fire-stop assemblies or enclosure of the pipe in fire-rated materials such as those shown in Figure 5.11. Vertical pipes, called *risers* (pressure pipes) or *stacks* (DWV) in plumbing terminology, are often enclosed in fire-rated shafts or chases.

Energy Efficiency

The primary consumer of energy in plumbing systems is the water heater. In commercial or institutional buildings built before about 1950, the water heater may have consisted of a storage tank with heat exchanger heated by a boiler. This design is relatively inefficient and necessitates running the boiler in the summer; it should be replaced by a new water heater. If the new use is residential apartments or condominiums, it may be desirable to install a small storage heater in each unit. If the new occupancy is commercial or institutional the choice will probably be a heater with storage tanks.

Instantaneous water heaters, also called *tankless water heaters* (see Figure 5.12), have sufficient capacity to heat the water as it flows to the point of use rather than heating it slowly and storing it until used. This design requires larger energy supplies—gas pipes or wires—but may save the heat lost through storage tank walls during periods of low use. Instantaneous heaters are usually located near the point of use such as under a lavatory or a shower, but larger central instantaneous heaters are becoming available.

Old hot water pipes should be checked for insulation as it was not uncommon to leave them uninsulated in the past. If the water heater is more than 75 feet from a fixture, it may be desirable to install a recirculating system to minimize the delay in getting hot water to remote fixtures.

Life-Cycle Cost

This analytical procedure is explained in more detail in Chapter 7, but it is discussed here in relation to decisions between plumbing alternatives. Often a component that is initially more expensive may save enough in operating costs to be less expensive over

FIGURE 5.12
Instantaneous or "tankless" water heaters are recent additions to the choices available to designers and owners. They may be good alternatives to traditional storage heaters.

its lifetime. To perform this analysis, the designer should have initial costs, expected lifetimes, energy-consumption rates, and fuel costs. Expected life and projections of replacement costs, labor costs, and fuel-cost escalation rates are difficult to predict and less certain than the initial and annual operating cost. Nevertheless, careful projections using the best available information can produce the optimal basis for decisions.

Sustainability

The most sustainable practice is usually to continue to use existing systems. In some cases of adaptive reuse, this may be possible, or it may be possible to continue to use parts of a system. In most cases it may be necessary to remove the existing and replace with new systems. If the old system has numerous pipe leaks, it probably is not practical to patch it. In the case of potable water, supply piping corrosion and scaling may have made the system no longer useful. Selection of low-water consumption fixtures will minimize potable water use. Collection of rainwater or gray water (wastewater generated from domestic activities such as washing dishes, taking baths, and the like) for subsequent use in flushing or landscape irrigation as shown in Figure 5.13 will further reduce potable water consumption. Rainwater collection and reuse has been a practice in the past, but now it is enjoying resurgence as a way to provide landscape irrigation and gray water for other uses.

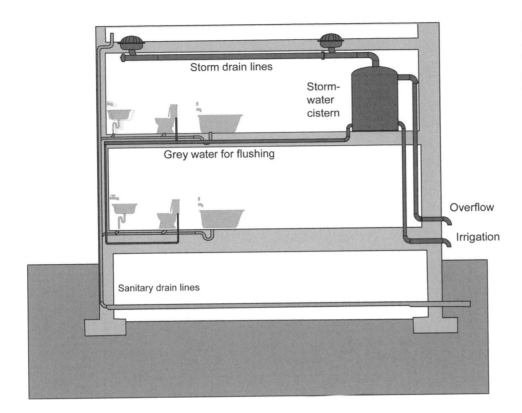

FIGURE 5.13
As concern for the potable water supply increases, other sources of usable, nonpotable water to replace it are emerging. One sustainable choice is a cistern to collect and store storm water for flushing toilets and irrigating landscaping.

Storm Drainage Systems

If the roof deck of an existing building is to remain in use, the roof drain system may be adequate for continued use. Figure 5.14 shows a new roof drain replacing an old one at the same location and connected to the existing piping. Cast-iron piping resists deterioration very well and has a service life of a century or more. It may be desirable to insulate horizontal rain leaders to prevent condensation dripping on finish materials during winter rains.

Potable Water Supply Systems

In addition to the corrosion and scaling mentioned earlier, existing potable water piping may not be able to deliver adequate flow by today's standards because of limited pipe sizes. On the other hand, waterless urinals and low-flush toilets have reduced the demand on supply piping. Threaded joints in steel pipe are very susceptible to corrosion and leaks. This is especially true when the piping is disturbed as parts of it are removed or new connections made.

Sanitary Drainage Systems

For storm drain systems, cast iron was the premium material for sanitary drains and can be usable for 100 years or more. Other pipe materials used for sanitary drains and vents also have very long useful lives. One of these is vitrified clay, which is a permanent but brittle material. It can suffer cracking due to physical impacts, shifting foundations,

FIGURE 5.14
In adaptive reuse projects, it is sometimes necessary to replace plumbing fixtures and fittings. Here a new roof drain replaces an old one at the same location. Note that the roof deck must be sound enough for continued service.

crushing, and other kinds of movement. Plastics such as PVC (polyvinyl chloride) appear to be relatively impervious to corrosion. This material, however, requires careful support and protection from ultraviolet radiation. Figure 5.15 shows a PVC sanitary drain installed during a 1980s remodeling. Methods of joining different pipe materials, such as plastic to cast iron, exist. This allows an adaptive reuse project to retrofit any existing runs of drain or vent pipe. The development of low-flush water closets and waterless urinals has decreased flow rates. This means that existing pipes can serve more fixtures, especially when codes require more.

Gas Piping Systems

Most natural or LP gas systems use black (not galvanized) steel pipe. Copper and aluminum tubing may also be used if the gas does not contain corrosive impurities. Neither of these gases is corrosive in itself, so except for gaseous impurities or water contamination in the gas, the interior of existing pipe is likely to be reusable. Where this pipe is exposed to weather, it can have external corrosion at threaded or welded joints. Plastic pipe may be used outside underground if listed for this purpose. Pressure tests should be performed on existing pipe to assure integrity. If pipe sizes of low-pressure systems are inadequate for intended new uses, it may be possible to increase the pressure and consequently the flow rate and thus reuse the pipe.

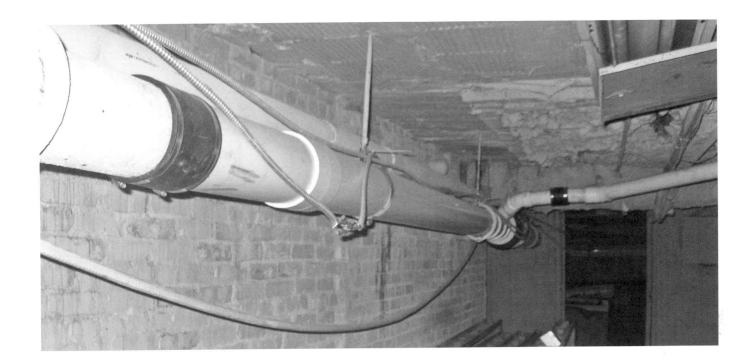

Fire-Suppression Systems

Sprinkler systems are carefully regulated and designed to deliver specific water flow rates over given areas. The requirements change with occupancy types, and thus a new use for a building will require investigation to assure compliance with new flow rates. If partitions are relocated and new partitions installed, sprinklers may also have to be relocated. In general sprinklers must be no more than 7.5 feet from walls and no more than 15 feet apart. Closer spacing may be dictated by minimum density requirements. Pressure in utility water systems may change over time and flow may not meet requirements after many years.

Most sprinkler systems use black steel pipe with threaded or grooved coupling joints. These are subject to the corrosion mentioned above and installers of new sections of pipe may find leaks appearing at previously tight joints as internally rusted pipes are disturbed. Corrosion in sprinklers systems is not as severe as in potable water systems, however, because the water in sprinkler piping is kept for years. Once the oxygen in an initial fill of water reacts with the pipe material, no further reaction takes place until fresh water is introduced. Valves and alarm systems have improved dramatically in recent years, so older signal systems will probably have to be upgraded.

FIGURE 5.15
Plastic pipe as well as cast iron can be spliced and continued in service. This photograph shows a 1980s PVC sanitary drain coupled with an approved rubber sleeve.

Selection of New Systems

Storm Drainage Systems

The shape of the roof dictates the type of storm drain system. A pitched roof probably has gutters at the eaves and downspouts to convey the water to the surface of the

FIGURE 5.16
Urinals and water closets use large quantities of potable water. Low-water use urinals have become available to reduce the volume of water required. This one flushes with less than a gallon of water.

ground outside. Most commercial and residential gutters are corrosion-resistant aluminum. Downspout discharge on the surface can cause erosion in some soils, and flow should be dispersed using rock beds or the downspouts connected to utility storm drains if available.

Low-slope or flat roofs usually have roof drains and internal rain leaders to carry the storm water to utility storm drains. The roof drains have domed strainers to minimize the possibility of blockage by leaves or other debris. Internal storm-drain piping may be cast iron or plastic. Pipe sizes can be as large as 12 inches in diameter, and space for horizontal sloping runs and vertical stacks must be allocated. These gravity flow lines take precedence over pressure flow lines or air ducts, so coordination between construction trades is important. It is prudent to insulate storm drains to prevent condensation on the exterior of pipes during cold rains. This is particularly important for pipes located over acoustic tile or gypsum board ceilings where drips and consequent stains ruin appearances. If the vertical stacks are in masonry chases, insulation can sometimes be omitted there.

FIGURE 5.17
An even more sustainable urinal is one that uses no water at all. Waterless urinals may have increased maintenance requirements, however.

Potable Water Supply Systems

New potable water systems from utility sources are very standardized and reliable. The main issues to consider are the pipe material, fixtures, and type of water heating. Copper is still the premium material for pipe sizes up to about two inches diameter; but its sometimes volatile price has led to searches for alternatives. The high price at this writing is causing serious theft problems in both new and renovation construction and in unprotected buildings. Chlorinated polyvinyl chloride (CPVC) pipe has been in common use for 30 to 40 years and has proven durable. But it is susceptible to distortion and sagging if not supported at close intervals. This is especially true of large sizes. Newer pipe material such as cross-linked polyethylene, polybutylene, and polypropylene are in current use.

Low-flush water closets have matured, and most flush reliably using one gallon of water. Low-flush urinals as shown in Figure 5.16 use less than one gallon per flush. Waterless urinals (Figure 5.17) eliminate supply piping entirely and are popular ways to conserve water. Water closets, urinals, and lavatories made of vitreous china are the optimal choice. Bathtubs and showers molded of fiberglass and acrylic materials are very popular, but cast iron tubs and tiled showers still remain serviceable and attractive options.

Sanitary Drainage Systems

Fitting new DWV systems into existing buildings, such as storm-drain systems, can be challenging. The requirement for gravity flow in these lines results in large pipe sizes and mandatory downward slopes that can create conflicts with structural members, ceilings, air ducts, and other pipes. Where new systems must be installed in buildings of two or more stories, stacking toilets and other rooms with plumbing makes the system more economical and minimizes these conflicts. In single-story buildings, the plumbed areas should be clustered as close together as possible. Of course, if existing DWV lines can be incorporated into new plans, this may offset the need to stack or cluster.

Materials for new DWV piping can be cast iron or ABS (acrylonitrile-butadiene-styrene) or PVC plastics. Cast iron has the advantage of attenuating the sound of flowing water better than plastic but is likely more expensive.

Gas Piping Systems

Natural and liquified petroleum (LP) gas systems are closely regulated and few decisions are left to the designer and owner. Piping is relatively small and can be run up and down as required to fit into existing structures. Where possible, it is preferable to run the pipe in accessible spaces rather than concealed inside walls.

FIGURE 5.18
Prior to the Americans with Disabilities Act, toilet rooms were smaller and were not accessible for persons in wheelchairs.

Fire-Suppression Systems

Fire-suppression sprinkler systems are the best protection available for people and buildings. They have proven effective in extinguishing fires with only a few sprinklers operating and reliable in function when properly maintained. These systems, like the gas and plumbing systems discussed in this chapter, are highly regulated by codes and few decisions are left to the discretion of designers and owners. The type of sprinklers—pendent, upright, concealed, and so on—is one such option. Whether to conceal or expose the horizontal piping is another.

Toilet Rooms

Required Facilities

Before plumbing codes required certain minimum fixture counts, designers and architects were free to use their judgment about the number and type of fixtures in their buildings. Since codes now list minimum facilities, the number required is generally larger. Recently recognition of the inadequacy of facilities for women in commercial and institutional buildings, for example, has resulted in a rapid increase in the number of water closets in women's toilets.

Handicapped Access

Another major influence on the space in toilets are the requirements mandated by the Americans with Disabilities Act (ADA) and the requirements of various state agencies for access for people who use wheelchairs or require other assistance to use water closets, washbasins, and other fixtures. Doors, passageways, and privacy stalls must be

FIGURE 5.19
Wheelchair-accessible toilet stalls with grab rails are now required. Existing toilet rooms probably will have to be expanded to meet the current codes.

FIGURE 5.20
Wheelchair-accessible toilet rooms are larger and more spacious than nonaccessible toilets.

FIGURE 5.21
Handicapped accessibility is one reason to upgrade existing toilers. Another is to improve the appearance of cramped, dark, and unattractive older toilets.

wider and space for turning radii (a five-foot circle) provided. Thresholds must be flat and ramps must circumvent stairs. Grab rails in stalls take even more space. Wheelchair accessible lavatories and urinals also need more space in toilets. It is apparent that toilets constructed before accessibility requirements, such as the one shown in Figure 5.18, will not suffice for today. In cases of adaptive reuse, such as this book covers, the changes will most likely include upgrading to meet codes current at the time of the new construction. This means meeting the extensive accessibility requirements (Figures 5.19 and 5.20).

Toilet Room Appearance

During most of the twentieth century, toilet rooms were considered to be utilitarian spaces with few amenities. They were designed as small as possible and frequently finishes were plain. As society became more affluent, toilets received more attention from designers. Consequently, toilets constructed in the latter third of the century are often larger and have higher-quality finishes. In evaluating a building for adaptive reuse, it is prudent to view the existing toilet in light of these developments. The marble walls shown in Figure 5.21 could be attractive, but the plain appearance, lack of mirrors, and dim lighting are unacceptable, compare with Figure 5.20.

Sustainability CHAPTER 6

Sustainability is a popular topic of discussion and a buzzword for building owners and designers. Is it only for new construction? Does it have any application to adaptive reuse? Is not leaving an existing building as it is the most sustainable course of action? What responsibility toward sustainability does a decision maker have? This chapter addresses these and other questions on the subject.

What Is Sustainability?

Climate Change

Since the 1980s the public has become increasingly aware of changes in the climate and the evidence that our planet is rapidly becoming warmer. In the geologic timescale, the earth appears to naturally and periodically cool and warm. These cycles are influenced by solar activity, orbital variations, volcanic activity, and other variables. The current warming trend is much faster than in past natural warming cycles, however. The United Nations (UN) has been studying the situation and its Intergovernmental Panel on Climate Change (IPCC) has issued a series of reports that conclude that it is very likely that gases resulting from anthropogenic (human) activities are a major factor in the warming process.

Our planet has an envelope of gases surrounding its surface. Some of these gases transmit incoming shortwave solar radiation (ultraviolet and visible light) but not longer-wave infrared radiation reflected from the earth's surface or originating on earth. These gases include water vapor, methane, nitrous oxide, and carbon dioxide. By admitting more incoming radiant heat and reducing escaping heat, these gases act as a blanket to warm the planet. The net result is that earth is about 43 degrees Celsius (C) warmer than if it had no atmosphere

Carbon dioxide occurs naturally and is necessary for plant respiration. It is also one of the products of combustion of hydrocarbon fuels such as wood, coal, and oil. If we burned only the wood we harvest and no fossil fuels, the earth would be able to absorb the carbon dioxide generated. However, fossil fuels are our major energy source, and their carbon has been locked up for millions of years. The earth cannot absorb the additional carbon dioxide released from these fossil fuels, and the resulting buildup appears to be a major factor in global warming. Carbon dioxide concentrations in the atmosphere have risen from about 280 parts per million (ppm) in 1900 to about 380 ppm in 2000.

The predicted effects of this warming are dire. Rising sea levels and increasingly severe storms, floods, and droughts are forecast. Loss of cropland and population displacement is possible. It is essential that humans reduce the amount of carbon emissions over the next few decades.

FIGURE 6.1
Candler Library at Emory University in Atlanta, Georgia, earned a Silver LEED Rating for a renovation project.

Growing Population

The population of the world has more than doubled from about 3 billion people in 1960 to about 6.6 billion in the past 47 years according to the U.S. Census Bureau (2008). Most of this growth has taken place in the developing countries, especially India, China, and Southeast Asia. This growth is expected to continue but at a diminishing rate. The world population will reach about 9.5 billion by 2050. Europe's population peaked in the 1990s and is now declining, and the United States population growth is slowing. A larger population means more demand for resources and energy.

Diminishing Resources

Natural resources such as minerals, fossil fuels, and water are limited, and ultimately the growing population will exert pressure on the supply. Oil is currently increasing in price as developing countries embrace the automobile culture. The price of many building materials is also increasing at the current time as demand increases. Some materials such as steel, copper, and aluminum already are extensively recycled; but many other materials that could be recycled are not being reused under current practice. In the long-range view, earth's resources are finite, and it will be prudent to use as few new resources as possible. Conservation in place is better than recycling or reusing materials and this is what adaptive reuse of buildings is all about. Emory University's Candler Library pictured in Figure 6.1 received a Silver LEED Rating after a major renovation. The Leadership in Energy and Environmental Design (or LEED) Rating System is described below.

Definitions of Sustainability

Many definitions of sustainability have been proposed. A generally accepted one is: Meeting today's needs without compromising the ability of future generations to meet their needs. The American Society of Heating, Refrigerating, and Air-Conditioning Engineers (ASHRAE) has drafted an Energy Position Document in which it describes sustainability as "a means to provide a safe healthy comfortable indoor environment while simultaneously limiting the impact on the Earth's natural resources."

While the use of energy and natural resources is a critical aspect of sustainability, the concept is broader than this. Protection of the natural environment, clean air, and clean water are important components.

Buildings and Sustainability

Building Energy Use

Energy is used to build a building, keep it comfortable and useful during its life, and to demolish it after it is no longer useful. The amount of energy consumed during this lifetime varies greatly from building to building. However, extending a building's useful life is almost always more sustainable than demolition and reconstruction. Responsible consideration of this subject should be part of every decision whether to adaptively reuse or to demolish and rebuild.

In February 2007, the *2010 Imperative* webcast by Architecture 2030, the environmental advocacy group, stated that in the United States we renovate 1.75 billion square feet of buildings each year, so we will renovate a total of 150 billion square feet by 2030. The 2030 Challenge presented during this webcast includes developing the ability to design new buildings for zero-net-energy use by the year 2030. For the renovated buildings, the goal is to reduce their energy use by 50 percent.

The U.S. Department of Energy (DOE) through its Energy Information Agency (EIA) publishes the Commercial Building Energy Consumption Survey (CBECS) of existing stock. The 2003 survey showed an overall average Energy Use Index (EUI) of 91,000 Btu/ft^2/yr for the United States. The American Institute of Architects, ASHRAE, U.S. Green Building Council (USGBC), and the Illuminating Engineering Society of North America (IESNA) have agreed that this will be the starting point for their efforts, in parallel with the 2030 Challenge, to reduce the EUI for new buildings to 36,000 Btu/ft^2/yr and the EUI for existing buildings to 50 percent of their previous use by 2010 and to net zero by 2030.

During Construction

Energy is necessary to produce building materials, bring them to the site, and erect them into a finished building. The amount of this energy is dependent on the selection of materials. A number of investigators have examined the embodied energy in various building materials.

During Operation

The energy to construct a building is overshadowed by the energy to operate it. This energy is that necessary for lighting, heating, cooling, and internal operations such as elevators, water heating, and equipment operation. It is greatly affected by the thermal efficiency of the building enclosure and the efficacy of the lighting, as well as the conscientiousness of the operators.

During Demolition

Too often buildings are simply knocked down with bulldozers or cranes and wrecking balls. In addition to actual demolition, energy is consumed in transporting the materials and debris to a landfill or other disposal point. The energy required is small in comparison with that needed to build and operate the building, but even the demolition energy can be avoided if the building is reused.

Materials for Buildings

Natural Resources

As noted above, valuable and finite natural resources may be consumed in the construction of a new building. While some materials have recycled content, it is rarely if ever 100 percent. Adaptive reuse can avoid most of the need for new materials, certainly more than demolition and rebuilding. Use of recycled materials is preferable to new materials. A natural resource that is becoming an issue in many parts of the world is water. Buildings use water for several purposes and not all of them require clean potable water. Figure 5.13 in the previous chapter shows a system for storing and using rainwater to flush toilets and irrigate landscaping. This system is encouraged by LEED points as described in this chapter.

Embodied Energy

Where new materials must be used, those with the lowest embodied energy should be selected. Embodied energy is difficult to quantify, but several organizations and individual authors have published lists. Hammond and Jones (2006) have produced a detailed database of embodied energy and carbon emissions using United Kingdom materials that is downloadable from the Internet. The Athena Sustainable Materials Institute offers free downloadable software to calculate the sustainability of North American materials and common assemblies.

Renewable Materials

Products made from rapidly growing plants such as bamboo are very sustainable and their use is recommended. Bamboo can be made into flooring, ceilings, and furniture.

There is some question about the energy and fuel consumption needed to transport the bamboo that is imported from Southeast Asia. Other rapidly renewable materials include cotton and wool insulation, cork, wheat and strawboard, and linoleum. Wood products, and particularly those harvested from forests managed sustainably according to the Forest Stewardship Council's principles, are responsible choices.

Local Materials

A considerable portion of the embodied energy for many construction materials is the energy used to transport the materials from the source to the project site. Often a more sustainable local material is overlooked in favor of customary material or material somehow considered more desirable. A return to more regional architecture would help to focus on local materials.

Reused Materials

Among the most sustainable choices in building materials is to reuse materials and assemblies salvaged from the building being adaptively reused or other buildings. This reduces landfill volume and air and water pollution from materials that are reused instead of discarded. It also minimizes embodied energy and environmental effects. Reused materials from other buildings can be selected to match the time horizon and style of a building that is to be adapted to a new use. Figure 6.2 shows steel joists salvaged for reuse after demolition of a building.

Postconsumer Recycled Materials

Another very sustainable practice is to choose materials that contain some postconsumer recycled content. Steel is an example that has 25 to 90 percent recycled content. Concrete made with fly ash from coal-burning power plants is another.

FIGURE 6.2
Steel joists have been removed from a building for reuse on another project. Reuse is a very sustainable process.

Demolition of Buildings

Toxic Materials

Some construction materials removed from buildings have toxic properties. Asbestos and lead are well-known examples that are regulated by laws. Other materials may also have toxic effects that are not regulated. Materials that are reused or recycled do not go into landfills and thus do not pollute groundwater.

Landfill Volume

In some communities construction debris composes a significant fraction of the waste taken to landfills. The practice of throwing away packaging materials, crates and boxes, scrap lumber, broken concrete, and so on should be examined for the possibility of other alternatives such as recycling. In addition to reduced resource use, the reduction in landfill volume can save costs. The U.S. Environmental Protection Agency (EPA) estimated in 2003 that construction debris totals about 135.5 million tons per year in the United States. Of this amount, they estimate that 0.2 million tons is waste from nonresidential new building construction, 9.8 million tons is debris from nonresidential building renovation, and 29.8 million tons is from nonresidential building demolition. Table 6.1 shows the breakdown of the waste materials.

Measuring Sustainability

In the late 1980s it began to be apparent that some method of measuring the sustainability of buildings was needed. The first systems of measurement were developed in Europe. Groups in the United States and Canada began work on similar systems in the early 1990s.

TABLE 6.1
Breakdown of construction and demolition debris. One goal of sustainable design and construction is to conserve and reuse building materials rather than to demolish and discard them.
Source: Sandler 2003, 51.

BREAKDOWN OF CONSTRUCTION AND DEMOLITION DEBRIS OVERALL	
http://www.epa.gov/CDmaterials/basic.htm	
Concrete and mixed rubble	40–50%
Wood	20–30%
Drywall	5–15%
Asphalt roofing	1–10%
Metals	1–5%
Bricks	1–5%
Plastics	1–5%

LEED®

In 1998 the USGBC published its first Leadership in Energy and Environmental Design Rating System. Since that time they have revised the original system and published five more rating systems with still more in the works. The rating system applicable to adaptive reuse is the USGBC's LEED New Construction and Major Renovation. The LEED NC Version 2.2 is the edition current at this writing. This system awards points in six categories:

- Sustainable Sites
- Water Efficiency
- Energy and Atmosphere
- Materials and Resources
- Indoor Environmental Quality
- Innovation in Design

By achieving 26 out of the possible 69 points a building can become Certified. Additional points earn higher ratings. The LEED NC 2.2 Reference Guide in Figure 6.3 is an invaluable tool in designing for LEED certification.

Of particular significance in adaptive reuse, LEED points can be earned by retaining 75 percent and 95 percent of existing walls and floors and by retaining 50 percent of existing interior nonstructural elements. Other points can be earned by reusing buildings in densely built areas, brownfields (i.e., properties in which the presence or potential presence of a hazardous substance, pollutant, or contaminant exists), and areas with existing infrastructure.

FIGURE 6.3
The LEED NC 2.2 Reference Guide is an essential tool for those involved in attaining a LEED rating for a major renovation project.

Why would one want to have a LEED-certified building? LEED certification indicates to the public the owner's commitment to ethical and responsible environmental citizenship. It shows willingness to invest in a sustainable future. It shows recognition of the impact of buildings on the environment and a desire to minimize that impact. It will bring public recognition to the building and probably increase its value.

Green Globes

Green Globes is an online sustainability assessment tool that has evolved from the original Building Research Establishment Environmental Assessment Method (BREEAM) system in the United Kingdom. It allows designers and owners to compare the sustainable performance of their buildings with best practices. It was developed in Canada as a less-expensive alternative to LEED. Green Globes is gaining popularity in the United States as well. It has also been harmonized with LEED so that they both have similar criteria. It enables users to rate their building online as they design. Third-party verification is available.

Pro Forma Analysis CHAPTER 7

The pro forma analysis, introduced in Chapter 1, is a standard part of any evaluation of a real estate purchase in which the economic feasibility of a business use or a redevelopment project is the desired outcome. Owner, developers, and other stakeholders in such purchases require that an investment produce a positive return.

The Purpose of a Pro Forma Analysis in Adaptive Reuse

The pro forma analysis allows the architects and developers to explore the rates of return by introducing different variables to assist them in making the right business decisions. For example, the pro forma, which is an automated computer workbook (e.g., Microsoft Excel), can run the numbers on projected square-foot costs and projected square-foot rental rates.

The pro forma's value is that it costs very little itself. It uses basic data to determine the feasibility of a project and with more refined construction estimates subsequent and ongoing economic analysis with even more accuracy.

As you can see, the pro forma simply plays the "what-if" game. You can look at relatively modest construction costs and then, by adding variables, more expensive construction costs. You can, for example, evaluate ranges and compare the rates of return using a more rigid or static rental rate. You can affix the construction costs at a certain class of construction that will produce a certain quality building and then vary the rental rates to see a minimum and maximum rate of return.

The first page—i.e., *worksheet*—of a pro forma presents the project variables. It is here that the user enters the required data so that the workbook can process the data and yield results over a spectrum of analyses that appear on individual worksheets. (The automated routines are called *macros*.) With certain numbers fixed such as interest rates, mortgage term, and mortgage ratio, you can then play *what-if* scenarios—by changing specific variable items and observing the generated returns. An example might be running the numbers for loft apartments in a former factory building and then the numbers for office units. Data can easily be obtained. For example, if the building is a possible purchase, the realtors or seller can provide the square footages. The party considering the purchase of the building will often have many of the numbers for the construction costs they intend to spend on the intended reuse. Experienced developers and architects can also provide data on how much costs will run given such variables as the quality of materials, construction methods, and what building codes require. Standard initial estimates of square-foot-construction costs are the product of experience. A feel for the costs can be achieved for the class of construction and building type.

This chapter explains and reproduces a typical pro forma analysis. The first sheet of the workbook includes the variables where the working numbers are entered. These include the following and require the most informed information possible:

Original Cost of Building The purchase price or book value (i.e., depreciation value) at the time a remodeling project begins.

Prime Interest Prime interest at the time of evaluation.

Mortgage Interest Interest rate on the permanent long-term mortgage.

Mortgage Term Length of the mortgage term in years. All pro forma data is set up on an annual basis. If the actual loan is to have monthly payments, the annual method utilized by this routine will produce adequate results.

Mortgage Ratio Ratio of the mortgage amount to the total project budget.

Annual Taxes Combined annual taxes, city and county.

Insurance, Annual Annual cost of fire, casualty, and liability insurance.

Utilities, Annual The annual cost of building utilities.

Janitorial, Annual The annual cost of janitorial services.

Maintenance, Annual Annual cost of miscellaneous repairs and preventive maintenance.

Construction Interest Rate Cost of money to pay contractors during the construction period.

Rental Rates Square-foot rental rates by floors to allow differentiation. The number of floors can be altered, up or down, with only a small effort.

Rentable Square Feet Rentable square feet by floors can be altered. The rentable square footage is a net. The corridors, stairs, mechanical rooms, and restroom square footages are not included in the rental computations.

Gross Square Foot The gross square foot for each floor is needed for construction cost formulas. This too can be altered up or down as needed.

Construction Costs per Square Foot Construction costs per square foot by floors is also set up to allow different quality or different degrees of construction (semifinish, etc.) as needed.

Initial Cost of Building including Land The initial or original cost of the building is shown a second time to allow the improvements and the land costs to be segregated for setting up the depreciation schedules.

Land Value and Value of Improvements Separate items as required by the spreadsheet.

In addition to the previous list, owner's equity, selling price, and present-value interest are also variables to enter. The owner's equity, however, is a figure pulled from a lower section of the pro forma and is not truly a variable. Income tax and capital gains rates are derived from the personal tax portfolio of the developer. Exhibit 7.1 is an example of a pro forma workbook for a commercial building rehabilitation project. Instructions follow for creating your own in a spreadsheet application such as Microsoft Excel.

	A	B	C	D	E	F	G	H	I
1	PRO FORMA WORKSHEET—COMMERCIAL REHABILITATION PROJECTS								
2									
3									
4	PROJECT TITLE—COMMERCIAL BUILDING (80 ft. x 100 ft.) NONHISTORIC								
5	Trial Number One								
6									
7									
8	(Variable Input		Orig. Cost Bldg. =		$1,000,000.00		Rental Rate (Fourth Floor) =		$15.00
9	Data, Above Line)		Prime Interest =		6.250%		Rentable SF (Fourth Floor) =		6400.00
10			Mortgage Intr. =		5.625%		Rental Rate (Third Floor) =		$16.00
11			Mortgage Term =		30.00		Rentable SF (Third Floor) =		6400.00
12			Mortgage Ratio =		0.95		Rental Rate (Second Floor) =		$16.00
13			Annual Taxes =		$80,000.00		Rentable SF (Second Floor) =		6400.00
14			Insurance Ann. =		$20,000.00		Rental Rate (First Floor) =		$30.00
15			Utilities, Ann. =		$12,500.00		Rentable SF (First Floor) =		6400.00
16			Janitorial, Ann. =		$10,000.00		Rental Rate (Basement) =		$10.00
17			Maintenance, Ann. =		$10,000.00		Rentable SF (Basement) =		3500.00
18			Const. Intr. Rate =		6.25%				
19									
20			CONSTRUCTION COSTS						
21			Cost/SF Roof Repl. =		$30.00		Gross SF/Roof =		8000.00
22			Cost/SF Fourth Floor =		$65.00		Gross SF/Fourth Floor =		8000.00
23			Cost/SF Third Floor =		$65.00		Gross SF/Third Floor =		8000.00
24			Cost/SF Second Flr. =		$65.00		Gross SF/Second Floor =		8000.00
25			Cost/SF First Floor =		$80.00		Gross SF/First Floor =		8000.00
26			Cost/SF Basement =		$55.00		Gross SF/Basement =		5000.00
27			Cost, Lobby Special =		$50,000.00				
28			Cost, Elevator (s) =		$50,000.00		Initial Cost of Building incl. land =		$1,000,000.00
29			Cost, Fire Stair (s) =		$30,000.00		Value of Improvements =		$750,000.00
30							Land Value (nondepreciable) =		$250,000.00
31									
32			Owner's EQUITY =		$212,520.63		(From Computations below)		
33									
34			SELLING PRICE =		$8,000,000.00		(Selling Price when held to end of sixth year)		
35									
36									
37			PV INTEREST =		6.25%		(INTEREST RATE for calculating PRESENT VALUE)		
38							at time of Sale.		
39			INCOME TAX RATE =		31.50%		(Standard Tax Rate for persons with substantial incomes)		
40									
41			RATE ON CAPITAL GAINS =		34.00%				
42									
43									
44									
45									
46									
47	PRO FORMA WORKSHEET USING DATA INPUT FROM TABLE ABOVE								
48									
49	NET OPERATING INCOME: (Net Operating Income is the Gross Rent minus Expenses)								
50				Dollars/ Sq. Ft.		Rentable	Gross Annual		
51				Rental Rate		Sq. Foot	Rent		
52	Gross Rent (Annual)			Varies, See Above		29,100	$527,800.00	Rent x SF, each Floor	
53	Vacancy Ratio			5% of Gross			$26,390.00	5% Vacancy	
54	Expenses:								
55	Taxes (Real Estate) =			Annual Cost (Manual Entry from above) =			$80,000.00		
56	Insurance =			Annual Cost (Manual Entry from above) =			$20,000.00		
57	Utilities =			Annual Cost (Manual Entry from above) =			$12,500.00		
58	Janitorial =			Annual Cost (Manual Entry from above) =			$10,000.00		
59	Maintenance =			(Annual Figures) =			$10,000.00		
60	Net Operating Income (NOI)			(Annual Figures) =			$368,910.00	(NOI = Gross Rent minus	
61								Expenses	
62	ECONOMIC VALUE: (Economic Value is the Net Operating Income divided by the Capitalization Rate.)								
63	Capitalization is the Prime Rate plus one =							7.250%	
64	ECONOMIC VALUE =			NOI/Cap. Rate =				$5,088,413.79	
65	If your TOTAL PROJECT BUDGET exceeds the ECONOMIC VALUE —The project is NO good —NO POSITIVE RETURN.								
66									
67									
68							Page No. 1		
69									

EXHIBIT 7.1
Pro forma workbook—commercial rehabilitation projects.

	A	B	C	D	E	F	G	H	I
70									
71	PRO FORMA WORKSHEET USING DATA INPUT FROM TABLE ON PAGE NO. 1 AND PAGE NO. 2								
72									
73	CONSTRUCTION ESTIMATE OF COSTS (Summary)								
74						Square Foot			
75	Basic Square Foot Estimate					37,000	$2,715,000.00	(Const. Cost = SF Cost x SF ea. Flr.)	
76	Misc. Additional Costs, Elevator, Fire Stairs, etc.						$130,000.00	(List of Additional Expenses)	
77	Architect's Fee: 8% of Total Construction Costs						$227,600.00	(8% is an Estimated Fee)	
78	Construction Interest: 50% of Total Const. Cost x One Year						$177,812.50	Cost of Construction Loan, One Year	
79	Initial Cost of Building, Land plus Improvements						$1,000,000.00	(Initial Cost of Property, Bldg + Land)	
80									
81	TOTAL PROJECT COSTS: (TOTAL PROJECT BUDGET)						$4,250,412.50	(Compare the Total Project Budget to	
82								the Economic Value)	
83									
84			RATIO OF ECONOMIC VALUE TO TOTAL PROJECT BUDGET				1.20	If RATIO is more than 1, the Project	
85								is good. If RATIO is less than 1,	
86								the Project is no good.	
87									
88									
89									
90									
91	DEPRECIATION VALUES								
92	Total Construction Costs (Total Project Budget)						$4,250,412.50		
93	Minus Land Costs of Initial Cost of Building						$250,000.00	(Land Costs subtracted here)	
94									
95	DEPRECIATION BASIS: Of Completed Project						$4,000,412.50	(Depr. Basis, 40-Year Ammort.)	
96	Depreciation per Year, Forty Year Straight Line Method						$100,010.31	(One Year's Depreciation)	
97									
98		Depreciation Sch.		Year 1	Year 2	Year 3	Year 4	Year 5	Year 6
99		Beginning Depr.		$4,000,412.50	$3,900,402.19	$3,800,391.88	$3,700,381.56	$3,600,371.25	$3,500,360.94
100		Depr. for Year		$100,010.31	$100,010.31	$100,010.31	$100,010.31	$100,010.31	$100,010.31
101		End Depr. (Basis)		$3,900,402.19	$3,800,391.88	$3,700,381.56	$3,600,371.25	$3,500,360.94	$3,400,350.63
102									
103									
104									
105									
106									
107	MORTGAGE INFORMATION: Permanent Loan Information Required						Computations within Spreadsheet, Info. Data on Page No. 1		
108	Mortgage Amount: Mortgage Ratio x Total Project Budget						$4,037,891.88	(Owner's Perm. Mortgage, 30 Yrs.)	
109	Owner's Equity: Amount required for Owner Investment						$212,520.63	(Owner's Equity, 5% Cash Collateral)	
110									
111		Interest Rate, Annual =			5.625%				
112		Ammort. Period, Years =			30				
113									
114		Mortgage Payment Calculated by Quattro Inboard Function							
115									
116			Annual Payment: (@PMT(Int., Period, Mtg. Amt.)					$281,675.47	Annual Payment	
117									
118									
119	AMMORTIZATION SCHEDULE (For First Six Years of Investment)						(Fully Automatic, no entry needed.)		
120									
121				Year 1	Year 2	Year 3	Year 4	Year 5	Year 6
122	Mortgage Balance (Beginning)			$4,037,891.88	$3,983,347.83	$3,925,735.68	$3,864,882.84	$3,800,607.04	$3,732,715.72
123	Interest For Year			$227,131.42	$224,063.32	$220,822.63	$217,399.66	$213,784.15	$209,965.26
124	Principal For Year			$54,544.05	$57,612.15	$60,852.83	$64,275.81	$67,891.32	$71,710.21
125	Total Annual Payment			$281,675.47	$281,675.47	$281,675.47	$281,675.47	$281,675.47	$281,675.47
126	Mortgage Balance (End of Yr.)			$3,983,347.83	$3,925,735.68	$3,864,882.84	$3,800,607.04	$3,732,715.72	$3,661,005.51
127									
128									
129									
130									
131									
132									
133									
134									
135						Page No. 2			
136									

	A	B	C	D	E	F	G	H	I
137									
138	**PRO FORMA ANALYSIS FOR BUILDING EVALUATIONS**								
139									
140	PRO FORMA ANALYSIS WORKSHEET (Based upon Sale of the Project after Fifth Year)								
141	(Fully Automatic, no input needed, Gross Income Increases at 2% per Year and Expenses grow at 5% per Year)								
142									
143		Year of Analysis		Year 1	Year 2	Year 3	Year 4	Year 5	Year 6
144									
145	a. Gross Income (Year)			$527,800.00	$538,356.00	$549,123.12	$560,105.58	$571,307.69	$582,733.85
146	b. Operating Expenses (Year)			$158,890.00	$166,834.50	$175,176.23	$183,935.04	$193,131.79	$202,788.38
147	c. Net Income (Before Tax)			$368,910.00	$371,521.50	$373,946.90	$376,170.55	$378,175.91	$379,945.47
148	d. Less Depreciation (Year)			$100,010.31	$100,010.31	$100,010.31	$100,010.31	$100,010.31	$100,010.31
149	e. Less Interest (Mort./Year)			$227,131.42	$224,063.32	$220,822.63	$217,399.66	$213,784.15	$209,965.26
150									
151	f. Taxable Income (Year)			$41,768.27	$47,447.87	$53,113.95	$58,760.57	$64,381.45	$69,969.90
152									
153	g. Plus Depreciation (Year)			$100,010.31	$100,010.31	$100,010.31	$100,010.31	$100,010.31	$100,010.31
154	h. Less Principal Payment (Yr.)			$54,544.05	$57,612.15	$60,852.83	$64,275.81	$67,891.32	$71,710.21
155	i. Cash Flow, Before Tax (Yr.)			$87,234.53	$89,846.03	$92,271.43	$94,495.08	$96,500.44	$98,270.01
156									
157	j. Less Income Tax (Year)			$13,157.00	$14,946.08	$16,730.89	$18,509.58	$20,280.16	$22,040.52
158	k. Plus Tax Savings (Year)			<<SUPPLY MISSING FORMULA FOR APPLICABLE CELLS>>					
159									
160	l. After Tax Cash Flow (Year)			$74,077.53	$74,899.95	$75,540.54	$75,985.50	$76,220.28	$76,229.49
161									
162									
163									
164	RATE OF RETURN COMPUTATIONS (By Several Methods)								
165									
166	Rate of Return: Net Income/			8.68%	8.74%	8.80%	8.85%	8.90%	8.94%
167	Max. Project Budget								
168									
169	Return on Equity Tax Flow			41.05%	42.28%	43.42%	44.46%	45.41%	46.24%
170	Before Taxes								
171	BTCF/Owner's Equity								
172									
173	Return on Equity Tax Flow			34.86%	35.24%	35.55%	35.75%	35.86%	35.87%
174	After Taxes								
175	ATCF/Owner's Equity								
176									
177									
178									
179									
180	PRESENT VALUE OF TOTAL AFTER TAX CASH FLOWS (ATCF) (End of year 1 and all other years brought to date)								
181									
182	Total ATCF, Actual			74,077.53	74,899.95	75,540.54	75,985.50	76,220.28	76,229.49
183		PV One Year		69,720.03	70,494.08	71,096.97	71,515.76	71,736.74	71,745.40
184		PV Two Years			66,347.36	66,914.80	67,308.96	67,516.93	67,525.08
185		PV Three Years				62,978.63	63,349.60	63,545.35	63,553.02
186		PV Four Years					59,623.16	59,807.38	59,814.61
187		PV Five Years						56,289.30	56,296.10
188		PV Six Years							52,984.56
189									
190									
191									
192		TOTAL PRESENT VALUES FOR FIVE YEARS BROUGHT TO DATE					$314,958.49		
193									
194									
195		SELLING PRICE AFTER FIFTH YEAR OF OWNERSHIP (After const. is completed, and building placed in service and producing income)							
196									
197		SELLING PRICE (PROJECT HELD FOR FIVE YEARS)					$8,000,000.00		
198		Less Depreciation Basis (Basis after 5 year holding)					$3,500,360.94		
199		Less Realtor Fee on Sales Price					$480,000.00		
200		TAXABLE PROCEEDS OF THE SALE (Net Proceeds From Sale)					$4,019,639.06	(100% Capital Gains)	
201									
202		INCOME TAX ON PROCEEDS FROM SALE					$1,366,677.28	(Current Rate from Page No.1)	
203									
204		NET PROCEEDS FROM SALE (Taxable Proceeds minus Income Tax)					$2,652,961.78		
205									
206									
207									
208									
209									
210						Page No. 3			
211									

	A	B	C	D	E	F	G	H	I
212									
213	TOTAL INVESTMENT VALUE OF THE PROJECT AND INTERNAL RATE OF RETURN								
214									
215									
216									
217		Total Present Value of Income Stream After Tax					$314,958.49	(PV of Income Stream after 5 Yrs.)	
218									
219		Present Value of Net Proceeds from Sale, After Tax					$1,959,233.96	(Net Proceeds/(1+PV Int)^5)	
220									
221		TOTAL PRESENT VALUE OF EQUITY INVESTMENT					$2,274,192.45	(PV of all Monies brought to Today)	
222									
223			Original MORTGAGE AMOUNT (at beginning point)				$4,037,891.88		
224									
225		TOTAL INVESTMENT VALUE (All PV's plus Original Mortgage)					$6,312,084.32		
226									
227									
228			INTERNAL RATE OF RETURN				36.03%	(Total Present Value of Equity	
229								Investment plus Owner's Equity)	
230								divided by Total Investment Value	
231									
232									
233									
234									
235									
236									
237									
238									
239									
240									
241									
242									
243									
244									
245									
246									
247									
248									
249									
250						Page No. 4			
251									

Creating Your Own Pro Forma Analysis

You can create your own pro forma analysis using Microsoft Excel, OpenOffice Calc, or another computer spreadsheet application. The formulas and narrative are indicated by cell numbers described below. Formatting, such as font sizes, boldface, and the like can be selected as desired. Microsoft Excel, for example, has many styles and style templates to create a workbook similar to the one in Exhibit 7.1.

To begin in Excel, click Format on the menu bar, select Properties, Row/Column to set the recommended widths for columns A through J. Instructions for your version of Excel and other spreadsheet applications may differ, so consult the appropriate help document to achieve the same or comparable results.

Column Widths

Column A   9.0 characters

Column B   9.0 characters

Column C   9.0 characters

Column D   15.83 characters

Column E   15.83 characters

Column F   14.67 characters

Column G   17.00 characters

Column H   15.83 characters

Column I   14.00 characters

Column J   11.67 characters

After you have set up the columns, enter the following information in the cell addresses that follow. Special instructions are shown in brackets ([]). Custom variable data may be inserted after you have finished and tested your model against the workbook illustrated in Exhibit 7.1.

Cells and Cell Ranges

Cell A1 PRO FORMA WORKSHEET—COMMERCIAL REHABILITATION PROJECTS

Cell A4   PROJECT TITLE—Commercial Building Nonhistoric, [your title]

Cell A5   Trial Number One

Cell A8   (Variable Input

Cell A9   Data, Above Line)

Cell C8   Orig. Cost Building =

Cell E8   1000000 (Your Cost of Real Estate, Cell is Formatted for $)

Cell G8   Rental Rate (Fourth Floor) =

Cell I8   15.00 [your projected rental rate, fourth floor or group of floors]

Cell C9   Prime Interest =

Cell E9   0.0625 [prime interest, cell is formatted for % and decimal at 2 places]

Cell G9   Rentable Rate SF = (Fourth Floor or Group of Floors)

Cell I9   6400 [cell is formatted for # number]

Cell C10   Mortgage Intr. =

Cell E10   0.05625 Interest Rate [cell is formatted for % and decimal at 2 places]

Cell G10   Rental Rate (Third Floor)

Cell I10   16.00 [your projected rental rate, cell is formatted for $]

Cell C11   Mortgage Term =

Cell E11   30 [cell is formatted for # number]

Cell G11   Rentable SF (Third Floor) =

Cell I11   6,400 [cell is formatted for # number]

Cell C12   Mortgage Ratio =

Cell E12   0.95 [cell is formatted for # number]

Cell G12   Rental Rate (Second Floor) =

Cell I12   16.00 (projected rental rate, cell is formatted for $)

Cell C13   Annual Taxes =

Cell E13   80000 [estimated taxes, cell is formatted for $]

Cell G13   Rentable SF (Second Floor) =

Cell I13   6400 [cell is formatted for # number]

Cell C14   Insurance, Ann. =

Cell E14   20000 [estimated insurance, cell is formatted for $]

Cell G14   Rental Rate (First Floor) =

Cell I14   24.00 (projected rental rate, cell is formatted for $)

Cell C15   Utilities, Ann. =

Cell E15   12500 [projected cost of utilities, cell is formatted for $]

Cell G15   Rentable SF (Ground Floor) =

Cell I15   6400 [cell is formatted for #]

Cell C16   Janitorial, Ann. =

Cell E16   10000 [projected cost of janitors, cell is formatted for $]

Cell G16   Rentable Rate (Basement) =

Cell I16   10.00

Cell C17   Maintenance, Ann. =

Cell E17   10000 [projected cost of maintenance, cell is formatted for $]

Cell C18   Const. Int. Rate =

Cell E18   .0625 [cell is formatted for percentage]

Cell G17   Rentable SF (Basement) =

Cell I17   3500 [cell is formatted for #Number]

Cell C20   CONSTRUCTION COSTS

Cell C21   Cost/SF Roof Repl. =

Cell E21   30.00 [cell is formatted for $]

Cell G21   Gross SF/Roof =

Cell I21   8000 [cell is formatted for #Number]

Cell C22   Cost/SF 4th Floor. =

Cell E22   65.00 [Cell is Formatted for $]

Cell G22   Gross SF/4th Floor =

Cell I22   8000 [cell is formatted for #Number]

Cell C23   Cost/SF 3rd Floor =

Cell E23   65.00 [cell is formatted for $]

Cell G23   Gross SF/3rd Floor =

Cell I23   8000 [cell is formatted for #Number]

Cell C24   Cost/SF 2nd Floor. =

Cell E24   65.00 [cell is formatted for $]

Cell G24   Gross SF/2nd Floor =

Cell I24   8000 [cell is formatted for #Number]

Cell C25   Cost/SF 1st. Floor =

Cell E25   80.00 [cell is formatted for $]

Cell G25   Gross SF/1st Floor =

Cell I25   8000 [cell is formatted for #Number]

Cell C26   Cost/SF Basement Floor =

Cell E26   55.00 [cell is formatted for $]

Cell G26   Gross SF/Bsmt. Floor =

Cell I26   8000 [cell is formatted for #Number]

Cell C27   Cost Lobby Spec. =

Cell E27   50000 [cell is formatted for $]

Cell C28   Cost Elevator(s) =

Cell E28   50000 [cell is formatted for $]

Cell C29   Cost Fire Stair(s) =

Cell E29   30000 [cell is formatted for $]

Cell G28   Initial Cost of Building incl. Land =

Cell I28   1000000 [cell is formatted for $]

Cell G29   Value of Improvements =

Cell I29   +I28-I30 [cell is formatted for $]

Cell G30   Land Value (non-depr.)

Cell I30   250000 [cell is formatted for $]

Cell CI32   OWNER'S EQUITY =

Cell E32   +G109 [cell is formatted for $]

Cell G32   [from computations below]

Cell C34   SELLING PRICE =

Cell E34   8000000 [cell is formatted for $]

Cell G34   [selling price when held to end of 5th year]

Cell C37   PV Interest =

Cell E37   .0625 [cell is formatted for percentage]

Cell G37   (INTEREST RATE for calculating PRESENT VALUE

Cell G38   at Time of Sale)

Cell A42   _____ [line across page]

Cell A47   PRO FORMA WORKSHEET USING DATA INPUT FROM TABLE
            ABOVE

Cell A49   NET OPERATING INCOME: Net Operating Income is the Gross
            Rent Minus Expenses.

Cell D50	Dol./SF
Cell F50	Rentable
Cell G50	Gross Annual
Cell D51	Rental Rate
Cell F51	SF
Cell G51	Rent
Cell A52	Gross Rent (Annual) =
Cell D52	Varies See Above
Cell F52	+I9+I11+I13+I15+I17 [cell is formatted to #Number]
Cell G52	+I8*I9+I10*I11+I12*I13+I14*I15+I16*I17 [cell is formatted to $Currency]
Cell H52	Rent × SF, each Floor
Cell A53	Vacancy Ratio =
Cell D53	Five Percent of Gross
Cell G53	+G52*0.05 [cell is formatted to $Currency]
Cell H53	5% Vacancy
Cell A54	Expenses
Cell A55	Taxes (Real Estate) =
Cell D55	Annual Cost (Manual Entry Above) =
Cell G55	80000 [cell is formatted to $Currency]
Cell A56	Insurance, Fire & Liab. =
Cell D56	Annual Cost (Manual Entry Above) =
Cell G56	20000 [cell is formatted to $Currency]
Cell A57	Utilities (Annual Cost) =
Cell D57	Annual Cost (Manual Entry Above) =
Cell G57	12500 [[cell is formatted to $Currency]]
Cell A58	Janitorial (Annual Cost) =
Cell D58	Annual Cost (Manual Entry Above) =
Cell G58	10000 [cell is formatted to $Currency]
Cell A59	Maintenance (Annual Cost)
Cell D59	(Annual Figures)
Cell G59	10000 [cell is formatted to $Currency]
Cell A60	Net Operating Income =
Cell D60	(ANNUAL FIGURES)
Cell G60	+G52-G53-G55-G56-G57-G58-G59 [cell is formatted to $Currency]

Cell H60	(N.O.I. = Gross Rent minus
Cell H61	Expenses)
Cell A62	ECONOMIC VALUE: (Economic Value is the Net Operating Income divided by the Capitalization Rate.)
Cell A63	Capitalization Rate is Prime Rate plus One
Cell H63	+E9+0.01 [cell is formatted to %Percent]
Cell A64	ECONOMIC VALUE =
Cell D64	N.O.I./Cap. Rate =
Cell H64	+G60/H63 [cell is formatted to $Currency]
Cell A65	If your TOTAL PROJECT BUDGET exceeds the ECONOMIC VALUE—The Project is NO Good—No POSITIVE RETURN
Cell F68	Page No. 1 [cell is formatted to General]
Cell A71	PRO FORMA WORKSHEET USING DATA INPUT FROM TABLE ON PAGE NO. 1 AND PAGE NO. 2
Cell A73	CONSTRUCTION ESTIMATE OF COSTS (Summary)
Cell F74	SF
Cell A75	Basic SF Estimate
Cell F75	+I21+I22+I23+I24+I25+I26 [cell is formatted to #Number]
Cell G75	+E21*I21+E22*I22+E23*I23+E24*I24+E25*I25+E26*I26 [cell is formatted to $Currency]
Cell H75	(Const. Cost = Cost/S.F. × S.F.)
Cell A76	Misc. Additional Costs, Elevator, Fire Stairs, Etc.
Cell G76	+E27+E28+E29 [cell is formatted to $Currency]
Cell H76	[list of additional expenses]
Cell A77	Architects Fee: Eight Percent of Total Construction Costs
Cell G77	(+G75+G76)*0.08 [cell is formatted to $Currency]
Cell H77	[8% is a comprehensive fee]
Cell A78	Construction Interest: 50% of Total Const. Cost × one-half year
Cell G78	((+G75+G76)*0.5*E17 [cell is formatted to $Currency]
Cell H78	Cost of Construction Interest
Cell A79	Initial Cost of Building, Land plus Improvements
Cell G79	+I29 [cell is formatted to $Currency]
Cell H79	(Initial Cost of Property, Bldg. + Land)
Cell A81	TOTAL PROJECT COSTS: (TOTAL PROJECT BUDGET)
Cell G81	+G75+G76+G77+G78+G79 [cell is formatted to $Currency]
Cell H81	(Compare the Total Project Budget to the
Cell H82	Economic Value)

Cell B84	RATIO OF ECONOMIC VALUE TO TOTAL PROJECT BUDGET
Cell G84	+H64/G81 [cell is formatted to #Number]
Cell H84	If RATIO is more than One, the Project
Cell H85	is Good. If RATIO is less than One
Cell H86	the Project is no good.
Cell A91	DEPRECIATION VALUES
Cell A92	Total Construction Costs [total project budget]
Cell G92	+G81 [cell is formatted to $Currency]
Cell A93	Minus Land Costs of Initial Cost of Building
Cell G93	+I31 [cell is formatted to $Currency]
Cell A95	DEPRECIATION BASIS: Of Completed Project
Cell G95	+G92-G93 [cell is formatted to $Currency]
Cell A96	Depreciation per Year, Forty Year Straight Line Method
Cell G96	+G95/40 [cell is formatted to $Currency]
Cell B98	Depreciation Sch.
Cell D98	Year 1
Cell E98	Year 2
Cell F98	Year 3
Cell G98	Year 4
Cell H98	Year 5
Cell I98	Year 6
Cell B99	Beginning Depr.
Cell D99	+G95 [cell is formatted to $Currency]
Cell E99	+D101 [cell is formatted to $Currency]
Cell F99	+E101 [cell is formatted to $Currency]
Cell G99	+F101 [cell is formatted to $Currency]
Cell H99	+G101 [cell is formatted to $Currency]
Cell I99	+H101 [cell is formatted to $Currency]
Cell B100	Depr. For Year
Cell D100	+G96 [cell is formatted to $Currency]
Cell E100	+G96 [cell is formatted to $Currency]
Cell F100	+G96 [cell is formatted to $Currency]
Cell G100	+G96 [cell is formatted to $Currency]
Cell H100	+G96 [cell is formatted to $Currency]
Cell I100	+G96 [cell is formatted to $Currency]
Cell B101	End Depr. (Basis)
Cell D101	+D99-D100 [cell is formatted to $Currency]

Cell E101	+E99-E100 [cell is formatted to $Currency]
Cell F101	+F99-F100 [cell is formatted to $Currency]
Cell G101	+G99-G100 [cell is formatted to $Currency]
Cell H101	+H99-H100 [cell is formatted to $Currency]
Cell I101	+I99-I100 [cell is formatted to $Currency]
Cell A107	MORTGAGE INFORMATION
Cell G107	Computations within the Spreadsheet, Info. Data on Page No. 1
Cell A108	Mortgage Amount: Mortgage Ratio × Total Project Budget
Cell G108	+G81*E12/100 [cell is formatted to $Currency]
Cell H108	(Owner's Permanent Mortgage, 30 Years)
Cell A109	Owners Equity: Amount required for Owner Investment
Cell G109	+G81-G108 [cell is formatted to $Currency]
Cell H109	(Owners Equity, 5% Cash or Collateral)
Cell B111	Interest Rate, Annual =
Cell E111	+E10 [cell is formatted to %Percent]
Cell B112	Ammort. Period, Years =
Cell E112	+E11 [cell is formatted to General]
Cell B114	Mortgage Payment Calculated by Quattro Inboard Function
Cell C116	Annual Payment: (@PMT(Mtg. Amt., Int., Period)
Cell G116	@PMT(+G108, E10,E11) [cell is formatted to $Currency]
Cell H116	Annual Payment (automatically generated)
Cell A119	AMMORTIZATION SCHEDULE [for first six years of the investment]
Cell G119	(fully automatic, no entry needed)
Cell D121	Year 1
Cell E121	Year 2
Cell F121	Year 3
Cell G121	Year 4
Cell H121	Year 5
Cell I121	Year 6
Cell A122	Mortgage Balance (Beginning)
Cell D122	+G108 [cell is formatted to $Currency]
Cell E122	+D126 [cell is formatted to $Currency]
Cell F122	+E126 [cell is formatted to $Currency]
Cell G122	+F126 [cell is formatted to $Currency]
Cell H122	+G126 [cell is formatted to $Currency]
Cell I122	+H126 [cell is formatted to $Currency]

Cell A123	Interest for Year
Cell D123	+D122*E111 [cell is formatted to $Currency]
Cell E123	+E122*E111 [cell is formatted to $Currency]
Cell F123	+F122*E111 [cell is formatted to $Currency]
Cell G123	+G122*E111 [cell is formatted to $Currency]
Cell H123	+H122*E111 [cell is formatted to $Currency]
Cell I123	+I122*E111 [cell is formatted to $Currency]
Cell A124	Principal for Year
Cell D124	+D125-D123 [cell is formatted to $Currency]
Cell E124	+E125-E123 [cell is formatted to $Currency]
Cell F124	+F125-F123 [cell is formatted to $Currency]
Cell G124	+G125-G123 [cell is formatted to $Currency]
Cell H124	+H125-H123 [cell is formatted to $Currency]
Cell I124	+I125-I123 [cell is formatted to $Currency]
Cell A125	Total Annual Payment
Cell D125	+G116 [cell is formatted to $Currency]
Cell E125	+G116 [cell is formatted to $Currency]
Cell F125	+G116 [cell is formatted to $Currency]
Cell G125	+G116 [cell is formatted to $Currency]
Cell H125	+G116 [cell is formatted to $Currency]
Cell I125	+G116 [cell is formatted to $Currency]
Cell A126	Mortgage Balance (End of Year)
Cell D126	+D122-D124 [cell is formatted to $Currency]
Cell E126	+E122-E124 [cell is formatted to $Currency]
Cell F126	+F122-F124 [cell is formatted to $Currency]
Cell G126	+G122-G124 [cell is formatted to $Currency]
Cell H126	+H122-H124 [cell is formatted to $Currency]
Cell I126	+I122-I124 [cell is formatted to $Currency]
Cell F135	Page No. 2 [cell is formatted to General]
Cell A138	PRO FORMA ANALYSIS FOR BUILDING EVALUATIONS
Cell A140	PRO FORMA ANALYSIS WORKSHEET (Based upon Sale of the Project after Fifth Year)
Cell A141	(Fully Automatic, no input needed, Gross Income Increases at 2% per year and Expenses grow at 5% per Year)
Cell B143	Year of Analysis
Cell D143	Year 1
Cell E143	Year 2

Cell F143	Year 3
Cell G143	Year 4
Cell H143	Year 5
Cell I143	Year 6
Cell A145	a. Gross Income (Year)
Cell D145	+G52 [cell is formatted to $Currency]
Cell E145	+D147*1.02 [cell is formatted to $Currency]
Cell F145	+E147*1.02 [cell is formatted to $Currency]
Cell G145	+F147*1.02 [cell is formatted to $Currency]
Cell H145	+G147*1.02 [cell is formatted to $Currency]
Cell I145	+H147*1.02 [cell is formatted to $Currency]
Cell A146	b. Operating Expenses (Year)
Cell D146	+G53+G55+G56+G57+G58 [cell is formatted to $Currency]
Cell E146	+D148*1.05 [cell is formatted to $Currency]
Cell F146	+E148*1.05 [cell is formatted to $Currency]
Cell G146	+F148*1.05 [cell is formatted to $Currency]
Cell H146	+G148*1.05 [cell is formatted to $Currency]
Cell I146	+H148*1.05 [cell is formatted to $Currency]
Cell A147	c. Net Income (Before Tax)
Cell D147	+D147-D148 [cell is formatted to $Currency]
Cell E147	+E147-E148 [cell is formatted to $Currency]
Cell F147	+F147-F148 [cell is formatted to $Currency]
Cell G147	+G147-G148 [cell is formatted to $Currency]
Cell H147	+H147-H148 [cell is formatted to $Currency]
Cell I147	+I147-I148 [cell is formatted to $Currency]
Cell A148	d. Less Depreciation (Yr.)
Cell D148	+G96 [cell is formatted to $Currency]
Cell E148	+G96 [cell is formatted to $Currency]
Cell F148	+G96 [cell is formatted to $Currency]
Cell G148	+G96 [cell is formatted to $Currency]
Cell H148	+G96 [cell is formatted to $Currency]
Cell I148	+G96 [cell is formatted to $Currency]
Cell A149	e. Less Interest (Mort./Yr.)
Cell D149	+D123 [cell is formatted to $Currency]
Cell E149	+E123 [cell is formatted to $Currency]
Cell F149	+F123 [cell is formatted to $Currency]
Cell G149	+G123 [cell is formatted to $Currency]

Cell H149	+H151 [cell is formatted to $Currency]
Cell I149	+I151 [cell is formatted to $Currency]
Cell A151	f. Taxable Income (Year)
Cell D151	+D149-D150-D151 [cell is formatted to $Currency]
Cell E151	+E149-E150-E151 [cell is formatted to $Currency]
Cell F151	+F149-F150-F151 [cell is formatted to $Currency]
Cell G151	+G149-G150-G151 [cell is formatted to $Currency]
Cell H151	+H149-H150-H151 [cell is formatted to $Currency]
Cell I151	+I149-I150-I151 [cell is formatted to $Currency]
Cell A153	g. Plus Depreciation (Year)
Cell D153	+G96 [cell is formatted to $Currency]
Cell E153	+G96 [cell is formatted to $Currency]
Cell F153	+G96 [cell is formatted to $Currency]
Cell G153	+G96 [cell is formatted to $Currency]
Cell H153	+G96 [cell is formatted to $Currency]
Cell I153	+G96 [cell is formatted to $Currency]
Cell A154	h. Less Principal Payment
Cell D154	+D124 [cell is formatted to $Currency]
Cell E154	+E124 [cell is formatted to $Currency]
Cell F154	+F124 [cell is formatted to $Currency]
Cell G154	+G124 [cell is formatted to $Currency]
Cell H154	+H124 [cell is formatted to $Currency]
Cell I154	+I124 [cell is formatted to $Currency]
Cell A155	i. Cash Flow, Before Tax
Cell D155	+D153+D155-D156 [cell is formatted to $Currency]
Cell E155	+E153+E155-E156 [cell is formatted to $Currency]
Cell F155	+F153+F155-F156 [cell is formatted to $Currency]
Cell G155	+G153+G155-G156 [cell is formatted to $Currency]
Cell H155	+H153+H155-H156 [cell is formatted to $Currency]
Cell I155	+I154+I155-I156 [cell is formatted to $Currency]
Cell A157	j. Less Income Tax
Cell D157	+D153*0.315 [cell is formatted to $Currency]
Cell E157	+E153*0.315 [cell is formatted to $Currency]
Cell F157	+F153*0.315 [cell is formatted to $Currency]
Cell G157	+G153*0.315 [cell is formatted to $Currency]
Cell H157	+H153*0.315 [cell is formatted to $Currency]
Cell I157	+I153*0.315 [cell is formatted to $Currency]

Cell A158	k. Plus Tax Savings
Cell D158	+ [cell is formatted to $Currency]
Cell E158	+ [cell is formatted to $Currency]
Cell F158	+ [cell is formatted to $Currency] FIX Me for IF Stmt.
Cell G158	+ [cell is formatted to $Currency]
Cell H158	+ [cell is formatted to $Currency]
Cell I158	+ [cell is formatted to $Currency]
Cell A160	l. After Tax Cash Flow
Cell D160	+D155-D157 [cell is formatted to $Currency]
Cell E160	+E155-E157 [cell is formatted to $Currency]
Cell F160	+F155-F157 [cell is formatted to $Currency]
Cell G160	+G155-G157 [cell is formatted to $Currency]
Cell H160	+H155-H157 [cell is formatted to $Currency]
Cell I160	+I155-I157 [cell is formatted to $Currency]
Cell A164	RATE OF RETURN COMPUTATIONS (By Several Methods)
Cell A166	Rate of Return: Net Income /
Cell B167	Max. Project Budget
Cell D166	+D149/G81 [cell is formatted to %Percent]
Cell E166	+E149/G81 [cell is formatted to %Percent]
Cell F166	+F149/G81 [cell is formatted to %Percent]
Cell G166	+G149/G81 [cell is formatted to %Percent]
Cell H166	+H149/G81 [cell is formatted to %Percent]
Cell I166	+I149/G81 [cell is formatted to %Percent]
Cell A169	Return on Equity Tax Flow
Cell D169	+D157/G109 [cell is formatted to %Percent]
Cell E169	+E157/G109 [cell is formatted to %Percent]
Cell F169	+F157/G109 [cell is formatted to %Percent]
Cell G169	+G157/G109 [cell is formatted to %Percent]
Cell H169	+H157/G109 [cell is formatted to %Percent]
Cell I169	+I157/G109 [cell is formatted to %Percent]
Cell A170	Before Taxes
Cell A171	B.T.C.F./Owners Equity
Cell A173	Return on Equity Tax Flow
Cell D173	+D162/G109 [cell is formatted to %Percent]
Cell E173	+E162/G109 [cell is formatted to %Percent]
Cell F173	+F162/G109 [cell is formatted to %Percent]
Cell G173	+G162/G109 [cell is formatted to %Percent]

Cell H173	+H162/G109 [cell is formatted to %Percent]
Cell I173	+I162/G109 [cell is formatted to %Percent]
Cell A174	After Taxes
Cell A175	A.T.C.F./Owners Equity
Cell A180	Present Value of Total After Tax Cash Flows (End of Year 1 and all other years brought to today.)
Cell A182	Tot. A.T. Cash Flows, Actual
Cell D182	+D160 [cell is formatted to $Currency]
Cell E182	+E160 [cell is formatted to $Currency]
Cell F182	+F160 [cell is formatted to $Currency]
Cell G182	+G160 [cell is formatted to $Currency]
Cell H182	+H160 [cell is formatted to $Currency]
Cell I182	+I160 [cell is formatted to $Currency]
Cell B183	PV One Year
Cell D183	@PV(D182,E37,1) [cell is formatted to $Currency]
Cell E183	@PV(E182,E37,1) [cell is formatted to $Currency]
Cell F183	@PV(F182,E37,1) [cell is formatted to $Currency]
Cell G183	@PV(G182,E37,1) [cell is formatted to $Currency]
Cell H183	@PV(H182,E37,1) [cell is formatted to $Currency]
Cell I183	@PV(I182,E37,1) [cell is formatted to $Currency]
Cell B184	PV Two Years
Cell E184	@PV(E183,E37,1) [cell is formatted to $Currency]
Cell F184	@PV(F183,E37,1) [cell is formatted to $Currency]
Cell G184	@PV(G183,E37,1) [cell is formatted to $Currency]
Cell H184	@PV(H183,E37,1) [cell is formatted to $Currency]
Cell I184	@PV(I183,E37,1) [cell is formatted to $Currency]
Cell B185	PV Three Years
Cell F185	@PV(F184,E37,1) [cell is formatted to $Currency]
Cell G185	@PV(G184,E37,1) [cell is formatted to $Currency]
Cell H185	@PV(H184,E37,1) [cell is formatted to $Currency]
Cell I185	@PV(I184,E37,1) [cell is formatted to $Currency]
Cell B186	PV Four Years
Cell G186	@PV(G185,E37,1) [cell is formatted to $Currency]
Cell H186	@PV(H185,E37,1) [cell is formatted to $Currency]
Cell I186	@PV(I185,E37,1) [cell is formatted to $Currency]
Cell B187	PV Five Years
Cell H187	@PV(H186,E37,1) [cell is formatted to $Currency]

Cell I187	@PV(I186,E37,1) [cell is formatted to $Currency]
Cell B188	PV Six Years
Cell I188	@PV(I192,E37,1) [cell is formatted to $Currency]
Cell B192	TOTAL PRESENT VALUES FOR FIVE YEARS BROUGHT TO TODAY
Cell G192	+D183+E184+F185+G186+H187 [cell is formatted to $Currency]
Cell B195	SELLING PRICE AFTER FIFTH YEAR OF OWNERSHIP (after construction is completed and building is placed in service)
Cell B197	SELLING PRICE (PROJECT HELD FOR FIVE YEARS)
Cell G197	+E34 [cell is formatted to $Currency]
Cell B198	Less Depreciation Basis (Basis after 5 year holding)
Cell G198	+H101 [cell is formatted to $Currency]
Cell B199	Less Realtor Fee on Sales Price
Cell G199	+G197*0.06 [cell is formatted to $Currency]
Cell B200	TAXABLE PROCEEDS OF THE SALE (Net Proceeds)
Cell G200	+G197-G198-G199 [cell is formatted to $Currency]
Cell H200	(100% Capital Gains)
Cell B202	INCOME TAX ON PROCEEDS FROM SALE
Cell G202	+G200*0.35 [cell is formatted to $Currency]
Cell H205	(Rate = 35%)
Cell B204	NET PROCEEDS FROM SALE (Taxable Proceeds minus Income Tax)
Cell G204	+G200-G202 [cell is formatted to $Currency]
Cell F210	Page No. 3
Cell A213	TOTAL INVESTMENT VALUE OF THE PROJECT AND INTERNAL RATE OF RETURN
Cell B217	Total Present Value of Income Stream After Tax
Cell G217	+G192 [cell is formatted to $Currency]
Cell B219	Present Value of Net Proceeds From Sale
Cell G219	+G204/(1+E37)^5 [cell is formatted to $Currency]
Cell H219	Net Proceeds/(1+PV Int.)^5
Cell B219	TOTAL PRESENT VALUE OF EQUITY INVESTMENT
Cell G219	+G217+G219 [cell is formatted to $Currency]
Cell H219	PV of all Monies brought to Today
Cell C223	Original MORTGAGE AMOUNT [at beginning point]
Cell G223	+D122 [cell is formatted to $Currency]
Cell B225	TOTAL INVESTMENT VALUE (All PVs plus original Mortgage)

Cell G225	+G221+G223 [cell is formatted to $Currency]
Cell D228	INTERNAL RATE OF RETURN
Cell G228	(+G221+E33)/G225 [cell is formatted to %Percent]
Cell H228	(Total Present Value of Equity Investment plus Owners Equity) divided by Total Investment Value
Cell F250	Page No. 4

Testing CHAPTER 8

Previous chapters have described walk-through observations for adaptive reuse. In certain cases, however, a walk-through is not sufficient. Simple tests may be necessary to learn more about the challenges and costs of reuse. Although testing has been covered earlier, this chapter goes into more detail about the kinds of tests and what deficiencies they reveal about a building's structures and its systems.

Introduction

Building assessment is a very involved process. Overall it can be achieved in stages or restricted to specialty areas. In stages the assessment is taken as far as needed for the intended purpose. To determine if a purchase is justified, the decision may only require certain data without the detail that comes from focusing on any one system. If the decision to purchase requires a more comprehensive investigation, the assessment is more involved and specialized to check the viability of each system. Outcome will determine if there can be continued use with rehabilitation and repairs or total replacement.

One area of specialized assessment is the structural fabric of a building, which can consist of masonry, cast iron, wrought iron, steel, structural concrete, or wood. This is going to acquire a greater degree of importance in the years to come. While code officials, developers, and bankers have their reasons for being wary of older buildings, such as the deterioration of various subsystems (plumbing, electrical, and mechanical) these structures are usually constructed better, made of better materials, and can last almost indefinitely with proper care. (These same subsystems are also subject to deterioration and have life cycles of their own. Generally the mechanical systems have shorter life cycles due to their involvement with multiple subsystems such as electronic controls, pumps, electric motors, fans, ductwork, or water-circulation piping and valves.) In contrast, modern buildings are constructed for optimum cost versus versatility. They are not only like an investment, they often are an investment; they have an expected life cycle of about 25 years for their return on investment before radical remodeling or destruction is required.

We are now seeing the end of the first life cycle, that is, the first quarter century of this era of the so-called "disposable buildings." Very often the company that enjoyed the benefits of a new building from the beginning has grown out of its space, moved to a new location, or gone out of business. If the structure is not reused, the building is either left to deteriorate or another lower-scaled business moves in.

Banks and mortgage brokers make it easier to construct a new building than remodel or rehabilitate an older one. The concept "new is better" is very much worked into the American corporate psyche. This is not the case, however, in many of the revived urban areas in large and even small American cities. But these kinds of businesses are smaller and do not require the repackaging that larger American companies use for everything that has to do with their "image," from the product and logo to the new corporate head-quarters. European companies do construct new buildings as a part of their corporate image and cultural awareness. At the same time, however, Europeans are very in tune with the concept of architectural conservation. (*Conservation* is the accepted term in Europe whereas *preservation* is a term unique to the American preservation movement.) Europeans are very careful to conserve and protect their districts and small towns that contain historical buildings. New construction, modern factories, and the like are care-fully placed not to disturb the historic environment.

Despite the cult of the new, change is taking place in many cities of all sizes. Many preexisting buildings are now finding new lives. Nineteenth-century department stores are becoming loft apartments. Old factories are being turned into trendy retail outlets and working spaces for small businesses. For this reason, an understanding of seem-ingly dated buildings as well as their components and capacities is crucial.

Masonry Walls

Handmade Brick

The strength of an individual brick is not as significant as the strength of the wall. His-toric walls made of handmade brick and lime-sand mortars are conservatively rated at 50 to 75 psi. It is expensive to test an existing brick wall, and the results are question-able. The strength of these historic walls would vary at almost any point along the wall. Thus it is impossible and impractical to test sections of the wall by cutting and remov-ing a 9-inch wide section of about 18 inches in vertical dimension. The cutting and re-moval often compromises the specimen, invalidating the results. Poul Beckman (1994, 33), one of the world's premier structural engineers, states that when the integrity of a wall is in question, there is justification in reducing the allowable stress.

Machine-Made and Modern Brick

The strength of an individual brick is appropriate for machine-made brick. The Amer-ican Society for Testing Materials (ASTM) C67–92a sets the procedure for testing a half brick as the sample. The result is the ultimate strength of the half brick as the test is car-ried to crushing failure. The ultimate compressive strength of the half brick is the ac-tual ultimate load divided by the area of the half brick. In handmade brick and lime-sand mortar, the safety factor averages about 25. One can allow a lower factor of safety on the machine-made brick and the brick-and-cement-based mortars as their relative strengths are very close (individual brick versus brick laid up in a wall). Most designers use a factor of safety of about 12.5 after careful verification of the condition of the wall.

Other Methods of Testing Masonry Walls

Other testing methods include the following:

Ultrasonic Testing If a masonry wall provides comparative strength and continuity data by analyzing the time of transmission through the wall in question versus a sound prototype, then ultrasonic testing can be used.

Pachometer This test is used to locate reinforcing in walls. The instrument is a magnetic detector that picks up rebar as a variation in the magnetic field.

Gamma Radiography Provides a photographic image of the interior of a masonry wall. Voids show as irregular patches and reinforcing as a light area.

Stone Masonry The same tests that apply for brick masonry apply. Ultrasonic tests can also be used to identify delaminations in stone masonry.

Metals: Cast Iron, Wrought Iron, and Structural Steel

Cast iron can usually be identified by its use as building columns. Some beams were once made of cast iron and their span would not exceed 10 to 12 feet. Cast-iron surfaces have a relatively coarse texture, almost like sandpaper, as the shapes were cast in sand molds. Cast iron has a high compressive-stress capacity and a very low tensile-stress capacity. Cast iron is rust resistant and will not deteriorate. Rust actually forms on the surface but becomes a protective cover.

Wrought iron, sometimes called *malleable iron,* was manufactured through a process called *puddling* in which the carbon was literally burned off in the furnace by superheating the molten metal with an oxygen-rich flame. Wrought-iron plates came from steam hammering to flatten the raw material into plates and thus create laminations as the flattened material was folded and rehammered several times to produce the desired size and thickness. The laminations are visible, especially after deterioration begins, through a monocular.

Structural steel, called *mild steel* in early periods of its production, were superior to wrought iron in that it had the same properties in tension and compression. Because the final shapes are hot rolled, there is equal strength throughout each section (e.g., angles or channels). Hot-rolled shapes do not fail at intersections of planes as often happened with wrought iron due to deterioration.

Wrought iron and steel can be identified by chemical analysis of small samples taken from drilling one-quarter to one-half inch cores through the material. The cores and the shavings can be analyzed for chemical content. For example, cast iron contains 2 to 5 percent carbon, wrought iron 0.1 to 0.5 percent, and structural steel approximately 1.2 percent. Early members would have been manufactured under fairly uncontrolled circumstances, and impurities such as sulfur and phosphorus can cause problems if they are present in too large a quantity. Those problems could be loss of strength and also excessive deterioration.

The following are further, nondestructive methods of metal evaluation to determine cracks, decay, flaws, and measures of strength.

Visual-Optical Use of borescopes, fiber optics, and panoramic cameras to identify surface defects, cracks, and corrosion pits.

Liquid Penetrant A liquid penetrant containing dye is drawn into defects by capillary action. Can be used on nonmagnetic metals only.

Ultrasonic Ultrasonic vibrations above 20,000 Hz can detect surface and subsurface defects, accurately measure thickness, and detect voids, cracks, porosity, and welding flaws.

Magnetic Particles Magnetic particles are attracted to magnetic lines of leakage force to detect cracks, seams voids, and the like to one-quarter inch below the surface.

X-Ray and Gamma Ray Such radiation can detect both internal and external flaws and voids or low-density areas as well as detect stress fatigue in welds and parent metal.

Eddy Current Eddy current can detect discontinuities, cracks, seams, and variations in alloys.

Test Specimen Test specimens can determine stress-strain data, yield strength, and ultimate strength. The sample must be large enough to provide usable data.

Load Tests Structure or parts of structure such as beams are loaded to a specified amount, or the design live loads, and deflections are monitored as a means of identifying maximum permissible loads.

Yield Stresses for Wrought-Iron and Structural Steels

Wrought-iron members	25,000 psi
Structural steel, prior to 1905	25,000 psi
Structural steel, 1905 to 1932	30,000 psi
Structural steel, 1933 to 1963	33,000 psi
Structural steel, after 1963	36,000 psi
Structural steel, after 1963, higher grade	50,000 psi

Concrete

The analysis of concrete structures is difficult in that the reinforcing elements are embedded within the concrete and cannot be identified without an examination of the original plans for the building. The concrete's strength is also a variable that is dependent upon not only the cement, sand, and stones but the proportions of the mix. The quality and quantity of water is also a critical component. Early concrete users were experimenting with mixes and reinforcing bars and bar patterns. These specialty bars, different for each engineer, were patented and sold. Concrete construction began to be standardized in 1928 with the issuance of concrete codes that addressed design, mixes, and placement as well as adopting a standard reinforcing bar.

The following test methods are applicable for concrete:

Tell-Tale Tell-tale measuring instruments consist of two target grids mounted on either side of a structural crack to obtain movement data for months or years.

Fiber Optics Detects internal cracks, voids, or flaws if path to surface exists and produces clear, high-resolution images.

Schmidt Rebound Hammer Concrete strength measured by rebound distance correlation to calibration curve.

Electrical Resistivity Electrical resistivity can determine on-grade slab thickness and locate reinforcing bars.

Magnetic Pachometers Magnetic pachometers can be used to detect reinforcing bars and determine their depth (up to 7–8 inches). The pachometer does not work on multiple layers of rebar or on welded wire fabric.

Ultrasonics Ultrasonics measures concrete thickness accurately but work only when both surfaces of concrete are accessible.

X-Ray and Gamma Ray Gamma ray and X-ray measure density of concrete and rebar location. This method works on concrete slabs where both sides are accessible.

Infrared Infrared tests through heat patterns to detect defects, voids, and cracks.

Load Tests The structure is loaded to a measured point or to design loads. Deflections are monitored and predictions of joint rotation and lateral movement are recorded for analysis.

Wood

Wood has been a major structural element, a furniture material, a wall décor, and a finishing material. It was the major element in windows and doors since Western Europeans began colonizing the Americas. Native Americans also utilized wood for building purposes. Wood is also used as a fuel for warmth and cooking, although not to the extent it was before. The Industrial Revolution and the introduction of fossil fuels such as coal, oil, and natural gas have changed the use of wood as a fuel for heating. Wood is a renewable resource, and if protected from fire, insects, and rot, it will last in buildings almost indefinitely.

The condition of a wood beam or column determines its ability to carry a load. The basic strength is in the uniformity of grain, density, and moisture content. The grain and density are inherent to the member and only differ with different species of wood. Green (wet, freshly harvested) timber to be utilized in finished products was traditionally air dried in sheds and barns until ready for use. During the colonization of North America, green, freshly cut logs were used to construct log houses and sheds as needed for immediate habitation. The air-drying process that takes years was not used then because the housing need was immediate. Kiln drying of construction wood started in the last quarter of the nineteenth century and continues to this day.

Water is a major cause of deterioration in buildings. It encourages the rusting of ferrous metals, the softening and loss of strength in gypsum board and acoustic tile, and the discoloration of many surfaces. Water infiltration is especially damaging to many kinds of wood. When wood is subjected to moisture either in wet-dry cycles or semi-continuous dampness, the moisture allows microorganisms and fungi to grow and digest cellulose, which all wood products consist of.

Only fire is more destructive than the effects of moisture. Kiln-dried and air-dried wood that is kept dried to 14 to 15 percent moisture content will not deteriorate or be subject to the kinds of fungal attack described in the following subsection. Tests in the United Kingdom have shown that at this constant moisture content, wood that has been in service for 200 years has not lost more than 1 to 2 percent of its strength. There are no studies to disallow continuing to use the same allowable stresses as used in the original designs. In fact, modern analyses have proven that the allowable stresses and design methods of earlier times are accurate and adequate. Sound judgment and experience must be utilized in the visual inspection of individual members and adjustment of allowable stresses if there is any reason for concern about any member. If a load test should show deflection in excess of that calculated for a given live load, the allowable bending stress or modulus of elasticity may have been liberal for the member or there may be reason to suspect the condition of the member. Columns can show a fair number of cracks of varying size and still be able to carry the design load. Beams can check (crack longitudinally) at the ends and still meet the requirements for bending and horizontal shear.

Signs of prior moisture deterioration, rot, or insect damage require a further intensive investigation. And moisture alone is insufficient to cause rapid decay in wood if the exposure to moisture is relatively short term. Moisture presence and a temperature above 72°F are both required for fungi to develop. Wet and dry rot are both the product of moisture intrusion and continuous dampness or periods of wet and dry on the surface of the timber.

Dry Rot and Mold

In spite of its name, dry rot is actually a result of too much water. It is caused by one or more of several fungi that chemically break down the cellulose that gives wood fibers their strength. It spreads to dry areas because the fungi are able to efficiently transport moisture from the wet areas to its extremities, reaching into dry areas. When wood structural or architectural elements are subject to frequent wet and dry conditions, the fungus finds an opportunity to begin colonies. The wood moisture content necessary for growth is about 28 to 30 percent. After it is established, fungi can continue to grow with moisture contents as low as 20 percent. If the water source is removed and the wood moisture content drops below this level, the fungus becomes dormant.

Dry rot attacks window and doorsills as well as frames and the building framing that surround them, as well as porches and decks. Wood structural members in contact with foundations that "wick" water upward are also common sites for dry rot. Other common locations are the floors below leaking plumbing fixtures. Dry rot has a characteristic appearance of shrinkage and leaves a checkered pattern. If this appearance and its attendant discoloration are present, a possible concealed problem may be indicated and the wood could be severely weakened.

Mold is also a fungus that grows when there is sufficient moisture. In general, mold fungus is present all over the world, including the inside of buildings. When mold encounters a cellulose food source, the presence of enough water, and temperatures normally found in buildings it will grow and spread. The exact quantity of moisture depends on the species, but it equates roughly to 80 to 90 percent air relative humidity over a period of days. Mold destroys its food source more slowly than dry rot. It discolors materials and becomes a human environmental nuisance by causing nasal and skin irritation and an allergic reaction in some individuals.

If a visual inspection reveals the presence of mold as in Figure 8.1, its presence should be taken very seriously. Once mold has developed a significant colony on porous materials, it can be very difficult to remove. Removal of the water source will stop growth and cause the mold to become dormant until water again is present. Nonporous materials can be cleaned with a mild solution of bleach. Porous materials will probably have to be removed. Serious mold conditions are best cleaned up by professionals. While the particular species of mold is probably not important to the problem, professional microbiologists or industrial hygienists can identify them if desired.

If mold is present, the first concern is to find the source of moisture. If the growth is on the exterior walls or a ceiling under a roof, a liquid water leak is the first suspect. If the mold is observed in a corner or in patterns that match exterior structural members, these areas may just be the coldest parts of the interior and, therefore, the areas with the highest relative humidity. The culprit may actually be the building's HVAC system. If this system cannot hold relative humidity below 60 to 70 percent, mold will probably grow. If the mold appears along the bottom of the exterior walls, the source of moisture may be rising damp from water rising through the foundations by capillary action. If there is no building defect that could cause sufficient water to promote mold growth, and the building has been vacant and unconditioned for a month or more, it

FIGURE 8.1
Visible evidence of mold growth can be seen on the gypsum board interior finish. Here improper exterior wall drainage and flashing allowed moisture to accumulate and provided favorable mold conditions.

may be that the lack of heating and cooling has resulted in increased relative humidity and facilitated the growth.

Insect Damage

In the southern half of the United States, and especially the southeast region of the Gulf Coast, termites cause significant damage to wood structures. To a lesser extent, prolonged infestations of carpenter ants and carpenter bees can also be harmful. A professional inspection by a pest control expert is the best course of action. However, in the course of a walk-through inspection, be alert for signs of termite activity. Termite damaged wood has a grayish appearance and is easily penetrated by a knife blade or ice pick as described above. Termites tunnel through wood and avoid paths in the open. They also feed off the cellulose. To cross an exposed surface, such as concrete block foundations, they construct mud tunnels on the surface, and the presence of these tunnels is a good indication of termites.

Wood Tests for Strength, Moisture Content, Rot, and Fungi

Visual Inspection

For decay, fungal rot, insect damage, and the like, determine the species, cause, and other extenuating circumstances. Inspect for possible locations of water infiltration or evidence of the same.

Dry rot can be visually identified if severe enough and on a visible surface. Additionally, a simple test can confirm its presence and give some quantitative estimate of the damage. This test consists of probing the wood with a pocketknife or ice pick as shown in Figure 8.2. Undamaged wood resists penetration more than an eighth of an inch or so, but rotted wood can be easily penetrated. A series of probes should show where the rot stops and sound wood begins.

FIGURE 8.2
Pocketknife being used to test wooden joists for soundness. Dry rot softens the wood and can be detected by this test.

Visual Stress Grading

Perform a visual inspection to determine the existence of *grading stamps* for allowable stress limits. Since grading stamps change frequently, enlist a structural engineer and the latest *National Design Specifications for Wood Construction* published by National Forest Products Association (NFPA) to interpret a grading stamp. A structural engineer can also perform visual inspections of knots, checks, shakes, and the like for deterioration or weakened areas.

Manual Probing

Determine the extent of decay or insect infiltration by pulling away decayed wood to determine the depth to sound wood.

Infared Imaging

Thermal imaging with an infrared camera can reveal differences in temperature in walls and roofs. Figure 8.3 shows three views of a wood-stud construction exterior wall. On the top left is a standard photograph, on the top right is a black-and-white infrared photograph, and on the bottom is a color infrared photograph. The studs have lower thermal resistance than the fiberglass batt insulation between them, so the inside surface is colder in these pictures. With an informed analysis, the temperature differences can be interpreted to estimate insulation values or water penetration into the building envelope.

FIGURE 8.3
A wood stud construction exterior wall as seen in a standard photograph (top left) and in infrared photographs (top right and bottom). In cold weather heat flows from the interior to the exterior of the wall through materials at different rates inversely proportional to their thermal resistance. Lower resistance materials are brighter in the infrared spectrum. This figure is also depicted in color in the color plates.
Source: Bob Melia and Barbara Melia Morris, Real Time Thermal Imaging, Mandeville, LA.

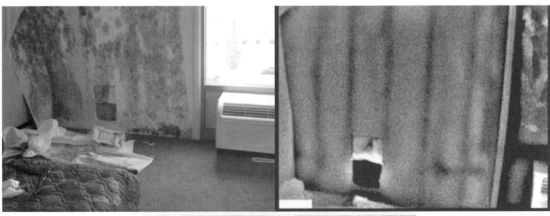

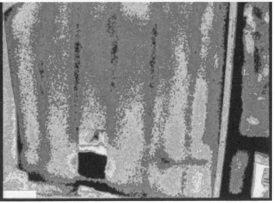

FIGURE 8.4
Water leaking into roof insulation lowers the thermal resistance of the roof and causes increased heat flow. The upper left corner photograph is a standard image of a roof, the upper right and lower images are black and white prints of an infrared image of the roof with the leak identified by the circle. In this view the brightness of the roof drain, the roof curbs, and the wet areas of insulation indicate the heat loss through these components. This figure is also depicted in color in the color plates.
Source: Bob Melia and Barbara Melia Morris, Real Time Thermal Imaging, Mandeville, LA.

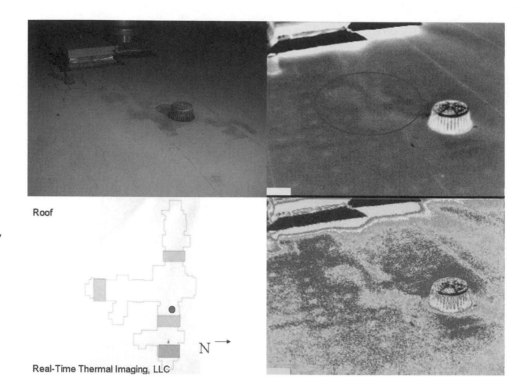

Roof

Real-Time Thermal Imaging, LLC

N →

FIGURE 8.5
Air flowing from floor to floor through unintentional passages in a multistory building is revealed by infrared thermography. The air transports heat that causes temperature differences visible on infrared film.
Source: Bob Melia and Barbara Melia Morris, Real Time Thermal Imaging, Mandeville, LA.

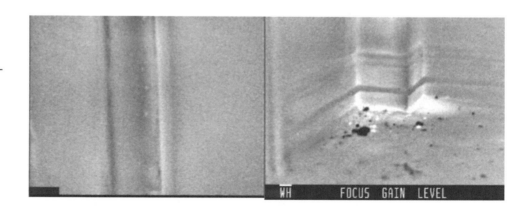

TIR image showing communication between floors through column

Real-Time Thermal Imaging, LLC

termite

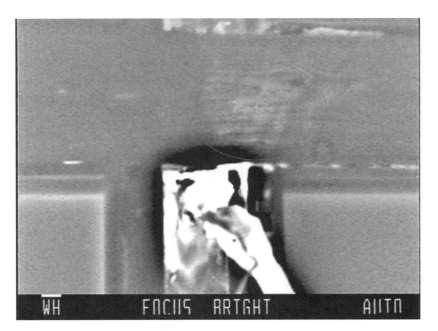

Warm air was injected into the beam to better articulate the damage

Real-Time Thermal Imaging, LLC   termite

FIGURE 8.6
This infrared thermal image
shows a wooden beam that
has been riddled by termites.
Image has been enhanced by
blowing hot air into the ter-
mite holes.
*Source: Bob Melia and Barbara
Melia Morris, Real Time Thermal
Imaging, Mandeville, LA.*

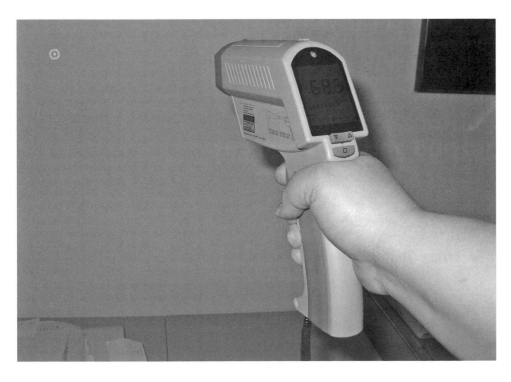

FIGURE 8.7
Hand-held infrared ther-
mometers can be used to
locate temperature discontinuities in building construction. Such discontinuities
might be caused by missing
insulation, wet construction,
air leakage, and so on.

Roof leaks are sometimes difficult to detect and analyze. An early indicator may be
water stains appearing on interior surfaces below a roof. Even then the exact location
of the leak is often hard to locate. An infrared camera scan of a roof from the outside
can often reveal the location of a leak—sometimes before it is detected. Figure 8.4 is a

photographic description of a roof with a leak. The upper-left corner contains a visual image of the roof, the upper right a black-and-white infrared image of the roof with the leak identified by the circle, and the lower right a color infrared image. In this view the bright colors of the roof drain and the roof curbs indicate the heat loss through these components. Figure 8.5 reveals air flowing from floor to floor through unintentional passages in a multistory building. Such air shafts can aggravate infiltration and consequent energy loss as well as convey smoke in a fire as well.

Another application for infrared thermal image testing is searching for termite damage. Figure 8.6 is a thermal image of a wooden beam riddled by termites. If the weather is mild or the damaged areas are located in the interior of the building, some method of developing a temperature difference is necessary for thermal imaging with infrared technology. In this case an ingenious solution was to blow hot air into the beam. Simple observation of the roof or walls with a hand-held infrared thermometer (Figure 8.7) may reveal some of the same information.

Strength and Rot Tests

Penetration Test for Rot The Pilodyn penetrometer can estimate the degrees of decay by measuring the range of penetration of a steel pin into the surface of the wood.

Ultrasonic Longitudinal Wave Propagation Meter This measures modulus of elasticity and strength. Discontinuities are measured by variation of velocity of longitudinal wave propagation between a transmitter and receiver on opposite sides of the tested member. The degree of decay is measured by establishing a modulus of elasticity that translates to the strength of the wood member.

Stress-Wave Propagation Equipment Such equipment measures modulus of elasticity and strength. Transmitter and receiver on opposite sides of member. Transverse wave velocity is influenced by inconsistencies in the wood member. Density and wave velocity are translated to modulus of elasticity.

X-Ray Using X-ray devices requires access to both sides of a member. Such testing can detect internal density variations, irregularities, decay, splits, knots, insect damage, and hidden members. X-rays also make a permanent record on film.

Moisture Tests

Dielectric Moisture Meters Such meters measure the moisture content in the wood. There are two types. A capacitance meter measures a change in oscillation frequency. A power-loss meter measures a loss of amplitude from an electric wave. Either type gives accurate measurement of the moisture content at or near the surface in wood.

Resistance-Type Moisture Meter This type of meter measures electrical resistance between two probes. Probes can be on opposite sides of a wood member as thick as three-quarters inch.

Electrical-Resistance Moisture Meter Moisture content is measured by a wooden probe inserted into a member. Two electrode faces measure the moisture content of the material. Such meters can be built into the structure for long-term monitoring. The probes can show long-term drift as strain gauges and can be used to develop a hysteresis plot.

Testing for Insulation Integrity and Air Leakage

If a building is to be adapted to a new use, an important consideration is the rate of heat flow through its walls and especially the roof. Further, if the interior finish is not going to be removed and replaced so that insulation can be visually inspected, some other way to evaluate the presence or absence of insulation is needed. Several techniques are available to do this.

Destructive Testing

Small diameter openings can be drilled through the finished surface for visual inspection. This can be done in unobtrusive places or behind baseboards if possible. A borescope will improve the ability to see more of the roof or wall interior cavity.

Infrared Imaging

Infrared thermal imaging was proposed as a means of locating wet areas of roofs and walls. It can also be applied to checking the thermal resistance of insulated roofs or walls. Figure 8.8 is composed of four images of the interior of a two-story lobby space in a building. The upper-right image is a normal photograph of the intersection of the ceiling and two walls. The upper-left image is a black-and-white thermal image showing two very dark areas. The lower-left image is a color thermal image in which the dark areas are now bright yellow. Bright yellow is indicated as cooler in the color temperature scale. These photographs were taken on a cold day, so the cooler areas are experiencing greater rates of heat loss than the warmer areas. The lower-right image was taken in the attic space above the lobby. Two spaces between ceiling joists, corresponding to the yellow rectangles, are seen to have no insulation installed while the adjacent areas have thick fiberglass batt insulation. While the cost of infrared photography makes it infeasible to casually survey a building, if water leaks are present or other problems are found it may be easy to completely scan the building while looking for the leak.

Heat Flow Meters

The rate of heat flow through building elements can be directly read using one of several commercially available heat-flux transducers. These consist of sensors that are applied to one or both surfaces of the building component as shown in Figure 8.9. The

FIGURE 8.8
Depicted in these photos is a two-story lobby space in a building viewed from the interior. The upper right image is a standard photograph of the intersection of the ceiling and two walls. The other three images are black and white prints of infrared thermal images showing two very dark areas. Brightness indicates cooler in the temperature scale. The lower right corner image was taken in the attic space above the lobby. Two spaces between ceiling joists, corresponding to the bright rectangles, have no insulation installed as contrasted with the insulated adjacent spaces. This figure is also depicted in color in the color plates.

Source: Bob Melia and Barbara Melia Morris, Real Time Thermal Imaging, Mandeville, LA.

Thermal image

Normal

Color thermal image

Real-Time Thermal Imaging, LLC

Missing insulation

1   thermocouple on outside surface
2   thermocouple on inside surface
3   heat flow sensor
4   heat flow meter
5   computer

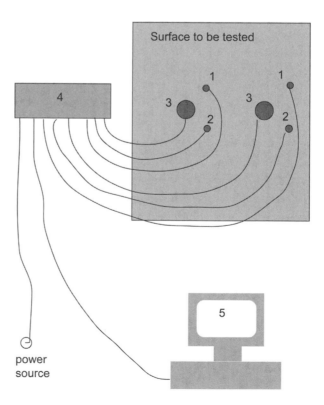

Surface to be tested

power source

FIGURE 8.9
A heat flow meter application measuring the rate of heat flow through a wall.

sensors send signals to a data logger that interprets the signals as rates of heat flow through a known area and between recorded temperatures. This data can then be mathematically converted to thermal resistance. This method does not produce laboratory grade results, of course, because of the three-dimensional nature of heat flow in real surfaces and the nonhomogenous character of construction elements. However, it can approximately identify the thermal resistances in an existing building.

Blower Door Test

Air leakage through the enclosure is a major transport mechanism for heat and moisture in buildings. This leakage is called *infiltration*. It is driven by wind and the difference in density between the air inside and that outside. This can be a source of the water that contributes to mold growth in summer. A detailed investigation of the performance of a building being considered for adaptive reuse should include this test. It is relatively inexpensive compared with others discussed herein. A blower door fits into the frame of an exterior door. It contains a fan and speed controls, pressure measuring instruments, and an airflow measuring instrument. (See Figure 4.26) The door is inserted and sealed tight to the frame. The fan is operated at different pressures and the airflow rate is read at each condition. The building volume also must be measured.

Air infiltration is expressed in *air changes per hour* (ACH), which is defined as building volumes of air per hour. Very old buildings and buildings with many openings such as warehouses are usually very leaky and experience infiltration rates in the range of .75 to 1 ACH. Typical office and school building construction from the period since 1975 may have infiltration rates in the range of .5 ACH. A very tight construction designed for low energy consumption may have an infiltration rate as low as 0.2 ACH. If the building is found to have an unacceptable infiltration rate, it can be reduced by replacing windows and doors, caulking around windows, caulking or sealing the joints where walls meet ceilings or floors, and closing the holes around penetrations such as electrical boxes, pipes, and wires and providing exhaust fans with automatic louvers.

Testing Electrical Systems

If the lights come on when the switch is thrown, that may be enough of a test to assume the electrical system is satisfactory. In some cases, however, appliances may not function, circuit breakers may trip, or sparks and smoke may emanate from the electrical panel. Such indications are sufficient reason to perform the following simple tests.

Testing Grounds

Electrical system safety is partially based on grounding of the neutral wire and the exposed metal components. A handheld receptacle tester (see Figure 8.10), which can be plugged into convenience outlets, is a handy device to verify proper wiring. It can indicate several types of faults including reversed polarity, an ungrounded neutral wire, or an open ground wire. The ground rod should be observed for any visual indication of loose connections, corrosion, or other faults. Major electrical components should have solidly connected ground wires.

FIGURE 8.10
An electrical receptacle tester to measure proper phase continuity and grounding.

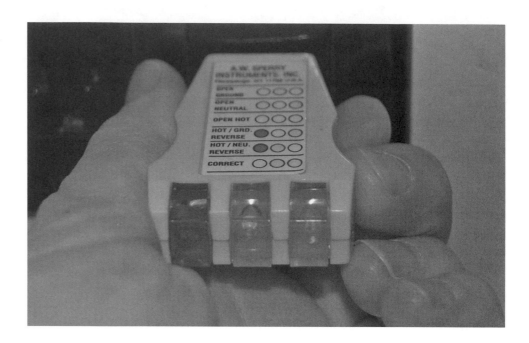

Testing Phases

Sometimes it is necessary or desirable to identify the specific phases to which a major electrical load is connected. Testers are available for this purpose.

Testing Voltage Drop

Electrical devices are designed to operate at slightly less than the nominal voltage. The tolerance is typically about 10 percent of the nominal voltage. Below the lower limit of tolerance the equipment experiences problems such as overheating or reduced output and efficiency. If some of the equipment in a building has symptoms like these the cause may be low voltage. This can be tested with a voltmeter, but the testing should be done with the equipment under load.

Testing Fire Alarm Systems

Fire alarm systems must be regularly tested under supervision of the local fire authorities. This testing may include sending alarms to the fire department, so tests must be carefully coordinated to avoid false alarm calls. The tests usually consist of activating an alarm input station and observing the audible and visual alarm notifications.

Testing Emergency Systems

Emergency systems in buildings are typically installed to provide lights or power for life safety in the event of a utility power failure. The standard kinds are described in this section.

Battery Exit Lights

Fire and building codes require that paths of egress from all rooms be illuminated so occupants can walk quickly and easily to the outside no matter whether it is day or night. For this purpose most buildings have lights that are powered both by normal utility electricity and by batteries. The majority have the batteries built into the fixture itself. An automatic transfer switch disconnects from the normal source and connects to the battery source if the voltage in the normal circuit falls significantly. The test procedure is to press the "test" button on the fixture and observe the light resulting.

Emergency Generators

Testing emergency generators is more complicated. These are internal combustion engines that drive electrical generators. Their fuel is gasoline, diesel fuel, or natural gas. They are activated by a drop in the normal electrical voltage and start automatically to restore power through a transfer switch. Testing can be done by manually activating the engine or by manually initiating the transfer switch and watching for the engine to start and produce power. Tests should occur regularly, and the engine should be exercised once a week.

Testing Mechanical Systems

Mechanical systems include the heating, ventilating, and air-conditioning systems that maintain comfortable indoor environments. They are expensive and vital to building function. When considering a building for adaptive reuse, if there is a possibility of maintaining the mechanical system then it should be tested. Tests should be for safety as well as performance.

Steam and Hot Water Heating Systems

The function of a steam or hot water system is to provide heat in the winter, and that is the best time to test if possible. If not, the tests should be conducted when the building is unoccupied to minimize occupant discomfort. A simple cold weather functional test would be to activate the whole system under automatic closed-loop control and observe each space for adequate heat. Other tests are more complicated.

Boilers

Boilers are regularly tested for safety by state or local inspectors. The test results should be available for review. Safety inspections can reveal incipient problems and trends so action can be taken before the problem becomes an emergency. Safety relief valves should be manually opened periodically to assure that they are not seized and can open. A significant cause of problems with steam boilers is loss of water from the system and resulting introduction of *makeup water*. As new water enters the system, it brings dissolved minerals. When the water evaporates as steam is generated, it leaves the minerals in the boiler, and they often form a layer of solid minerals or "scale" on the boiler tubes. (Figure 5.3 shows scale in a potable water pipe that would be similar to that in a water tube boiler.) A laboratory chemical analysis of the water is necessary to evaluate the scaling potential of the water. If scaling is a problem, or a potential problem, a treatment system must be installed. If scaling has already occurred, it must be removed by chemical or mechanical means.

Testing that complies with the American Society of Mechanical Engineers (ASME) Boiler and Pressure Vessel Code is beyond the scope of this book. To informally test performance, several parameters must be measured, and there must be some way to dispose of the heat produced. The parameters for steam boilers are steam pressure and either steam or condensate flow rate. Some systems have flow meters installed; but most probably do not. Strap-on ultrasonic flow meters can be used without cutting the pipe if desired. The flow rate can be translated to pounds per hour and this, along with the pressure, can be compared with the boiler's rating.

Performance of hot water boilers is somewhat easier to measure. Water temperature in and out and water flow rate are needed. Most systems have thermometer wells in the piping. If they do not, insulated strap-on thermometers can substitute. As with steam boilers, if water flow meters are not installed, strap-on ultrasonic flow meters may be substituted. In the case of both steam and hot water boilers, any additional information that can be compared with the above data will help confirm and reduce uncertainty in the test. Such information might be rate of fuel flow, water flow or temperature measurements in other locations, and so on.

Piping

Hydronic piping can be tested for leakage at 1.5 times the working pressure or 100 psig, whichever is higher. The pressure can be generated by pumping, utility pressure, heating, or other means. Fuel oil and natural gas piping should be tested using the appropriate National Fire Protection Association (NFPA) code procedures.

FIGURE 8.11
A centrifugal water pump performance curve. Pressure is the vertical axis and flow rate is the horizontal axis. The parallel curves are the performance of different impeller diameters. These curves help in checking for proper operation of pumps.

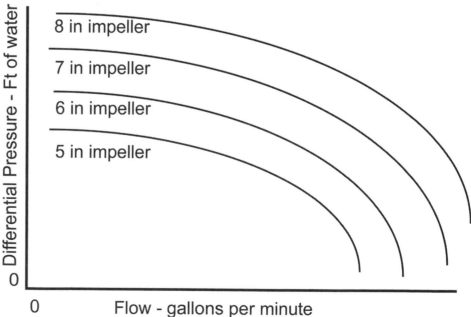

Pumps

Centrifugal water pump performance is rather easy to test. Pump manufacturers can provide performance curves for each pump if given its model and serial number. The curves are characteristically shaped as in Figure 8.11.

Terminal Units

This term covers many types of equipment including space-located heat or cooling devices from cast-iron radiators to variable-volume air controllers. Several of them will be discussed individually or in groups. Steam or hot water cast-iron radiators, convectors, or baseboard heaters are not likely to need detailed performance testing. If they heat when the heating medium is available, that is usually sufficient. It is more likely that the control valve or trap should be checked for proper operation. If the heating terminal is not warm but the supply pipe is, the valve can be manually opened, and if the result is still no heat, the valve may be the problem. A faulty steam trap will probably not permit condensate to flow through, and the result is a cold heating terminal.

Fan-coil units are another common form of terminal. Figure 8.12 shows a typical vertical fan-coil unit, and Figure 8.13 shows the interior with the access panel removed. Again, a heating or cooling performance test is not usually needed for a unit of this type. If it does not heat or cool, the problem is probably in the fan or the water control valves. Manual operation or electrical testing may locate the difficulty.

Air system terminals for such systems as double-duct, reheat, and variable-volume systems are almost always located above ceilings. They act to regulate airflow in some manner under control of a thermostat located in the occupied space. Many now have airflow meters built in and so actual performance can be tested. If a flow meter is not available, a pitot tube traverse can be taken to measure airflow rate. Otherwise the control function is probably the only test needed. Move the thermostat set point to the minimum and observe the resulting action in the terminal. In a double-duct system, the damper should move to admit only hot air. In a reheat system, the damper should close to the minimum position, and the reheat coil should activate. In a variable-volume system the damper should close and the heat source, usually a separate system, should activate.

Controls

Heating, ventilating, and air-conditioning (HVAC) system controls include the system of electric, electronic, or pneumatic devices that work together to operate the system.

Direct-Expansion Cooling Systems

Direct-expansion refrigeration is identified by the location of the cooling coil in the airstream from the occupied space. These systems are usually small and their units and control systems relatively simple.

Window and PTAC Units

Window units are the very smallest type of air-conditioning units. *Packaged terminal air-conditioning systems* (PTAC) are larger units that serve a single room. They extend

FIGURE 8.12
A typical vertical cabinet fan-coil heating and cooling unit.

FIGURE 8.13
Removal of the front panel reveals the interior of a vertical cabinet fan-coil heating and cooling unit with its fans, coils, filters, and controls.

through an exterior wall and have air-cooled condensers on the outside. Neither one of these units is very complex, so testing consists of operating the controls switches to determine whether the unit runs and cools (and heats, in the case of heat pumps). Other checks might include observing the filters, observing whether the condensate drains freely and, whether the outdoor coil is clean, and looking for possible rain leaks.

Rooftop and Split Direct-Expansion Units

These are larger unitary equipment that might range from 2 to 15 tons of cooling capacity. Even larger units are available. Field-fabricated refrigeration systems are required to be pressure tested when installed, whereas packaged units are not field-pressure tested unless a leak is noticed. Testing these units, like their smaller cousins, consists of operating the thermostat and observing the results. Also, like the smaller units, checking filters, condensate drainage, and cleanliness of the outdoor coils are easy to perform. These large units usually have some form of heating capability. It may be a gas furnace or an electric heater, or the unit may be a heat pump. Switching the thermostat to the heat position will verify it operation.

Ductwork

Air ducts should be tested for blockage, excessive dirt accumulation and leakage. Serious faults such as blockages can be caused by collapse, which is sometimes the result of workers crawling or climbing over ducts, or by internal insulation falling across the duct, by control dampers that vibrate out of position or come loose from their mountings, or by fire dampers that close accidentally. A simple test is just to feel the air coming out of grilles, registers, or diffusers with a hand. Air velocities and flows in buildings are sufficient to be readily felt against the skin.

More elaborate tests require measuring the air velocity with a pitot static tube and water manometer. First, holes are drilled in the duct wall, and the tube is inserted into the airstream. The cross section of the duct is divided into nine or more small areas and a reading is taken at the center of each area. The readings are averaged and converted to velocities and then to airflow rates. If original drawings are available, the readings can be compared with design figures. Another technique for measuring airflow rates and duct leakage is to read the flow rate from each grille, register, or diffuser with a flow hood. A flow hood is a fabric funnel that directs the airflow into an array of small pitot tubes that have an automatic airflow rate meter and readout.

Duct leakage can be evaluated by closing the ends of a section of duct and pressurizing it with the fan. It can be quantified by measuring the flow into the duct. Large leaks can be felt with the skin. If desired, the Air Moving and Conditioning Association (AMCA) provides test procedures for formal tests. If dirt and dust accumulations in the duct become a problem, the ducts can be cleaned by professional duct cleaners.

Fans

Centrifugal fans in HVAC equipment can be performance tested by measuring the airflow with a pitot tube traverse and the pressure across the fan. The fan speed in *revolutions per minute* (rpm) can be read with a strobe or mechanical counter. Fan-motor power can be read by measuring the electrical current flow to the motor, and this can then be converted to horsepower. These readings can be compared with manufacturer's data to evaluate the fan. Nonducted propeller fans are difficult to test because the airflow rate cannot be read.

Chilled Water Cooling Systems

Larger buildings are frequently cooled by indirect refrigeration using a stream of chilled water at about 45°F to distribute "cool" around the building. This requires a large central refrigeration system to chill the water and some other components special to this system. Hydraulically it is similar to the hot water heating system described earlier.

Chillers

The packaged refrigeration system is called a *chiller*, and its function is to cool a stream of water from about 55°F to 45°F. The heat removed from this water is discharged into another stream that carries it to a cooling tower. A chiller is probably the most expensive single component in the HVAC system. Its capacity can be roughly measured by reading inlet and outlet chilled water temperature, inlet and outlet condenser water temperature, and the flow rate of each. The results can be compared with manufacturer's data. Formal tests can be performed in accord with Air-Conditioning and Refrigeration Institute (ARI) procedures. Considerable knowledge in this field is needed to test chillers without causing damage.

Cooling Towers

Cooling towers are the large bulky structures that expose the water from a water-cooled condenser to the ambient air. By dividing the water stream into small drops, the heat exchange between water and air is enhanced. The cooled water is then recirculated to the condenser. The first step in testing a cooling tower is to visually inspect it. Look for corrosion, missing or misaligned fill (the slats or lattices that water trickles over as it courses down through the tower), algae in the basin, and leaks.

Since the water in the tower is continually exposed to the atmosphere, it becomes aerated and chemically active. Also, since some of the water evaporates (~2 percent) during each cycle, any dissolved minerals in the remainder become concentrated and can be deposited in the hottest part of the loop, the condenser. The deposited minerals are called *scale* and form a layer of material inside the tube (like the water pipe shown in Figure 5.3). This material insulates and retards heat flow, the temperature in the condenser rises, and chiller efficiency is reduced. Scaling can be detected if the condenser pressure is higher than expected for the tower water temperature entering the condenser. If scale is present, it must be chemically or mechanically removed. The water should be laboratory tested for scaling potential, and if it is strong enough, a chemical treatment plan should be implemented or an automatic treatment system installed.

A rare hazard, but one that can be dangerous, is the possibility that *legionella* could propagate in the tower basin. Legionella is the bacterium that causes Legionnaire's Disease. A laboratory analysis of the water should include testing for this microbe. Proper water treatment will control it.

Controls

The controls found on chilled water systems are usually sophisticated whole building systems that integrate the operation of all components in the HVAC system and sometimes other building systems as well. Systems installed before the 1990s were probably pneumatic compressed air systems, since these were the least expensive controls available to modulate the operation of valves and dampers. In the 1990s direct digital controls became affordable and have since come to dominate the market.

Pneumatic controls need to be calibrated every year or so since they tend to drift. Although Table 4.1 shows the expected life of a pneumatic control system to be 20 years, air compressors, air dryers, and sensing devices wear out and may have to be replaced more quickly. Run the air compressor first to assure an adequate air supply. A control system should first be tested in small increments such as a room thermostat and its controlled terminal or a fan and its speed controller. This can be done in closed-loop mode by adjusting the set point and observing the results. Calibrate as you go, if possible. Once the individual local branches are operating and calibrated, more sophisticated portions, such as weather-related sensors and resets from other components can be tested.

Electronic direct digital controls commonly have a central interface with a dedicated computer or at least a connection for a laptop. It is much easier to test systems from a central port like this.

Other Systems

Kitchen Ventilation

Kitchen ventilation systems found in restaurants, school cafeterias, and the like are relatively low-tech compared to the central control systems discussed above. These systems remove the airborne contaminants and heat produced by cooking operations. They also provide makeup air to replace that exhausted from the space. A simple first test is to simply turn on the fans and look for them to exhaust air without depressurizing the space. Visual inspection of the grease filters and fans to check for cleanliness and grease buildup is recommended. The equipment must be performance tested for exhaust and makeup airflow and proper operation, capture, and containment by smoke or steam when installed. This test can be repeated if necessary. When cooking equipment is changed its ventilation requirements change, so be aware of the effect of changes. In addition to simple exhaust and makeup, kitchen ventilation systems have fire-suppression systems that must be maintained and tested under fire code officials' supervision.

Testing Plumbing Systems

The plumbing systems are defined in this book as the potable water supply; the *sanitary drain, waste, and vent* (DWV); the storm drainage; and the fire-suppression sprinkler systems. Some plumbing system tests were mentioned in Chapter 3. This chapter describes the tests in more depth.

Testing Water Pressure and Flow

Potable water usually is supplied by a public or private utility through underground mains. The water is frequently delivered at pressures higher than necessary or desir-

FIGURE 8.14
Potable water supply system pressure can be easily tested with a pressure gauge at a hose faucet.

FIGURE 8.15
To test a water heater safety-relief valve, lift the manual lever to discharge a small amount of water through the valve.

able. The acceptable range is typically 60 to 90 psig. Most buildings have *pressure reducing valves* (PRV) in the line where it enters the building. The first test is to read the pressure at the nearest accessible point and set the PRV to the desired pressure. Figure 8.14 shows a pressure gauge attached to a hose faucet to measure pressure.

Some plumbing fixtures such as flush valves will not operate if flow and pressure are inadequate. Operate the fixtures on the top floor most distant from the service entrance to verify performance. Flush several in quick succession. If inadequate, increase the pressure at the PRV and test again. Pressure can be read on the top floor by attaching the gauge to hose faucets, if available, or to a lavatory supply line. If the pressure is adequate when no fixtures are in operation but drops severely when flowing, the problem is likely to be either undersized piping or pipe area reduction due to scale formation (see Figure 5.3). If necessary to actually test flow rates, water meters can be borrowed or rented or flow can be diverted into a bucket of known capacity and the time to fill measured.

Most commercial buildings are now required to have protection from the backflow of water from the building to the utility lines if pressure is lost. This takes the form of a set of valves that discharge water to a visible drain rather than permit backflow. These should be tested annually and when installed or after repairs in accord with procedures outlined in American Society of Sanitary Engineers (ASSE) standards.

Water heaters are subject to the pressure of the water supply system. In addition, they can add pressure as they heat water and it tries to expand. If a backflow prevention valve does not allow pressure to be relieved back to the utility system, either a small expansion tank or a relief valve, or both, must do this job. The water heater relief valve must be manually operated frequently to verify its ability to open and relieve pressure as shown in Figure 8.15.

Testing Drainage Flow

Sanitary DWV systems are susceptible to blockages because they transport solids with very little pressure—only that due to gravity at small slopes—available. Velocity must be kept high enough to prevent the deposition of solids. Everyone is familiar with stoppages in lavatory and water closet drains and the resulting mess. The problem is aggravated if the stoppage is downstream from several fixtures and the overflow through a fixture or a floor drain is copious. Fortunately, access points called, appropriately enough, cleanouts are required at maximum intervals of 100 feet when drain lines change direction.

A simple adequacy test is to flush several of the highest fixtures at the same time and look for overflows. If a more severe test is desired, a hose can be inserted into a vent on the roof or a cleanout and turned on. Be cautious, because a hose can overwhelm even a properly designed drain system. Finally, an old but still workable test is to flush a ball down a top level water closet and watch for it to emerge at a cleanout outside the building. If signs of blockage are found, it is now feasible to have a video camera inserted into the pipe and extended for considerable distances. This can also be done in the sewer outside.

Storm-water systems can also be tested with hoses flowing into the roof drains. Here there is a smaller hazard, because there are no openings from the rain leaders into the building.

Testing Leakage

Supply Systems

Test water supply piping for leakage with water at 1.5 times working pressure or 50 psig, whichever is greater. Watch for pressure loss during the test, which indicates leakage. Visually observe the pipe where possible for slow leaks. Air tests are also permitted except not for plastic pipe, as it is brittle under air pressure and can explode.

DWV Systems

To leak test a DWV system, install pipe-closure bladders at fixtures and any other openings in the section to be tested. Fill the system with water to the height of the highest vent in the section or pressurize with air to 5 psig (not for plastic pipe) or smoke test at 1 in water gauge (WG) air pressure. Observe the water level or pressure gauge for a decrease. Also observe the pipe where visible to check for small leaks or smoke leakage.

Testing Sprinkler and Fire-Suppression Systems

Fire-suppression sprinkler systems are carefully regulated by the National Fire Protection Association (NFPA) and by local fire code officials. In general, tests of sprinklers should be performed by code officials or licensed contractors. The systems have integral inspector's test valves and drains for the purpose of flow-rate testing. Among the tests required are flow and pressure at the standpipe connections on the roof, flow and pressure at remote areas, and flow and pressure at the nearest hydrant (for evaluating changes in the utility system).

Bibliography

A58 Committee. 1945. "The American Standard Building Code Requirements for Minimum Design Loads." In *Buildings and Other Structures,* A58.1–1945.

Abrams, D. P. 1992. *Masonry Structure.* Boulder, Colo.: Masonry Society.

American Concrete Institute (ACI). 1988. *Building Code for Masonry Structures.* ACI Publication No. 530 -88, Section 6.3. Detroit, Mich.: ACI.

———. 1989. *Building Code Requirements for Reinforced Concrete.* ACI Publication No. 318–89. Detroit, Mich.: ACI.

———. 1941. *Reinforced Concrete Design Handbook.* Detroit, Mich.: ACI.

American Institute of Steel Construction. 1930. *Manual of Steel Construction.* 1st ed. New York: American Institute of Steel Construction.

———. 1939. *Manual of Steel Construction.* 3rd ed. New York: American Institute of Steel Construction.

Athena Sustainable Materials Institute, *AthenASMI.com,* http://www.athenasmi.ca.

Baker, I. O. 1892. *A Treatise of Masonry Construction.* 7th ed. New York: John Wiley & Sons.

———. 1910. *A Treatise on Masonry Construction.* 10th ed. New York: John Wiley & Sons.

Beckmann, P. 1994. *Structural Aspects of Building Conservation.* New York: McGraw-Hill.

Beedle, L. S. 1964. *Structural Steel Design.* New York: Roland Press.

Bell, W. E. 1857. *Carpentry Made Easy, or The Science and Art of Framing.* Philadelphia: Howard Challen.

Bethlehem Steel Co. 1962. *Bethlehem Structural Shapes.* Catalogue S-18. Bethlehem, Pa.: Bethlehem Steel Co.

Birkmire, W. H. 1894. *Skeletal Construction in Buildings.* 2nd ed. New York: John Wiley & Sons.

———. 1898. *The Planning and Construction of High Office-Buildings.* 2nd ed. New York: John Wiley & Sons.

Bray, D. E., and D. McBride. 1992. *Nondestructive Testing Techniques.* New York: John Wiley & Sons.

Building Officials and Code Administrators International, Inc. 1987. *BOCA National Building Code, 1987.*

Cambria Steel Co. 1919. *A Handbook of Information Relating to Structural Steel.* 12th ed. Philadephia, Pa.: Cambria Steel Co.

Carnegie Steel Co. 1893. *Pocket Companion.* Pittsburgh, Pa.: Carnegie Steel Co.

———. 1913. *Pocket Companion.* 16th ed. Pittsburgh, Pa.: Carnegie Steel Co.

———. 1920. *Pocket Companion.* 21st ed. Pittsburgh, Pa.: Carnegie Steel Co.

———. 1923. *Pocket Companion for Engineers, Architects and Builders.* 23d ed. Pittsburgh, Pa.: Carnegie Steel Co.

Comer, J. P. 1942. *New York City Building Control.* New York: Columbia University Press.

Concrete Reinforcing Steel Institute (CRSI). 1978. *CRSI Hand book.* 3rd ed. Chicago: CRSI.

Condit, C. W. 1964. *The Chicago School of Architecture: A History of Commercial and Public Building in the Chicago Area, 1875–1925.* Chicago: University of Chicago Press.

Cowie, J. 2007. *Climate Change, Biological and Human Aspects.* Cambridge: Cambridge University Press.

Dunham, C. W. 1939. *The Theory and Practice of Reinforced Concrete.* 1st ed. New York: McGraw-Hill.

Ferguson, P. M. 1973. *Reinforced Concrete Fundamentals.* 3rd ed. New York: John Wiley & Sons.

Ferris, H. W., ed. 1978. *Historical Record, Dimensions and Properties: Rolled Shapes,* New York: American Institute of Steel Construction.

Fitzgerald, R. W. 1967. *Strength of Materials.* Reading Mass.: Addison-Wesley.

Franklin Associates. 1998. "Characterization of Building-related Construction and Demolition Debris in the United States, Report Number EPA530-R-98–010." Washington D.C.: U.S. Environmental Protection Agency.

Freitag, J. K. 1895. *Architectural Engineering.* 1st ed. New York: John Wiley & Sons.

———. 1909. *Architectural Engineering.* 2nd ed. New York: John Wiley & Sons.

Gay, C. M. 1947. *Mechanical and Electrical Equipment in Buildings.* 2nd ed. New York: John Wiley & Sons.

Green Globes. 2008. *Green Building Initiative,* http://www.thegbi.org.

Hamlin, T. 1953. *Architecture through the Ages.* Rev. ed. New York: G. P. Putnam's Sons.

Hammond, G., and C. Jones. 2006. "Inventory of Carbon and Energy." Department of Mechanical Engineering, Bath University.

Harper, R. H. 1985. *The Evolution of the English Building Regulations.* London: Mansell.

Holness, G. V. R. 2008. "Improving Energy Efficiency in Existing Buildings," *ASHRAE Journal* 50 (January): 12–26.

Hool, G. A., and N. C. Johnson. 1929. *Handbook of Building Construction.* New York: McGraw-Hill.

Hool, G. A., N. C. Johnson, and S. C. Hollister. 1918. *The Concrete Engineer's Handbook.* 1st ed. New York: McGraw-Hill.

Hool, G. A., and W. S. Kinne. 1923. *Foundations, Abutments and Footings.* 1st ed. New York: McGraw-Hill.

———. 1924. *Steel and Timber Structures.* New York: McGraw-Hill.

Huntington, W. C. 1929. *Building Construction.* 1st ed. New York: John Wiley & Sons.

International Correspondence Schools (ICS). 1899A. *The Building Trades Handbook.* 2d ed. Scranton, Pa.: International Textbook Co.

———. 1899B. *A Treatise on Architecture and Building Construction.* Vol. 2, *Masonry, Carpentry, Joinery.* Scranton, Pa.: Colliery Engineer Co.

———. 1905A. *Fireproof Floor Systems.* Scranton, Pa.: International Textbook Co.

_____. 1905B. *Loads in Structure; Properties of Sections; Materials of Structural Engineering; Beams and Girders; Columns and Struts; Details of Construction: Graphical Analysis of Stresses. International Library of Technology.* Vol. 51. Scranton, Pa.: International Textbook Co.

———. 1905C. *Statics of Masonry, Heavy Foundations, Retaining Walls, Fireproofing, Roof-Truss Design, Wind Bracing, Specifications.* Vol. 52 of *International Library of Technology.* Scranton, Pa.: International Textbook Co.

———. 1908. *Operations Preliminary to Building, Limes, Cements, and Mortars, Excavation, Shoring and Piling, Foundations, and Others.* Vol. 34C of *International Library of Technology.* Scranton, Pa.: International Textbook Co.

———. 1911. *The Concrete Engineer's Handbook.* 1st ed. Scranton, Pa.: International Textbook Co.

———. 1912. *The Building Trades Handbook.* 2nd ed. Scranton, Pa.: International Textbook Co.

_____. 1919. *Hollow Tile and Fireproofing.* Scranton, Pa.: International Textbook Co.

———. 1923A. *A Fireproofing of Buildings, Stair Building, Ornamental Metal work, Builders' Hardware, Roofing, Sheet-Metal Work, Mill Design.* Vol. 33C of *International Library of Technology.* Scranton, Pa.: International Textbook Co.

———. 1923B. *Operations Preliminary to Building: Limes, Cements, and Mortar; Excavating, Shoring, and Piling; Foundations; Stone Masonry; Concrete Construction; Areas, Vaults, and Retaining Walls; Carpentry; Mechanics of Carpentry; Joinery; the Steel Square.* Vol. 30C of *International Library of Technology.* Scranton, Pa.: International Textbook Co.

———. 1924. *Design of Beams.* Vol. 11E of *International Library of Technology.* Scranton, Pa.: International Textbook Co.

_____. 1928. *Reinforced Concrete Construction.* Scranton, Pa.: International Library of Technology.

———. 1960. *The Building Trades Handbook.* 8th ed. Scranton, Pa.: International Textbook Co.

Irace, F. 1988. *Emerging Skylines: The New American Skyscrapers.* New York: Whitney Library Design.

Jandl, H. W., ed. 1983. *The Technology of Historic American Buildings.* Washington, D.C.: Foundation for Preservation of Technology.

Johnson, J. B., C. W. Bryan, and F. E. Turneaure. 1894. *The Theory and Practice of Modern Framed Structures.* 3rd rev. ed. New York: John Wiley & Sons.

Ketchum, M. S. 1918. *The Structural Engineer's Handbook.* 2nd ed. New York: McGraw-Hill.

———. 1924. *The Structural Engineer's Handbook.* 3rd ed. New York: McGraw-Hill.

———. 1921. *The Design of Steel Mill Buildings.* 4th ed. New York: William T. Comstock.

Kidder, F. E. 1900. *Carpenter's Work.* Vol. 2 of *Building Construction and Superintendence.* 3rd ed. New York: William T. Comstock.

———. 1902. *The Architects' and Builders' Pocket-book.* 13th ed. New York: John Wiley & Sons.

———. 1904. *The Architects' and Builders' Pocket-book.* 14th ed. New York: John Wiley & Sons.

———. 1905B. *Strength of Beams, Floors and Roofs.* New York: David Williams.

———. 1912. *The Architects' and Builders' Pocket-book.* 15th ed. New York: John Wiley & Sons.

———. 1905A. *Mason's Work.* Vol. 1 of *Building Construction and Superintendence.* 7th ed. New York: William T. Comstock.

Kidder, F. E., and H. Parker. 1949. *Kidder-Parker Architects' and Builders' Handbook: Data for Architects, Structural Engineers, Contractors, and Draughtsmen.* 18th ed. New York: John Wiley & Sons.

Lord, A. R. 1928. *A Handbook of Reinforced Concrete Building Design, in Accordance with the 1928 Joint Standard Building Code.* 1st ed. Detroit: American Concrete Institute.

Mahan, D. H. 1885. *A Treatise on Civil Engineering.* Rev. ed. New York: John Wiley & Sons.

Mazria, E., and K. Kershner. 2008. "2030 Blueprint: Solving Climate Change Saves Billions." *Architecture 2030* (7 April), http://www.architecture2030.org.

Merriman, T., and T. H. Wiggin. 1947. *American Civil Engineer's Handbook.* 5th ed. New York: John Wiley & Sons.

Moxon, J. [1703] 1975. *Mechanick Exercises, or, the Doctrine of Handy-Works.* 3rd ed. Scarsdale, N.Y.: Early Industries Assn.

Mulligan, J. A. 1942. *Handbook of Brick Masonry Construction.* 1st ed. New York: McGraw-Hill.

National Forest Products Association (NFPA). 1988. *National Design Specification for Wood Construction.* Washington, D.C.: NFPA.

———. 1991. *National Design Specification for Wood Construction.* Washington, D. C.: NFPA

O'Rourke, C. E. 1940. *General Engineering Handbook.* 2nd ed. New York: McGraw-Hill.

Patton, W. M. *A Practical Treatise on Foundations.* 1st ed. New York: John Wiley & Sons.

Paul, C. E. 1916. *Heavy Timber Mill Construction Buildings.* 3d ed. Chicago: National Lumber Manufacturers' Association.

Peters, T. F. 1987. "The Rise of the Skyscraper from the Ashes of Chicago." *American Heritage of Invention and Technology* 3 (Fall 1987): 14–22.

Peterson, C., ed. 1976. *Building Early America: Contributions toward the History of a Great Industry.* Radnor, Pa.: Chilton.

Phoenix Iron Co. 1906. *Handbook of Useful Information, Tables, Rules, Data, and Formulae Appertaining to the Use of Steel.* Philadelphia, Pa.: Phoenix Iron Co.

Ramsey, C. G., and H. R. Sleeper. 1936. *Architectural Graphic Standards.* 2nd ed. New York: John Wiley & Sons.

Reid, H. A. 1907. *Concrete and Reinforced Concrete Construction.* 1st ed. New York: Myron C. Clark.

Ricker, N. C. 1912. *A Treatise on the Design and Construction of Roofs.* 1st ed. New York: Myron C. Clark.

Rivington. 1899. *Elementary Stage.* Part 1 of *Notes on Building Construction.* London: Longmans, Green.

Rock, David. 1979. "Building Conversion and Rehabilitation, Reusing Buildings—A New Arts and Science." In *Building Conversion and Rehabilitation: Designing for Change in Building Use*, ed. Thomas A Markus. London and Boston: Butterworths.

———. *Advanced Stage.* Part 2 of *Notes on Building Construction.* London: Longmans, Green.

Sahlin, S. 1971. *Structural Masonry.* Englewood Cliffs, N.J.: Prentice Hall.

Sandler, K. 2003. "Analyzing What's Recyclable in C&D Debris." *BioCycle* 44, no, 11 (November): 51–54.

Schneider, H. E. 1930. *Practical Wind Bracing.* Buffalo, N.Y.: Lancaster Press.

Shedd, T. C. 1934. *Structural Design in Steel.* 1st ed. New York: John Wiley & Sons.

Sprague, P. E. 1983. "Chicago Balloon Frame." In *The Technology of Historic American Buildings,* ed. H. W. Jandl. Washington, D.C.: Foundation for Preservation Technology.

Thurston, R. H. 1892. *Materials of Construction.* 5th ed. New York: John Wiley & Sons.

Timoshenko, S. P. [1930] 1983. *History of Strength of Materials.* New York: Dover.

Trautwine, J. C. 1888. *The Civil Engineer's Pocketbook.* 13th ed. New York: John Wiley & Sons.

Turneauré, F. E., ed. 1908. *The Cyclopedia of Civil Engineering.* Chicago: American School of Correspondence.

Turneauré, F. E., and E. R. Maurer. 1914. *Principles of Reinforced Concrete Construction.* 2nd ed. New York: John Wiley & Son.

United Nations Intergovernmental Panel on Climate Change, Climate Change (IPCC). 2007. "Synthesis Report."

U.S. Census Bureau. 2008. "World Population Information," *International Data Base,* http://www.census.gov/ipc/www/idb/worldpopinfo.html.

Urquhart, L. C., and C. E. O'Rourke. 1941. *Elementary Structural Engineering.* 1st ed. New York: McGraw-Hill.

Voss, W. C., and E. A. Varney. 1926A. *Architectural Construction.* Vol. 2, bk. 1, *Wood Construction.* New York: John Wiley & Sons.

Voss, W. C. and E. A. Varney. 1926B. *Architectural Construction.* Vol. 2, bk. 2, *Steel Construction.* New York: John Wiley & Sons.

White, C. E. 1932. *Hollow Tile.* Part 1 of *Hollow Tile and Fireproofing.* Scranton, Pa.: International Textbook Co.

Wilson, F. 1984. *Building Materials Evaluation Handbook.* New York: Van Nostrand Reinhold.

Index

ML   1/10